7 ANCIENT KEYS TO HAPPINESS

A 90 Day LESSON-A-DAY GUIDE TO ACHIEVING INNER BLISS

ISBN 1453602623 (paperback)
EAN-13 9781453602621.

To my dear niece Sara, I'm writing this for you, to help you navigate your ship through the rough waters of life and to steer you towards an island of beauty, true happiness, fulfilment and love.

Contents

SMELL EVERY ROSE

KEY #1- SEE THE GOOD

PART 1 – SEEING THE GOOD BY LEARNING THE ROPES

SMELL EVERY ROSE

KEY #1- SEE THE GOOD

PART 2 - SEEING THE GOOD IN OUR PAST

SMELL EVERY ROSE

KEY #1- SEE THE GOOD

PART 3 - SEEING THE GOOD IN PEOPLE

SMELL EVERY ROSE

KEY #1- SEE THE GOOD

PART 4 - RIGHT NOW AND IN THE FUTURE

CLIMB EVERY MOUNTAIN

KEY #2 - OBJECTIVITY

CLIMB EVERY MOUNTAIN

KEY #2 - OBJECTIVITY

THE DYNAMICS OF JUDGING OBJECTIVELY

LOVE EVERY DAY

LOVE EVERY DAY

KEY #3 – COMPASSION

LOVE EVERY DAY

KEY #4 – GIVING

LOVE EVERY DAY

KEY #5 – BONDING

LOVE EVERY DAY

KEY #6 – CONTENTMENT

LOVE EVERY DAY

KEY #7 – TRUTH

END OF CONTENTS

Introduction

Imagine winning 1 billion dollars, an Olympic gold medal, being elected President, becoming rich, famous, admired, loved and honoured by everybody - all on one day. Take all that pleasure you would feel and multiply it by every day of your life. When you master the keys to happiness, you will be able to experience this level of pleasure – AND MORE every day.

There are 7 ancient keys to having this level of inner-happiness. Unlock the secrets!

People who have harnessed the power of happiness have become more successful and motivated, achieved major goals and developed charisma. If you can master the art of happiness you will be a more effective boss, employee, spouse, parent and friend. You will also simultaneously acquire more direction in life, persistence, vitality, drive, patience, enthusiasm, magnetism, inner-greatness, distinction, confidence, courage, self-esteem and true fulfilment. People love happy people and happy people are constantly blessed with good things happening to them. Happiness is THE most powerful tool for business, relationships and life!

Happiness – The Inside Story.

If we look around the world, we see a mass of humanity all searching for the same thing – happiness. A human being seems to need to pursue happiness as though it is a life necessity, like air, or water etc. In fact, most of society is based on catering for this human drive. We search for it in food – looking for new and exciting taste sensations; clothes – trying to find that outfit that brings out the best in us; relationships, music, art, success, money, spiritual experiences and popularity etc. We hope by fulfilling our needs, wants, desires or even whims we will attain this ultimate goal called happiness.

This book was written as a guide for those searching for the real thing – a long lasting, constant and continuous state of being.

But in order to get this pleasure we need to realize one important thing – Happiness is a CHOICE. Happiness is not a happenstance, it is not something that if the right stars move into the right alignment then boom we will be happy, it's not a case of meeting the right girl/boy, it's not a case of whether we get the promotion or anything external to us.

Happiness is NEVER dependant on other people. We may have people in our lives that are extremely challenging and frustrate us immensely – but they are not the ones that decide whether we are happy or not. People may be placed in our lives to help us work on our inter-personal relationships. If we can use challenging people and situations as a springboard for developing ourselves into better people and bettering our personal character traits (such as patience, unconditional love, assertiveness etc) then we will be happy to have had the opportunity to meet these difficult people – because they would have helped make us into better people.

Developing the inner feeling of happiness is completely up to us. Other people cannot be the determiners of whether we are happy. It's only how we choose to react or view these people that determine our state of mind. We can choose to be upbeat and positive in the face of other's negativity and poor behaviour. We can choose not to give them power over us and not to let their influence undermine our peaceful, joyful outlook.

Happiness is a CHOICE, an internal choice whereby we can choose to make the most of our lives and be proactively joyful. Passively waiting around for happiness to descend upon us will NEVER bring lasting happiness. We have to work for it and the harder we work to be happy, the more happiness we will be able to cultivate.

So let's choose to be happy! We can choose to be happy. We can choose to turn our lives around and make them into joyful experiences – every day. We can choose to live a life we love and to love the life we live. It's all up to us. We only live once. We can make it a great life with no regrets.

In order to get the most pleasure out of life we need to wake ourselves up. We all fall asleep in the humdrum comings and goings of our lives. If we can wake ourselves up and see that every second of life offers us the most unbelievable opportunity to turn it into a blissful moment – then we can start to really taste the joy of living.

Once we are awake, trying to live life to the fullest, we can start to think about what we can do that will give us the greatest pleasure in that moment....

Nothing can beat a tried, tested and successful recipe. Grandma's old sponge recipe always tastes the best. An old good wine has nothing with which to compare. So in our search for ultimate happiness, we can go looking for such a recipe and if we look back far enough we will find an ancient recipe for happiness.

Everybody has heard of the story of Noah and the Great Flood. Even societies that were not influenced by Judaic-Christian-Muslim influences have old archaic versions of a story about a man who was saved from a big flood. It is a universally known story. However, very few people know that after the flood, Noah was given 7 Commandments (No NOT the 10 Commandments – that happened much later.) From these 7 Commandments we can derive 7 timeless principles which are the ancient keys for achieving happiness. Many will notice that we find some of these keys in every single culture in one form or another, which is proof of their timeless wisdom. These ancient keys have been used for thousands of years by all different people. For the first time, '7 Ancient Keys to Happiness' has collated all 7 of these keys into one succinct, hands-on, do-it-yourself guide to happiness.

Using these 7 ancient keys to happiness we are going to be guided through an exciting, pre-tested and successful path to bliss. So get ready to open your mind to a different and ancient reality and join us on this mystical path to the City of Happiness.

———

The 7 ancient keys to happiness can be divided into 3 main principles, thus this book is divided into three main sections.

Section 1:	**SMELL EVERY ROSE**	
	Key #1 (i.e. See the Good in Everything)	
Section 2:	**CLIMB EVERY MOUNTAIN**	
	Key #2 (i.e. Judge things Objectively); and	
Section 3:	**LOVE EVERY DAY**	
	Keys #3to #7 (i.e. Love Yourself)	

Overall the book consists of 90 days of wisdom and growth. Each day there is a 'Give it a Go!' exercise which is a practical thing for us to do to help drive us towards attaining success and happiness. After doing this exercise we are given an opportunity to rate it. By doing this we'll quickly be able to remember which exercises were the ones that hit our buttons and gave us increased levels of happiness. When we know which exercises work best for us we can go back to them again and again for bigger boosts of happiness.

Since it's hard for most people to be disciplined enough to do the exercises there is a little 'Why should I?' pep talk after each 'Give it a Go!', which explains why we should try out the exercise and what we hope to gain by doing it.

Meeting the Quiet Voice

Before we begin our journey to discover the 7 keys to happiness and before we learn how to smell every rose, climb every mountain and love every day, we need to get in touch with that part of us that helps us reach for the stars, follow our dreams and be the type of person we love and can be proud of. Let's meet our tour guide - The Quiet Voice...

Day 1
Getting in touch

It had been a hard day. I woke up in the morning, crawled out of bed, ran into the shower, and then sat in front of my wardrobe trying to find something to suit the mood I was in, something that projected the image I wanted to portray, something that would be me. I put on my makeup, eye makeup to make my eyes look bigger, foundation to make my face look more smooth and tanned, blush to show a little bit of youthful exuberance and lipstick to bring out my passionate side. I rummaged around the kitchen for something that was tasty, and would keep my body looking and feeling good. Then I set out for the shopping centre. I talked and laughed with my friends all day whilst shopping. 8 hours later I returned home, with some new goodies that called out a promise of making me more fulfilled. Then I collapsed in front of the computer looking for something light to lift my mood, as I ate dinner. I watched a show, where the person said, "So are you happy? Do you know what you are living for?" I thought for a little bit, "Yeah I'm happy – I think. I don't really know why I'm living and I don't care!" A few hours later I retired but I couldn't fall asleep. All I could think of was "Yeah I'm happy and I don't care why I'm living." But there was a voice in my head that kept saying it over and over. The voice was getting louder and more panicky. It was like I was trying to shout down an opposing voice. I felt tense, and I was breathing quick shallow breaths. I shouted out aloud, "Yeah, I'm happy, and I don't care! Why are you bothering me?" Then I heard it, it was a small voice inside my head, it was barely audible it whispered, "No, I'm not happy. I'm completely miserable. Help - I want to live!"

We all have times in our lives when we hear that quiet voice. Sometimes it's the quiet voice of wisdom and insight, whereas other times it could be the quiet voice of discontent that tells us that we are leading futile lives. When it's the quiet voice of discontent we tend to ignore it or we might try to distract ourselves. We may do this because we secretly fear that there is no solution to our vague feelings of discontent or answers to our quest for meaning

However, if we tune into listening to this quiet voice, we will discover that it will lead us on paths of self-discovery and true delight. It takes courage not to run away. It takes courage to ask ourselves questions and to hear our inner answers.

We all have a deep reflective part of us that is full of wisdom. It is full of true goodness and it is that part of us that gives us the tools to attain the deepest most long lasting feelings of pleasure. This reflective part of us is not the selfish "I need", "give me" voice that says 'chocolate cake is delicious so give me 5 pieces'; instead it's the one that really looks after our interests. It might say, "have some," but only for the right reasons - the chocolate cake looks delicious, we haven't had any for 3 months and if we are too tough on ourselves we'll start rebelling against our healthy eating resolution - so it recommends we have some (maybe ½ a piece) and really enjoy it!

Some people who have tried to find their deep reflective quiet voice, have expressed frustration saying, "I sat on my bed and waited, and nothing happened." When we ask them "What are you thinking whilst you sit quietly waiting for the wellsprings of wisdom to open up." These people may say they were thinking thoughts like, "This is silly". The thought "This is silly" is the not the quiet voice we are trying to tune into. The thought "This is silly" is the shallow, impulsive, noisy voice that so often distracts us from being able to listen to our quiet voice. In order to get in touch with the quiet voice, we need to learn to ignore the distractions that this noisy voice will throw our way.

In this book, when we talk about voices we are not talking about REAL voices that we hear, the voices are not external to us. Normally crazy people only hear such voices. The voices we are talking about are really THOUGHTS. We are thinking all of the time. These thoughts can be divided into categories – shallow wants and desires, analysing information and making decisions we need to make etc (we call this 'the noisy voice') and there are deeper thoughts (we call this 'the quiet voice').

Some people prefer to call the quiet voice the thoughts of the good conscience, intuition, a flash of inspiration, or deep and meaningful revelations. We are thinking them already - they are not going to be something 'new and exciting'. However, what may be new is that we all have DIFFERENT types of thoughts and these can be categorised, prioritised and even channelled. Tapping into how we think is the beginning of self-knowledge. Once we understand how we work, we can then manipulate, control and use our inherent awesome powers to have a wonderful life.

Give it a Go!
Sometimes at the beginning of getting in touch – we need to turn it all off, in order to turn the quiet voice on. It means turning off the phone, the computer, the TV, the radio, the books, and the mindless chatter that goes on inside our heads.

Try lying on your bed, look at the ceiling or close your eyes and ask yourself a question e.g. "What's my life about? Or 'Am I happy?" The noisy voice may rush in to answer, let it have a little turn, and then tell it to be silent, and wait for the quiet voice to respond. Try turning off for at least 15 min.

I tried this exercise _____ times.
I would rate this exercise as:

1	2	3	4	5	6	7	8	9	10
(not so good)				(Average)					(Spot on)

Why Should I?
Getting in touch with ourselves is the first step to achieving anything in life. If we learn to know who we really are, what makes us tick and what gives us real pleasure then we are able to 'feed' ourselves with all the things that ultimately bring us happiness. Imagine if we bought a fern and cactus from a shop and swapped around the care instructions, there is no doubt that both the fern and the cactus would die, as the fern needs plenty of water and little sunlight whereas the cactus needs little water and much sunlight.

We human beings are such unique creatures and the care instructions for one person will be totally different to that of another. We need to understand ourselves to know how to care for ourselves and how to provide ourselves with the nourishment we need to bring out the best in us. However, since no two people are alike we can't turn to anybody else to tell us how to operate ourselves and care for ourselves optimally. Sure we can (and should) ask others for advice and ideas, but ultimately we are the only ones that know when the advice we are given is applicable to us.

Each person has internal care instructions for themselves hard wired into their personality, which means each person in this world has the ability to find out who they are and how to maximize their potential. The care instructions are deep within us, embedded in our consciousness, intuition or felt at times of inspiration. When we learn to reflect deeply and get in touch with who we are we can start the journey of self discovery. Discovering what you like, what drives you, what motivates or de-motivates you, makes you into a formula 1 race car driving towards your goals at top speed.

Conversely when we are afraid to ask ourselves deep and meaningful questions and run away from that part of ourselves we weaken our ability to take hold of the wheel and drive ourselves where we want to go. We go about directionless and end up not using even half the amount of potential we have.

So the first step towards achieving happiness is to recognise we have a part of ourselves that is deep, reflective, wise, worth listening to and consulting. If we can learn how to sit down and get in touch, then we will have discovered the most powerful tool for success in anything in life. We can use this tool for the rest of our lives, any time and in any situation to help us achieve any goal.

When we learn how to tune into our quiet voice we will have also discovered our best advisor, friend, user manual, care instructions, life coach and life-long companion.

Reading a book about upgrading our levels of happiness will make us happier in the short term but for long term benefits we need to put into practice what we've learned. Go on try out the exercise, it won't take long and you'll benefit from it greatly.

Go on – Get to know yourself – Give it a Go!

Day 2
Learning to Listen

Once we have discovered the deep reflective quiet voice inside we can start learning to listen to it – even when we are not all alone without any distractions.

"My friend called me up and asked if I wanted to come out with her. I did want to. But I had already said to my mother that I would help her do some spring cleaning that day. I had a choice. Either I could push my mother off, or I could take a raincheck with my friend. I really didn't know what to do, so I asked my quiet reflective voice. The noisy voice rushed to answer, "Go with your friend, you'll have more fun, and you're not your mother's slave anyway", but I waited patiently for the quiet voice, and it said, "take a raincheck" (with your friend).

The more we tune into listening to that quiet voice, the more we get in touch with the "real me". And when we learn to listen to the "real me's" advice, the more we start to feel an inner calmness and happiness.

"I used to feel my emotions were like a tornado hovering over the ocean, with waves crashing, with power and speed on the shore. Now, when I try to visualise how I am emotionally feeling, a scene of the sea shore still appears but, the water is very calm – more like a lake, with tiny ripples as waves."

"I think all of this sounds foolish, we live in the real world, how is escaping into my thoughts going to get me more money, power or prestige."

Money, power and prestige are not synonymous with happiness. However, as we all know - it doesn't mean we live in bliss if we DON'T have them, but it also doesn't mean we ARE happy if we DO have them - they don't bring us lasting happiness ON THEIR OWN. Money, power and prestige are like cars that we can use to drive us towards happiness. But if we are just driving around, not knowing where we are supposed to be going then we won't arrive at our destination, and we might get very frustrated and lost. It is a bit pointless spending all our time and effort in upgrading and improving our cars, without actually knowing where we are planning to drive them. By learning to listen to our inner voice, we'll be turning on the GPS navigation system in our car. Our deep reflective quiet voice will lead us towards happiness. Listening to our quiet voice is not escaping into our thoughts; it is bringing our thoughts out into the open. The quiet voice is always there, and is talking to us – we just need to tune in and it will guide us towards a life of bliss.

Give it a Go!

It's time to get quiet again. Let's reflect and ask ourselves, "What can I do today to increase the levels of joy I feel in my life?" and wait for the quiet answer.

Write down the answer you received:

_____

I tried this exercise _____ times.
I would rate this exercise as:

1	2	3	4	5	6	7	8	9	10
(not so good)				(Average)					(Spot on)

Why Should I?

We are actually more wise, knowledgeable and intuitive than we realize. We all have a part of ourselves that knows us very well. Deep down we have hunches or inklings about what will bring us to true joy. When we learn to listen to ourselves, we will start hearing some amazing and insightful answers that we JUST KNOW are right.

When a person is feeling serene and relaxed their brain is fired up into more creativity and profound thought. Often when we stress ourselves out, we are actually blocking all of our neural pathways with 'urgent, beware, be on guard, quick, hurry, I must...' messages and these shallow recurring thoughts use up our brain power, drain us of our thinking ability and turn us into robots walking the treadmill of life.

In order to develop our creativity and ability to think outside the box of our current problems and existence, we need to free our mind from the humdrum routine of life that we constantly preoccupy ourselves with.

When we take the time to teach ourselves to slow down, relax and reflect, we can then start using that amazing gift of our brain to help us. With deep reflective thought we can actually come up with most of the answers to all of our problems. So instead of suffering our problems we can use our brain to solve our problems.

All we need to do is believe we have it within us. You are smart, you are creative, you are a genius at being able solve your problems, and you are able to bring yourself to a place where you feel genuinely happy, energised and satisfied with your life.

The only way we can develop this firm belief in our abilities is to become proactive and practice tapping into our deep inner wisdom. The more we can practice asking ourselves deep and meaningful questions, the more we will realize that good quality answers bubble up from within. Eventually we will be able to rely on these answers and trust our quiet voice.

Only by experimenting with this idea and finding that it really works, will we develop the faith and trust in our ability to access a higher wisdom within ourselves whenever we want. When we know that we have this power within us we will never feel totally lost, alone, out of our depth or completely overwhelmed – no matter what situation we happen to be in. When we learn to ask ourselves deep questions and we just KNOW we will receive great responses we develop a confidence in our own decision making and in our ability to determine our own path in life.

Go on - Learning to listen to your deep reflective inner voice will bring you unimaginable rewards – Give it a Go!

Day 3

Keeping in touch

"I found it," Kate said, "I listened for a few days, and finally I heard it. I have a problem though – I don't want to do what it said. It tells me to be responsible and I want to be carefree. It tells me to tell the truth, when I want to tell a little white lie – it's a pest! "

Have you ever really wanted something, and you worked really hard to achieve it, and finally you got it? It could have been a good grade on a test, winning an athletics competition, or getting the lead role in a play. The feeling of victory or success was made so sweet not DESPITE the hard work that was put in but BECAUSE of the hard work that was invested. Listening to our soft quiet voice doesn't mean instant happiness, but it's starting the climb up the mountain. It's not easy to climb a mountain, but the higher we climb the more beautiful the view is. When we sit down to practice the piano, its hard work, it's boring, it's a pest! But the result, the beautiful sounding melody that floats from the instruction of our fingers, fills the air and raises our spirits and we feel that all the hard work is worthwhile. Learning to listen to our quiet voice will take effort, but we need to keep going and keep trying. The more we make this voice our friend and listen to what it is saying, the more we will soar to heights of happiness.

"I don't like the voice because it makes me feel guilty."

Sometimes the quiet voice tells us to do many good and kind things that are simply inconvenient or are just not what we feel we are prepared to do at this time in our lives. Then when we don't live up to what it says we should be, we might feel like a failure or feel guilty. But if we listen closely, it's not the quiet voice that calls us a failure, or tells us that we are bad – it is that loud rapacious one. When we've done things that hurt somebody's feelings the quiet voice says, 'go make up and apologise', but the loud voice shouts 'you're hopeless, no good, bad etc...'

The quiet voice wants to point us in the right direction – and it is not necessarily possible for us to be there straight away. That's ok. We are not perfect, and we shouldn't expect ourselves to be perfect. So if our quiet voice tells us we should set up an institution for disabled people, we don't have to feel bad if we don't go out and do it. What we need to know is that there is some place inside us that cares for disabled people and would like to help them out – how we express this desire immediately could be simply by helping a person who needs our assistance to cross the road.

If the quiet voice is persistent with grand desires – then we should follow the path that will lead us there. However, we may find that we will reach a point of satisfaction and not desire to follow through with our original grandiose plans (e.g. of setting up an Institute for disabled people.) If we are doing small acts that are similar to our original plan e.g. helping a disabled person once a week, we may notice that we no longer desire to set up that Institute. Why? Because the quiet voice's grand plans are sometimes wild fantasies based on an unfulfilled need we have deep inside. It's a bit like when we are starving hungry - we fantasize about many different types of food or drinks, but when it finally comes time to eat we are too full to eat even half of what we fantasized about having. The same principle may apply to our quiet voice grand plans. Once we start feeding our deep needs, we may find that our original grand plans become sidelined. But we should never sell ourselves short, if our quiet voice really craves for us to set up an institution – then eventually, step by step – we'll get there. We just need keep asking the quiet voice what to do next, keep up the dialogue and keep listening.

Give it a Go!

Try taking one small step towards something that your quiet voice says to do.
Today I will try to take one step towards:

_____

I tried this exercise _____ times.
I would rate this exercise as:

1	2	3	4	5	6	7	8	9	10
(not so good)				(Average)					(Spot on)

Why Should I?

Life is not a spectator sport. Every person in this world has grand dreams, goals and wishes/resolutions for a better life. What between the winners and the losers, the achievers and the dreamers is ACTION (and persistence to keep on doing those actions.) If we have worked hard and taught ourselves how to access our deep wisdom then we are completely foolish to ignore its good advice, especially since we know deep down that its advice is perfect for us. It's like an alcoholic having a revelation that all of his problems are due to his addiction but not having the inner strength to do anything about it. Knowing HOW to solve our problems doesn't make them go away, just like knowing how to make a million dollars doesn't make us a millionaire. Only by going out there and putting our knowledge into practice do we start to accrue the benefits of that knowledge.

If we've gained some clarity in what we really would like to do with our lives, then we need to chase that dream, hunt it down, take hold of it with both hands and make it a reality. Losers are full of regrets, lost dreams and 'I should have, could have...' statements. Upbeat, happy people are full of the joy of living, trying (regardless of whether they succeed or not), and a can-do attitude.

Success is not achieved over night. Success also isn't always measured by achieving our original dream or goal – but success IS being able to make and appreciate the small steps needed in order to reach our goal. Success is when we get up from a fall and try again. Success is when we beat that part of ourselves that wants to give up and resign itself to mediocrity. Success is when we keep dreaming, hoping and planning for a better future (whilst simultaneously appreciating all that we have right now.)

So it's time to get up and go. Dust off those old dreams, reflect deeply on what you really want out of life and who you really want to be and take a step towards being a success TODAY. You might find that it will be the first of many steps leading you to a life of success and happiness.

Go on – Take your first steps towards achieving lost dreams - Give it a Go!

Day 4

Two are better than one

Now I'm going to take you on a journey to true bliss. On the journey, reflect and ask yourself "Is this true?" and if it is, then ask yourself, "What should be done with this information?" and wait to hear a quiet answer.

As with all cruises, they are best done whilst enjoying the company of people we like. The friends a person chooses, the work/school associates and the family which we have been born into (or marry into) all form a basis of whom we interact with regularly. They are often the ones who can cheer us up or conversely give us the biggest challenges to maintaining our equanimity.

So the first step in navigating towards a more blissful existence is to learn the ability to make good friends and keeping them.

Who is a good friend? Ask your quiet voice.

When on the journey of life, we need to have friends who will help us, be there for us, guide us, inspire us, encourage us and most of all - love us. Nothing great has been achieved alone. There is always a team of two or more. Ask any successful person, and they will say they were helped by others on the way.

Everybody needs a friend (or more) if we want to grow as a person and get the most out of our journey in life, if we want to grow as a person, we need friends to talk with, to help us, to grow with us. Friendship is based on sharing – sharing what we have with them, and their sharing with us. Friendship is based on love – loving them for who they are (not needing them to change in order to justify our love), and for them to love us for who we are (warts and all).

"I had heaps of friends; I was one of the most popular girls in my class. However, last year when a new girl came to class, she turned them all against me, and now nobody wants to talk to me."

True friends stick by us. They aren't our friend because of what we give them, or because everyone else is, or to gain social standing by being associated with us. True friends are attached to us with an invisible bond of love. They are the ones who will be there for us even when it is really inconvenient or embarrassing.

"I have a friend who gets herself into trouble, and waits to see if I'm going to bail her out."

A good friend is a giver not a taker. A good friend knows her worth. She knows that she is a likeable person. If a person puts themselves into a position of need, to test their friend, then this person doesn't really feel he/she is lovable. A person who doesn't honestly think they are lovable is incapable of loving – because we can only give to others what we own. If we don't own love (and the first love is self love), then we can't give it to anyone else.

"I don't know if I have a good friend."

As said earlier, everyone needs friends, and if we don't have suitable friends – then we can MAKE FRIENDS. This means helping our to-be friends by teaching them how to be a good friend and a good person. How do we do this? By choosing a person who looks like they have some qualities we admire. Befriending her (or him) and then teaching him/her to see their good qualities - point them out, compliment him/her etc... This way we will be building a friend for ourselves.

The best way to go through life is with a friend. And the best way to go through learning this book is with a friend. We can call up a friend and ask him/her if they want to do this with us. Each day we can speak on the telephone (or meet together) and go through the pages of the book. Each day we could read a different 'Day', talk about the ideas and do the Give it a Go! exercise. We could do the exercises together, grow together and be happy together.

Give it a Go!

1. Get quiet and ask yourself "Who would make a good lifelong friend?"

2. See if you can do this book together with a friend.

I tried this exercise _____ times.
I would rate this exercise as:

1	2	3	4	5	6	7	8	9	10
(not so good)				(Average)					(Spot on)

Why Should I?

Have you ever tried to diet, but just gave up - not because you didn't want to lose the weight, but because it was just too hard to keep up the momentum? Achieving true inner-happiness is like any type of change and is going to require persistence, dedication and determination. One of the BEST ways to keep up our great resolutions is to have a support group. In particular, it's a great idea to get together with a buddy or a friend and work on bettering ourselves and our levels of contentment. Two people are more powerful than one. Although one plus one normally equals two, when it comes to working on something together with another person, one plus one equals heaps more than two.

With a friend we are able to maintain our momentum to achieve our goals. We will have a person to discuss any difficulties or share any inspirations. We will catch our friend when he/she falls and he/she will catch us when we are falling. We can help each other, encourage each other, support each other and grow together – not just growing by achieving our goals, but we will grow as a person and our friendship will blossom and deepen as a result of sharing a common goal and experience.

So let's do ourselves a favour, call up a friend that we think will also want to work on maximizing their happiness and joy and see if we can do it together, it will be much more fun.

Go on – Enjoy doing this book with a friend – Give it a Go!

Day 5
Starting the Cruise

Before we start on the journey towards the City of Happiness together we need to make sure we're all looking at the same map, and all heading in the same direction.

- *"I think happiness is a state of complete euphoria, like living on cloud 9 constantly."*
- *"I think happiness is a quiet soft feeling of contentment."*
- *"I think happiness is the thrill of wild excitement running through your veins constantly."*

If we are aiming for a state called 'Happiness' we need to know what it is we think we are trying to achieve. This book will lead us along the path towards different types of feelings we categorise as happiness. But the ultimate goal is to reach a level of constant, continuous inner-bliss.

In order to reach this goal of inner-bliss we are going to be learning lots of new, exciting and interesting information and tools. This book is a full-on, hands-on happiness workbook. It's designed for people who seriously want to be happy. We will be able to attain mind-blowing levels of inner-peace, enthusiasm and zest for living by taking each day seriously and doing the Give it a Go! exercises.

In order to be willing to put in the effort, we must be clear that we want the results. So it's good to write down what we hope to achieve by reading the book. Think about it before we start, because that way we will become hyper-focused to head toward attaining this great level of bliss. Think about what Happiness means to you and how you could see your life as different if you lived with a feeling of happiness. The more we think about it, the clearer it will become to us that happiness is something we deeply desire and it's ours for the taking.

"If I lived in a state of happiness, I would be more patient, loving and kind to my children."

"I think one of the biggest benefits to me working on being happy is that I will have more friends."

"I want to be happier because I've had enough of getting depressed and wasting my life away."

There are areas of our lives that will start to shine when we are able to maintain a happy disposition. We all have the inner wisdom to know how much better our lives will be when we master the state of inner-bliss. Once we can see how our lives will improve as a result of working on increasing our levels of happiness, we will be excited and committed to learning this valuable skill.

You can do it! Your life will never be the same once you have tasted the sweet tranquil waters of bliss. So Come on – Let's Go – All Aboard – We're OFF!

Give it a Go!

1. What does Happiness mean to you?
   _____
   _____

2. Write down 3 ways your life would be different if you lived in a state of happiness.
   - _____
   - _____
   - _____

I tried this exercise _____ times.
I would rate this exercise as:

1	2	3	4	5	6	7	8	9	10
(not so good)				(Average)					(Spot on)

Why Should I?

The first exercise helps us gain clarity on what we want to achieve when we say we want to be happy. Sometimes we think we want something without even knowing what that 'something' is. This first exercise will help us work out what we think happiness is all about, and then we can start really shooting towards it. Also when we start defining what we believe happiness is we can assess whether we are trying to reach a real and attainable goal. For example if somebody thinks happiness is having 10 billion dollars, millions of admiring fans and enough time in their day to lie in bed for 18 hours. Then they will never reach happiness, because even if they reach their goals they will be disappointed to find out they still haven't acquired happiness.

When trying to define what happiness means to us, we would be wise to project into the future and think deeply. If we can envisage ourselves living our lives according to our definition and having a feeling of complete satisfaction and bliss – then our definition is probably a good one. Before we shoot for the stars, it's good to know which star we are trying to reach.

The second exercise is a great way to feel the power of happiness. It is there to focus us on how our lives would be different if we mastered living in the state of bliss.

It's great to dare to dream, because if the dream is vivid and desirable enough we will be fortified to keep striving until we make it a reality. When we are clear that happiness will transform our lives substantially we will have the determination and stamina needed to reach our goal.

If we can think of three tangible ways that improving our levels of happiness will enhance our lives, we will automatically start to focus on being happy and our lives will become better – without doing anything. It's an amazingly powerful tool. Just using our imagination to dream of a better life, sets the wheels in motion for us to have a better life.

When we've finished reading the book, it may be a good idea to revisit this day and see how much our lives have changed. We may be pleasantly surprised to discover that our lives have improved dramatically especially in the three ways we have identified in this exercise.

Go on – Start the Journey to the City of Happiness - Give it a Go!

SMELL EVERY ROSE

KEY #1- SEE THE GOOD
(THE SKELETON KEY THAT OPENS ALL DOORS)

PART 1 – SEEING THE GOOD BY
LEARNING THE ROPES

Introduction

In any book written about increasing one's levels of joy and happiness the first step is to learn how to see and focus on the good things in our lives. Since Happiness is a choice, we can choose to live happy lives by learning to see what's so good about life. We can train ourselves to see the cup as half full, not half empty and to see the silver lining behind every cloud. Accustoming ourselves to stop, notice, appreciate and even smell the roses, makes life more pleasant.

In any society around the world where we find people of elevated consciousness (e.g. Spiritual advisors and guides, guru's, mentors and life coaches etc.) we will find one consistent message – See and focus on the good things in life! This is the first and most important of the Ancient Keys to Happiness.

Seeing the good in everything is the skeleton key that opens all doors. Every block we have in our lives is due to not being able to see the good that lies within the situation. Once we learn the art of extracting the good from every experience, situation, person or interaction etc. we will find we are able to sail smoothly and happily through life – wherever life happens to lead us.

When we learn to see the good in our lives we learn to see a great world, we learn to have elevated levels of consciousness, we react with people and our environment more positively and we will become great people who are delightful to be around. We even develop the ability to be happy and content when everyone else around us is drowning in darkness and misery.   The more we can see good in our lives, the more we can start relating to the world through this prism and the more success and true bliss we will experience.

Day 6

First stop

The first stop in the journey of life towards bliss and happiness is to know how to recognise the goodness and sweetness that already exists in our lives. We all need to learn to smell the roses. If we have ever watched people smell roses we would have seen a person focus on the beauty of the flower, carefully position their nose and then take in a deep breath. We can also do this with life – we can focus on the good in our lives, carefully draw close to that goodness (whilst simultaneously being careful not to be pricked by the thorns of life), and then inhaling and enjoying the beauty of living.

There are some things in our lives that don't really look like roses on the outside. We have some situations that don't look 'pretty', but even then we can still learn to enjoy them. These situations are more like oysters than roses. Many things in life are like oysters, they may look hard and cold on the outside, disgusting and smelly on the inside, but in fact there are pearls of magnificent beauty contained within them. When we train ourselves to search for the pearls and cast aside the oyster, in every part of our lives we will be on the way to true happiness.

"The alarm went off. `Uhhhh.  7:30am Monday morning.  I hate Mondays. Maybe I'll just stay in bed a bit longer – maybe Monday is just a bad dream that will go away when I wake up again... 7:45am. Uhhh. It really is Monday!?' I dragged myself out of bed bemoaning my fate. `Why do I have to go to that horrible place every weekday?' On my wall was a picture, a deep sea ocean picture with colourful fish, coral and a few oysters. `Oysters', I thought , "what pearl is in this situation? I hate Mondays!' Then I started to think what life might be like if I couldn't get out of bed, or if I really didn't have a place to go on Mondays. Imagine if I was expelled from school, or fired from my job – then I would feel even worse. As I put my shoes on my feet, I thought, "I'm glad I've got shoes", then I thought ,"I'm glad I've got feet!" When I started thinking this I noticed my body didn't feel so heavy, and that getting ready was less of a

chore. When I started looking for the pearls in EVERYTHING that I did, I started to feel very wealthy."

———

"I can't imagine thinking `how lucky I am to have feet' would make me feel any better. Yeah - I've got feet - hurray! So? Everybody else also has feet and they're miserable. "

It's not what we've got, but how much we focus on enjoying what we have that will bring happiness. The whole aim of the 'happiness game' is to learn how to focus on the good and keep focused on the good. It is completely irrelevant whether other people also have what we have as to whether we are enjoying ourselves or not.

"I had been hanging out to get a triple decker ice-cream cone with chocolate syrup, cream and nuts on top. Every time I thought about it my mouth watered, and finally I arrived at the ice-cream parlour. I ordered my dream ice-cream and just as I went to give it my first lick an old friend that I hadn't seen for years came up to me and we started to chat, reminisce and enjoy each other's company. When it was time for us to bid each other farewell, I left the shop, only to realize that I had eaten my ice-cream all up, and I don't even remember doing it. Ahhh! I felt so frustrated, I had been waiting so long to savour the experience, and in a few minutes of not paying attention it was all gone. "

When we focus on what we have and appreciate it we instantly start to feel happy. The more intensely we can focus on the good things that we are currently enjoying, the happier we become. Conversely, when we get distracted and forget to focus on all the good we have, we have missed out on the opportunity of fully enjoying that moment of life.

"One day I decided to blindfold myself for half an hour. I walked around like this, trying to do what I normally do. One thing that really bothered me was that I couldn't see other people's faces. When another person smiles at me it makes such a difference to me. I only then started to really appreciate the gift of eyesight that I have."

Give it a Go!

Let's tune into seeing all the beautiful roses that are in our lives.
Try to sit down for 15 minutes and write down a list of all the good
things you have. These may fit into the following categories:
1) Physical – e.g. head, nose, mouth, clothes, shoes, car;
2) People – friends, family and acquaintances (past or present);
   and
3) Emotional – an appreciation of music, the ability to feel
   emotions such as love.

See if you can add 5 new ones to each of the categories each day for the
next week.

(If you are really brave – try putting the list in priority order e.g. friends
would come before shoes, head would come before car etc.)

I tried this exercise _____ times.
I would rate this exercise as:

1	2	3	4	5	6	7	8	9	10
(not so good)				(Average)				(Spot on)	

Why Should I?

This exercise is a training exercise to help us build up our positive
thinking muscle. If we can take time out to actually list, categorise and
or prioritise all of the good things we have in our lives, then for those 15
minutes we are working out and training ourselves to NOTICE the good
things.

The main skill in achieving happiness is to be able to consistently
maintain AWARENESS. This exercise enables us to become aware of our
blessings. The more we think about the great things we have in our
lives, the more we will appreciate them and the more positive we will
feel.

A person who does regular training exercises becomes a top notch, super
fit athlete. The more we can work at this exercise the more proficient we
will become and easier it will become for us to turn ourselves around
from being in a negative mood into being in a positive mood.

PART 1 – LEARNING THE ROPES

I have personally seen this exercise transform people from unhappy, negative worriers into up-beat, positive, successful people. Some really committed people have made journals and for YEARS done this exercise and as a result have had major personality and life changes for the better.

Another advantage of concentrating on the good in our lives is that we can actually INCREASE the amount of good in our lives by doing this. **Whatever we concentrate on happens more often.** This is particularly obvious when we are talking about interpersonal relationship. For example, if we want an employee to show more initiative – then all we need to do is wait for a time when he/she actually does show some initiative (even if it's only a very minute amount) and praise him/her, focus on how much we appreciate their initiative, how much we recognise this as a latent talent in them, how good it was for us and how much we appreciated their efforts. That employee will naturally start showing more initiative more often. The same applies with children. If we want our child to eat with their fork, then anytime they even (accidentally) touch their fork, we should NOTICE it, comment on it and praise them e.g. 'I see you have your fork in your hand – Well Done!'

The principle of: 'Concentrate on the good and the good will increase', also applies to other things in our lives. Just try it out and you'll see for yourself. The more we notice and appreciate how many material blessings we have the more they will increase. If we notice and appreciate those that we love then our love for them will increase. If we notice and appreciate the good in ourselves then that part will naturally begin to shine forth more.

(This principle works the opposite way around as well. The more we focus on the negative the more that will also increase. E.g. if we notice and comment on somebody's faults, or what's wrong with our life then things start to get worse. This is a great lesson to learn: Concentrate on the Good and Ignore the Bad – and we will have a great life!)

If we really want to upgrade our lives– then it is great to start by upgrading the way we view our lives. This exercise is guaranteed to make us more positive people and make the good in our lives increase.

Go on – Become a positive person today - Give it a Go!

Day 7

When Good goes Stale

"When I first get something new, I'm excited and I feel pleased and happy but the feeling doesn't last."

When we have something new our full attention is focused on the object. We look at it, we think about it, and how good it is in our eyes we also on some level believe that it is going to give us that illusive feeling of happiness and satisfaction that we are searching for. However, as the newness wears off, we tend to take our minds off how good it is. We start to see its imperfections and we start to realize that it isn't going to be that all-encompassing provider of joy that we hoped it would be. We do this over and over again – chasing around looking for something that will give us lasting happiness, only to discover in the end that lasting happiness only comes from within.

"I find that I have a great time when I meet new people, but after being with them a while, their charm just wears off."

We get used to things; it's the way we are made. If someone makes a beeping noise, at first it's noticeable and eventually it fades into background noise. All of our senses become dulled by a constant feeling. Who feels the pressure of air on our skin? Who hears the birds tweeting during the day? Who notices the old billboard that hasn't changed for a few months? Who can smell the distinct odour of their own home? We are desensitized to the world around us, and the only way to re-sensitize ourselves, is to make a conscious effort to remain focused and to tune into the good in our lives.

"When I want to appreciate my health, I think of a time last year when I had to go to hospital and how sick I felt."

Sadly sometimes the best way to re-sensitise ourselves to the good we have is to contrast it with times when we didn't have it. The saying 'you don't know what you've got until it's gone' can ring true. However, we are not doomed to under- appreciation, we can learn to appreciate.

How much effort goes into learning how to appreciate wine? People take wine appreciation courses, just to learn how to appreciate a simple beverage. Just like people who learn how to appreciate wine become wine connoisseurs, we can become LIFE Connoisseurs. People who are wine connoisseurs don't get bored of wine, in fact, the more they train themselves to enjoy it, and the more often they use this skill to enjoy it, the more they will be excited to taste another drop. We as Life Connoisseurs can learn to appreciate every experience, every possession, every relationship, just by making a conscious effort to focus on appreciating what we have whilst we are participating in enjoying it.

Give it a Go!

Pick one of the following:
1. An experience (e.g. eating an apple);
2. A possession (e.g. your bed); or
3. A relationship (e.g. your best friend)

and try and become a connoisseur of the thing you have chosen for a day.

For example, if you chose your bed. Notice how the blankets feel on your body. How the pillow holds your head at a perfect angle. How the sheets are crisp and smell fragrant. How the cotton sheet is smooth but airy, the blanket is warm and the doona looks fluffy and inviting. Etc...

I tried this exercise _____ times.
I would rate this exercise as:

1	2	3	4	5	6	7	8	9	10
(not so good)				(Average)					(Spot on)

Why Should I?

If we can notice something good in our lives in more detail or from a slightly different angle then an aura of 'newness' envelops what we are concentrating on and we start to really notice it.

Imagine if Coke advertised its products in the same way, with the same tunes, the same packaging and the same advertising angle – we would be so bored and tired of Coke, we would go out and buy something else, just for a change. But Coke doesn't advertise like that. If we analyse how it advertises the same product for years on end we'll find that it's with new tunes, new images, slightly new flavours, new packaging and always exciting messages for the next generation.

We can be better than Coke's top advertising executives, we can learn how to be LIFE's advertising guru. If we could take all the good things in our life and appreciate them on a deeper level then we will be living life to the fullest, experiencing its benefits more often and never getting tired or bored with living. With a bit of creativity we can turn our lives into one, new, exciting, upbeat adventure every day.

Wouldn't it be great if we could look at life through the eyes of an artist? – see all of the details, textures, shades, lighting etc... we would see a different world altogether. Let's try looking at a tree as through the eyes of an artist (or as a tree connoisseur), how would we start to draw it? What would we notice about the bark on the tree, the sap, the individual shape of each leaf etc...? There is no doubt that if we can develop our ability to see life through a detailed lens, appreciating life like a connoisseur, then we will experience a deeper pleasure in living than we have ever felt before. If we were to compare a wine connoisseur to an alcoholic, there is no doubt that the wine connoisseur enjoys wine thousands of times more than an alcoholic, despite not drinking even half as much wine.

If we can master the technique of being a connoisseur of life then we will be able to experience heightened levels of pleasure in our relationships, career and life. Simultaneously we will succeed in develop our creativity, 'out-of-the-box' thinking ability, and optimism, which will in turn transform us into highly successful, talented and happy people (and if we're in sales, we'll develop the ability to sell snow to the Eskimos!)

Why not learn to become a connoisseur of life? Let's enjoy life to the max. If we can try out this technique, we'll see that it will open our eyes to the beauty of a world that we've previously 'drank' but never fully appreciated.

Go on – Get a new lease on life - Give it a Go!

Day 8
It is all up to us.

No-one, no matter how well meaning they are, has the power to make us happy. Just like nobody can use our eyes and see for us, nobody can use our minds and create happiness within us.

"When someone gives me a present, or shows that they care for me, then I feel happy – this demonstrates that other people do make me happy."

It's not what others are doing to or for us that makes us feel happy, it is how we interpret what they are doing. If someone gave us five dollars to help buy a drink because they saw we were thirsty, we would feel cared for, loved and important enough for someone to notice us. If however, the same person threw the money at our feet, and gave us a disgusted look, we may have interpreted that as an insult, and if we did interpret it as an insult we would feel unimportant, burdensome to others and this would produce in us feelings of sadness. However, the objective fact is that someone gave us five dollars. It's not the money that made the good feeling but what it meant to us.

We can choose how we are going to interpret any situation. It depends on us whether we will see things in a good light or a bad light. In the example of the person throwing the money at us, we could choose to view it positively and in that case we could have thought – 'Oh this person really doesn't see my value – he thinks I'm a nothing, I know I'm a valuable person, it's a shame he's so blind to the real me, but even though he doesn't appreciate me, at least he was kind enough to give me five dollars, and that's fantastic – I can now have a drink.' Any situation can be viewed in a positive or negative way, it's up to us to decide how we are going to interpret what happens to us.

People can say or do things that make it easier for us to think happy uplifting thoughts, but essentially they are not the ones that make us happy.

"I was given a black crayon, I could choose to make a dark gloomy picture, or I could use the colour to make a pleasant warm picture. The crayon was a gift: what I chose to draw with it was my choice."

When we try and attribute bad motives into another's gift, we are turning a potential present of happiness into one of sadness – it's up to us.

"My mother gave me a dieting book! I knew I could be offended and think, she thinks I'm fat, ugly and worthless, but instead I chose to make this a happy moment and thought, "My mother cares so much about me, she cares about how I look. I know she loves me and I love her. She wouldn't have deliberately given me this present to make me feel bad; she did it because she thinks it will eventually bring me to a level of greater health and happiness."

We have so many people in our lives that care for us. However, they don't have the power or ability to make us happy. They may try hard to make us happy, but it doesn't matter what others do or say to us, in the long run we are the only ones that can create that state of bliss in our minds.

Give it a Go!

1. Reflect and ask yourself "Is there anyone in my life that I'm really waiting for to make me happy? *E.g. I thought I would be happy if I wasn't single, but now I'm married I still don't feel happy. I thought I would be happy if I quit my job, but now I'm self-employed, I'm still not happy. I thought I'd be happy if my children behaved themselves, but now they've grown up and left home, I'm still not happy. I thought I would be happy if my parents got off my back and stopped nagging me, but now I've left home, I'm still not happy.*
2. The next time we hear ourselves blaming someone (by either thinking or saying 'It's your/his/her fault'), resolve to stop, turn things around and ask "How can I see the good or positive side of this situation?"

I tried this exercise _____ times.
I would rate this exercise as:

1	2	3	4	5	6	7	8	9	10
(not so good)				(Average)				(Spot on)	

Why Should I?

This exercise is so empowering. When we realize that we are the only ones responsible to make ourselves happy, then we can give up waiting around for happiness. Happiness is at our doorstep. It's there within our reach, it's a power we possess. Nobody can give it to us and nobody can ever take it away from us once we have learned how to do it.

When we give up expecting others to change in order to make us happy, we start to make our own efforts, concentrating all of our powers inwards and effecting a change on ourselves – and that will bring us to happiness. We will also have better inter-personal relationships, because we will stop expecting others to provide us with the impossible. It is impossible for one person to MAKE another person happy. We can only do whatever is in our power to do things to please another person. However, happiness is a state of mind as is the ability to appreciate the things we have. Only we have the power to control our minds and make ourselves happy. Nobody else can do this for us – regardless of how hard they try.

When we stop expecting others to make us happy, we can start appreciating those people for WHO they are and the efforts they make to bring pleasure into our lives. Once we learn to appreciate people for who they are we will find our ability to love others naturally increases. Our interactions with others will become more positive and people will actually start to like us more. Not expecting others to provide us with happiness gives us charisma. It frees us from being 'enslaved' to others for the expectation of reward, and it makes us powerful, independent individuals.

So let's take control of our lives, free ourselves from the power others have over us and throw away any excuses that stand in our way of being happy. Our ticket to self empowerment is just one exercise away.

Go on – Take charge of your happiness today – Give it a Go!

Day 9
Living in the Real world

"I live in the real world. No rosy coloured glasses. It's no use trying to fool myself into wishing things were better – I see them as they are."

When we look at white polka dots on a black background, what do we see? White polka dots of course. Imagine somebody said they didn't see white polka dots they only saw black swirls – who would you say is viewing the picture properly? They are both correct, the picture is made up of the white dots and the black swirls in the background. In fact there are some people born with learning disabilities that make them see a book with the white of the paper at the foreground and the black writing as a background sea of black colour. Nobody would say these people are reading what is in front of them correctly. We live in a world of good things. The bad or dark parts of our lives are the swirls in the background that give definition and shape to those good things. Who is living in the real world? Those that only see the black swirls or those that see the good white polka dots?

When we live in the real world all of a sudden we begin to see big white polka dots of goodness all around us, and in each person we meet. Goodness exists, and to deny that it is there because we also see things that we don't like amounts to not living in reality. Another person might say, "Ugliness exists, and to deny it amounts to not living in reality." But we are not denying ugliness exists, we are just saying that if we have a choice about which we wish to concentrate on, it is better to choose to concentrate on the goodness, because this will make us happy. Concentrating on the black background swirls will make us miserable – it will make us so miserable that we won't even notice the white polka dots – and that is certainly not living in reality.

"I thought I was smart and perceptive if I could see through other people's veneer of respectability. Then I realised that I was even smarter and more perceptive if I could see past others' faults and find what was good and kind in them."

We can use our intelligence and perception to help us have a more miserable life, or we can use it to bring us unbelievable bliss - the choice is up to us. And we must know that we are making a choice. Even choosing not to choose is a choice. If we don't actively work on living in the real world of goodness, then we risk choosing by default or habit to live in the unreal world of misery.

Give it a Go!

Think about a problem you have in your life at the moment. Now try and see what goodness lies within this problem. See the problem as the black background and the goodness as the white polka dots.
e.g. My child has been in hospital for 3 days. The goodness I see in this is I've noticed so much kindness has been extended to me by so many people, I appreciate my child so much more and we have grown closer as a result of this incident.

I tried this exercise _____ times.
I would rate this exercise as:

1	2	3	4	5	6	7	8	9	10
(not so good)				(Average)					(Spot on)

Why Should I?

If we think happiness is an 'escape' from reality, then we'll play with the idea of being happy but won't seriously work on it. But happiness is not an escape - it is reality. Everything in life has goodness within it. Even the most trying, hard or painful circumstances have hidden benefits.

Living a happy life is possible. It's not escaping, it's really living it up. Imagine we met a slave and we explained to him about the lifestyle a rich free person can have. We might say to him 'you can wake up whenever you want, eat whatever delicacies you desire, you can buy whatever catches your fantasy, take 3 month vacations to beach side resorts where you play games and go swimming all day. All you need to do is run away from your master, get some lucky breaks and this could be your lifestyle'. In most cases the slave will not be able to hear our advice. He would think 'that's not living in reality, that's too far-fetched, I don't deserve that....' However, if the slave could appreciate that in fact such a lifestyle (or something similar to it) was within his reach, he would run away

TODAY. We are only motivated to aim towards a goal if we really think it is 'reality', achievable and desirable.

Happiness is desirable and it is achievable – even when we are burdened down by our problems. We can be smiling, happy, energetic and full of joy regardless of the circumstances of life. If we can deeply believe this, we will work, think, contemplate and open our eyes to see the goodness that is in EVERYTHING.

This exercise helps us see life in a different light. We are not doomed to always concentrate on the black swirls in our picture of life. We can choose to re-look, re-focus and re-see the life circumstances we have. We can choose to see the white polka dots of goodness that are hiding in our lives and we can bring that image to the forefront of our focus and thinking. Goodness is there and it is living in reality to notice it. Let's be brave enough to run away from being enslaved to viewing hardships 100% negatively. Let's break free and see the silver lining to every cloud in life.

Go on – Lighten up your life and expand your horizons - Give it a Go!

Day 10
The Energizer

"If I'm happy – I won't be motivated to achieve anything, I'll just sit around being happy with everything I have. If I feel discontented I'm motivate to strive and drive for a better future."

Happiness is not complacency. Happiness is energising. Happy people are more likely to have the self-confidence to keep going and pursuing their dreams. Negative people give up before they even start.

To some extent it is true that if we are hungry we will go looking for food. However, if we get to the point that we are starved we don't even have the energy to go to the refrigerator. A little hunger is good. A happy person can still be hungry. A happy person still has goals and ambitions – she/he is just more likely to attain them.

Sara and Jane both wanted to make it into a top university course. Sara was confident that if she put in the effort she would succeed. She told herself positive statements such as "You can do it", "Keep going, you're doing well", "Look how far you've come – almost there", "Life is great, I'm enjoying this journey." Jane on the other hand was a bit of a pessimist (she called herself a realist), she would say things to try and motivate herself like "You're so hopeless, you'll never get anywhere in life, if you don't try harder. Hurry up you lazy loafer! I hate studying, I hate school, and I can't wait 'till I leave this dumb place". Who do you think has the stamina to keep going? Who do you think will be able to go the distance and follow through with her goal, and who do you think will retire to bed with a blanket over her head to try and escape the battlefield of life?

"But speaking aggressively to myself works, it motivates me. It stops me being lazy and gets me up to move."

Negative motivation doesn't last the distance. It may work for a small amount of time, but it doesn't keep us going in the long run. And on top of that, negative motivation harms us and lowers our levels of self-esteem. Imagine if we had someone constantly yelling at us the way some people yell or speak to themselves – we would tell them to "Go Away! And leave me alone." So why do we sometimes do it to ourselves? We need to learn to speak to ourselves the way we would like a loving caring friend to speak to us e.g. *"Come on, you really should get up and do your homework. I know it's unpleasant, but you'll feel so good when it's done. It's no point avoiding it you're going to have to do it anyway, so let's do it now, and then we can have some fun."*

Give it a Go!

Stop and pause. It's time to pat ourselves on the back and motivate ourselves by using the kind and loving side of our personalities. We could say something like: *"Well done. I've been learning this book on happiness now for 10 days. I can see I've been persistent and dedicated in trying to reach my goal of attaining inner-happiness. I'm enjoying the process of becoming happier and I'm confident that I'll eventually reach a state of bliss. I'm going to keep going and I'm going to succeed."*
OR *"I'm proud of myself for sticking to the diet, I felt really tempted to have ice-cream and chips but I didn't. Well done for me! If I keep this up I'll feel healthier and have more energy."*

The more often we can pat ourselves on the back, the more motivated, happy and encouraged we will become.

I tried this exercise _____ times.
I would rate this exercise as:

1	2	3	4	5	6	7	8	9	10
(not so good)				(Average)					(Spot on)

Why Should I?

Thinking happy thoughts makes a person happy. It's as simple as that. The more we look at the good in our life, the happier we are. The happier we are the more energy we have, the more successful we are and the more patience we develop. Happiness is the answer to almost all of our problems. When we are happy we are more sociable, friendly and likeable. When we are happy our brains work better and we become smarter, more creative and successful. Have you ever noticed that when we are in a good mood how much easier EVERYTHING is? When we are happy chores take less time, the day doesn't drag, people seem much more friendly and even the sky looks more attractive.

One of the biggest challenges to happiness is when we think negative thoughts about ourselves, or call ourselves mean names. Self criticism can lead to depression.

This exercise gives us a feel for motivating ourselves with good and kind words. When we practice this regularly we will begin to feel great about ourselves and we will become highly motivated. Using a holistic happiness approach to motivating ourselves will bring us to levels of happiness that are higher than we've ever felt. We will also notice that we will become motivated and have the stamina to keep going with and achieving our goals.

There is a nursery rhyme 'Sticks and Stones may break my bones but names will never hurt me' – it is complete nonsense! It should be written 'Sticks and Stones may break my bones but names can completely destroy me.'

Many people with childhood scars are hurt mostly by what somebody SAID to them (or about them), more than what was DONE to them. It is an absolute fallacy if we think we are better off by motivating ourselves to achieve our goals with nasty comments, name calling and other negative motivational techniques. Using these negative techniques may mean that sometimes we will win the battle of achieving a specific short term goal, but we'll lose the war – we won't be able to maintain a happy motivated disposition if we continually put ourselves down. When we learn to positively motivate ourselves we will not only win the battle and achieve our short-term goals, but we will win the war and be an upbeat, motivated, energetic, ball of fire – LONG TERM.

It's time to practice being a positive, successful self-motivator. You'll appreciate this technique and love yourself forever if you learn how to do this well.

Go on – You can do it - Give it a Go!

Day 11

Conditional Contentment

Listen carefully to others talk and they will reveal what they think is standing in their way of achieving true fulfilment from life. E.g. "If I had a million dollars I would travel around the world". So the person really wants to travel, she thinks that travelling around the world will enrich her life and only the lack of a million dollars is what is standing in her way. But the lack of money is only an illusory obstacle in her way. If we were to ask her 'What's stopping you? – It doesn't cost a million dollars to go overseas'. She may discover that it wasn't a lack of money that deterred her from fulfilling her dreams. If we were to track down what she really wants by going deeper we could ask her "Why do you want to travel so much?" She might answer "Because I like meeting interesting people." If so, then instead of waiting for the few opportunities to go travelling she could work out how to meet interesting people today or every day. If we were to ask her "Why do you want to meet interesting people? " She might answer "Because it gives me insight into how different people think." So now we see that she really enjoys understanding the thinking patterns of different people. By asking her deeper and deeper questions she will eventually discover the main underlying desire that is driving this fantasy to travel around the world. Once she has discovered what is really driving her, she can follow her desires and dreams TODAY without the million dollars.

"If I had a million dollars I would buy all my relatives a new house and car." So he really wants to give something to his family members to make them happy. He doesn't have to wait to have a million dollars to do this he could buy them something he can afford that they will love, or give them some more of his time.

"If I had a million dollars, I'd quit my job and I would volunteer for meals on wheels to help the elderly and infirm." So she really wants to help the elderly and infirm. Why not volunteer on Sunday for 1 or 2 hours?

PART 1 – LEARNING THE ROPES

We all have layers of excuses for why we are not doing what we really want to do with our lives. We need to recognise that most of the time all obstacles are illusions and the things we are awaiting for us to be happy aren't going to bring us real happiness. Only honestly looking at what we want to get out of life and pursuing it – with NO excuses - will make us achieve our goal.

Everyone has excuses. What is your excuse, that's getting in the way of you living a great life?

Fill in the blank.
"When I've got _____ I'll be happy"

Now read carefully because it is really true that we all make excuses for why we are not happy.

Pauline was in a designer clothes shop. She saw a cute jacket, and she thought, "If I buy that, I'll look so good, people will admire me, they will think that I'm really something – that will make me happy." Now imagine she bought the jacket, it looked good on her, people admired her and for a few days she felt she was really "something". However, two months down the track the jacket doesn't do it for her. The jacket manufacturer is trying to sell the illusion of happiness, and Pauline was gullible enough to believe it. Before Pauline bought the jacket she was sure that she would be happy if she only had it. A few months later she realized it was just not true.

If Pauline was more in touch with what really makes her happy, she would have seen that she was expecting the jacket to give her a feeling of importance. Why should she wait to be able to afford the jacket to feel important? She could work on feeling important without the expense, and the results would be more long-lasting. Every person is important. We just need to get to know and appreciate ourselves more to realize how important we are.

We all have excuses for why we can't be happy and we all chase illusions thinking they will make us happy. We don't have to live this way. We can free ourselves from our conditional contentment and be determined to live a happy life today (even if we are lacking things that we think will make us happy.)

Give it a Go!

It's time to get quiet again and ask yourself:
1. "What would I really like to do with my life if I had all the money I needed?"

_____

_____

Analyse the answer, and try and work out what you are really searching for that you think will make you happy. Then ask yourself:

2. "What can I do now (given I don't have the money) to live my dream?"
Write down your answer(s):

_____

_____

_____

_____

_____

_____

I tried this exercise _____ times.
I would rate this exercise as:

1	2	3	4	5	6	7	8	9	10
(not so good)				(Average)				(Spot on)	

Why Should I?

Most people have excuses or blocks that hold them back from living life to the fullest. This exercise is aimed at getting past our 'I can't' excuses that we legitimately think stand in the way of us achieving our goals and being satisfied with our lives. A lot of people think they can only be happy if they have money, but there are plenty of people who have money, or a great relationship, or great kids, or a successful career and are still miserable. Happiness is not based on what we have.

When we can get in touch with what we really want to do with our lives (despite our lack of funds), we will start to discover that we actually do aim for more than a big bank balance. We have dreams and desires to be a certain type of person or to live a certain lifestyle. We can chase those dreams despite our lack of funds.

PART 1 – LEARNING THE ROPES

This exercise will open up our minds to alternative possibilities. It will make us into pro-active achievers. No longer will we be sitting around waiting for something or somebody else to come along and fix up our problems – we can live a life we love – with our problems!

All problems are really illusions. Problems are just there to see if we can maintain our drive and focus to keep forging ahead to achieve the type of life or goals we are working on. Problems are like hurdles to be joyfully jumped over, just as an Olympic track athlete jumps over his/her hurdles on the way to achieving gold. Imagine an athlete who refused to run when the starting gun went off because 'there are all of these hurdles in the way – if the officials just moved them out the way then I'll run, and I'll win the race'. We would laugh at such an athlete and we would say to him 'you fool, the only way you are going to win a gold medal in this hurdle race is to embrace the challenges, jump over them and sprint to the finishing line.'

The race of life is full of hurdles, don't let them stand in your way or let them scare you away from achieving your goals. Use this exercise to recognise these hurdles for what they really are (illusions in your way, preventing you from reaching your goals) and just go for it.

Go on – Jump every hurdle in life with Joy - Give it a Go!

Day 12

You owe it to yourself & others

Positive people make better friends, better spouses, better parents, better children, better workers, better bosses, and better human beings. If we don't want to be happy and upbeat for our own sake – do it for everyone else in humanity.

Would you prefer to be served by a miserable sales clerk or a happy one?

A miserable sales clerk is likely to be slow, mean and rude, whereas, a happy sales clerk enjoys her job, is pleasant, helpful and friendly. Happy people treat others better than depressed people.

When we are feeling depressed and we are focusing on the negative things in our lives, we tend to be grumpier and lash out at others more readily. Enjoying our own life is a great way to help everyone else enjoy their lives.

With most things in this world, the more we have of something and the less somebody else has of it, the better off we are. E.g. if we have lots of money and everyone else doesn't, then we can buy more things. With being happy and upbeat however this is not the case. The more others feel positive and joyful, the more this rubs off on us and actually helps us feel happier too. The happier we are, the more we interact with others in a way that makes it easier for them to be happier, in turn the more this helps us to be happy. It's a cycle. (Unfortunately misery is spread in the same cyclical way – unless someone makes a conscious effort to break the cycle.)

"I can't be happy, my mother always criticizes me and then even though I was in a good mood, the negative atmosphere in the home just gets me down."

It is really hard to maintain a positive outlook when we are surrounded by negative people, we will discuss how to deal with this more in the next sections. However, by just remaining firm in our resolve to be a positive, encouraging and a joyful person and behaving that way even when others don't, will have some positive effect on our environment. It rubs off, just keep persisting. People love happy people because deep down everyone wants to be happy and if they see that we are happy they will want to be near us - so some of our 'happy sparks" might lighten up their lives and warm their hearts.

Give it a Go!

Make a commitment to yourself that: "From today onwards I will walk on the path of trying to see and speak about the goodness in everyone and everything - past, present and future."

You may want to write out this declaration and post it on the fridge.

I tried this exercise _____ times.
I would rate this exercise as:

1	2	3	4	5	6	7	8	9	10
(not so good)				(Average)				(Spot on)	

Why Should I?

Making a commitment to work on a goal, strengthens our resolve, encourages us to keep trying to achieve it, keeps the goal at the forefront of our mind and ultimately helps lead to achieving our goal. If we can read out aloud our commitment statement every morning, we will find that throughout the day that statement will resound in our mind and it will encourage us towards our goal.

The idea of writing out a commitment statement (or a goal statement) is a great tool to help us succeed in life, we don't have to use the statement recommended above, we can feel the power of this exercise by adapting it to any goal. However, this book is a book to achieve the most exalted levels of inner contentment so making a commitment to this goal is one step on the way to achieving it.

In order to retrain our brain to think positively we need to practice frequently. This exercise helps us keep this goal in mind and to slowly develop into a positive person.

If we can write up a commitment to ourselves to see the good and resolve to read that commitment out loud every day for 2-3 months we will find that throughout the day we will naturally look for opportunities to look for the good in people and situations and this will increase our levels of happiness. We will achieve our goal and we may even find our levels of inner-bliss exceed our expectations.

Go on – commit yourself to at least 90 days of solidly focusing on your goal of happiness – Give it a Go!

Day 13
Making Good Better

What if we look in the mirror, and we don't exactly like what we see. Yes we can see our good points, but we can also see that we could be a lot better.

"I know I'm generally a nice person. I make an ok friend because I'm not mean or nasty. I don't go out of my way to hurt anyone's feelings. However, some days I'm not that nice. There are days where I really should wear a red warning sign around my neck telling others to "Stay away – I bite!" When I look at myself honestly like this, I know that I'm not really the kind of person I would like to have as a friend."

When we see things about us that we don't like, it's ok because we are not doomed to always be the type of person we are today. We can work on ourselves and become the type of person we want to be.

"I can't change. I was born like this, my mother was like this and I'll probably die like this."

There is a big secret to life, listen carefully and you will understand. Whenever we do or say anything it is because on some level of our consciousness we really WANT to do or say the thing. What makes our limbs move is a message sent from the head, the message says, "I want to move my leg" and my leg moves. Whatever we really want to do, (provided it is really possible) we will achieve. This means if we really want to change we will. The secret is learning how to want to do it.

"I don't want to change. It's too much bother – I'm comfortable being imperfect me."

When we think it's too much effort to do something that we KNOW will make us happy, then we are listening to that noisy inner voice. The quiet one says, "why not, I want to get the most out of life, I want to live life to my potential, I want to be the best me that I could ever be. This is my life, and I've only got one shot at it – I don't want to waste it." It takes effort to change. It takes effort to change a bed sheet, but the bed is more pleasant to sleep in. It takes effort to change our clothes, but the clean ones feel more respectable to wear. Everything in life takes an effort – the best thing about changing ourselves is that it gives us energy when we do it. When we can look back on what we used to be like and compare that to what we are like now, we feel good, energized, accomplished and satisfied.

"I had a bad day, I was in a bad mood and I snapped at everyone today. I alienated my friends and my dog won't even come near me! I want to change - I just don't know how."

There are days when we will feel low. This is the way we are made, we have ups and we have downs. We are like waves in the ocean – with high waves and low troughs. Accepting the fact that we are having a low day, and that we will have them in the future, helps us cope with them when they come because we won't be shocked that another low day has come. We can even learn how to prepare to handle these low days when they come. The best way of preparing for a low day is to plan ahead. Before we are feeling low, we need to ask ourselves, "How should I look after myself when I'm feeling low?" and listen to the quiet answers.

"I know when I feel low I get angry easily and I say nasty things for no good reason. So one day, when I was in a good mood, I imagined myself in an angry mood and then I floated above the angry mood, and I stopped myself saying something nasty. I replayed this image in my mind many times. When I did eventually hit a bad mood day, I found it so much easier to cope with – I floated above my angry mood and didn't say anything I regretted. I felt like I was just performing a play that I had rehearsed many times over – I was a star!"

Give it a Go!

Now it's time to dream a great dream. It is a dream of who you could really be. We call this person the 'Ultimate me'. The "ultimate me" is the type of person you envisage yourself as if you could dream what the best you would look like. What you really would like to be, how would you like to interact with life/people etc? How would you like your friends, family and associates to describe you? What would you like written on your tombstone, or said at your funeral?

Reflect and ask yourself, "What would the ultimate me look like?" Write it down, and keep it in a safe place. *E.g. The ultimate me would get up early every morning to see the sun rise and greet a fresh new day. I would smile readily, greet everyone warmly and be open and friendly. I would be giving and caring and everyone would know they could turn to me whenever they needed anything. I would give my children quality time with me every day and I would treat my wife like a princess...etc.*

I tried this exercise _____ times.
I would rate this exercise as:

1	2	3	4	5	6	7	8	9	10
(not so good)				(Average)					(Spot on)

Why Should I?

This exercise is one of the most powerful ones we could ever try. When we can paint a picture of ourselves in a way that makes us see all of our inherent capabilities, desires and dreams realized then we will know who it is that we are trying to become. If we have a goal that is tangible, able to be visualized and concrete we will have a desire to become like that image. Our desire will be so strong that we will charge towards that goal at top speed and steam roll anything that gets in our way.

When we can sit down and write out who it is that we would really like to be, what type of person we would like to become, what character traits we wished we could develop, then we will be able to envision a 'me' that we just love. The stronger this image is the more powerfully we will be affected. Because once we can see our 'ultimate me' we will instinctively, without really much effort on our behalf make choices, decisions and changes that enable us to make our vision a reality.

The power of this exercise is not going to be apparent straight away, but if we write down a detailed 'Ultimate Me' description and then look back on that piece of paper in 3 or even 6 months, we will be blown away by how much we have changed to become like that person we wished we were.

Go on – you'll never regret doing this one - Give it a Go!

SMELL EVERY ROSE

KEY #1- SEE THE GOOD
(THE SKELETON KEY THAT OPENS ALL DOORS)

PART 2 - SEEING THE GOOD IN OUR PAST

PART 2 – SEEING THE GOOD IN OUR PAST

Day 14

De Já Vu

Most people we see walking around on earth have emotional baggage. It might be hidden from our immediate view but if we look hard enough, or talk to enough people we will discover most of us carry around a heavy load of negativity based on past experiences. Life doesn't have to be that way. We can free ourselves of our emotional baggage. We can choose to just put the bag down and walk away. However, in order to be able to do this we might need to learn some techniques.

One technique with coping with pain in our past is to ignore it and know that it's now gone and nothing can change it so just get on with life. Each time a sad memory revisits our mind we can just say to ourselves 'that was the past, but now I choose to focus on happy thoughts', then think about things that make us happy.

At other times it may be better to use a technique of re-visiting the past and turn what was a very sad memory into just an unpleasant one, or even a neutral memory. The ability to re-visit the past is like opening up the emotional baggage we are carrying and throwing out some of the items in there or trading the items in for lighter ones.

"I've heard about re-writing my past; it sounded a bit unreal. After all I can't change what happened to me – so why try and fool myself?"

When we re-write our past, we aren't actually changing the facts of what has happened. We are however changing our interpretation of the facts. For example, imagine we see somebody walking into a shop and taking a few items off the shelf and then walking out. We may feel very upset with this thief, and may harbour resentment towards him (especially if it was our parents' or friend's shop). However if we found out 10 years later that the 'thief' was actually the shop's most important customer, who had been given permission to come and select a few items free of charge, our feelings towards him would change immediately. The facts are the same, but the emotion we feel based on this incident has changed.

"But what if new information regarding a person's hurtful behaviour doesn't come to light?"

Then we need to try and work out what information we overlooked in order to see the good in the person, even when she/he has done something hurtful.

"My life is good now. I have a loving family, a good job, and lots of friends. However, when I think about my past, I feel sad and angry. I was bullied a lot at school and made to feel like a complete nothing. I try to look at my life and think my past has gone, but it still drags me down."

In this example we can see the bullies in school for who they are – children! Children who were immature, insensitive and unaware of the horrific damage they were doing to the victim. Bullies are also usually extremely insecure people, who feel the need to show their control over others because they feel so out of control of themselves and their environment. Don't get this idea wrong – WE ARE NOT CONDONING THE BEHAVIOUR, we are just trying to see it in a way that shows the other side of this hurtful situation. When we see the other side we notice that these bullies were completely wrong in what they did, but they aren't the 100% embodiment of evil we used to think they were. In fact an important point to understand is; it was really that **they** had a problem (emotionally or psychologically) **not the victim**. If a baby would kick us we wouldn't feel any lingering emotional hurt towards the baby (even if the kick really hurt), because it's just a baby. When we see the bullies as big babies with problems, we can start to let go of the emotional scars. This realization is balm to our hurt emotions, and helps us move on in life.

When we revisit our past, we try to see how the hurtful situations were really due to the perpetrator making a mistake. Try to take the heat out of the hurt, by honestly attempting to understand his/her behaviour and seeing the perpetrator as a broken person with problems, but basically a good person.

Give it a Go

1. Think about someone who has hurt your feelings in the past. Now try and feel sorry for them. Feel sad that they have such bad character traits, are bitter, mean or insensitive to others. See this person for who they are: a person with problems, faults and failings. We can then feel happy that we don't suffer from such bad character faults. We can see the hurt they inflicted upon us as a reflection of their failings and not a reflection of who we are or of how valuable and lovable we are.
2. Next try and see the person who hurt you as a basically good person who doesn't see themselves as bad, wicked or horrible, but sees themselves as a decent human who occasionally makes mistakes. Try and see this person in the same way that they view themselves.

(A lot of people have issues with their parents. Some people may want to try seeing one of their parents as basically a person who wants to be good but because of various reasons has made many mistakes. Try and understand the situation from the parent's point of view, with his/her background and own set of rationalizations for the behaviour.)

I tried this exercise _____ times.
I would rate this exercise as:

1	2	3	4	5	6	7	8	9	10
(not so good)				(Average)				(Spot on)	

Why Should I?

Wouldn't we all love to get rid of unproductive hate, resentment and anger? Imagine being able to take all of our past hurt feelings and throwing them out the window. Imagine having the self confidence of knowing whatever anybody has done or said to us was no reflection on our value as a person. Imagine having the capacity to see the ugly faults of others and not feeling hatred for them but feeling bad or sad for them because they have such emotional problems which lead them to behave in such poor ways.

When a person doesn't treat us as well as we would like to be treated we have two choices. We can choose to be MAD. We could become full of anger, hatred, revenge, guilt, depression or any other reactive negative feeling. Or we can choose to be SAD for them. When we choose to be sad, we don't get caught up in negative emotions. The other person's behaviour remains external to us. It is like we are wearing an invisible coat of armour and anything unpleasant bounces off us. We choose not to internalize or accept the other person's negativity, instead we bounce it right back by thinking 'this negativity is a big problem – but it's their problem, not mine, I just have to make sure I do whatever I can to avoid it happening again.' And then we choose to be loving and caring by thinking 'It's a shame this person owns so much negativity, it must be hard for them. With a problem like that they'll find it so much harder than me to have real happiness and joy in their life.'

Choose to be Sad not Mad, because sad takes away the heavy baggage we are carrying. When we choose to be Mad it is like we take somebody else's heavy problems and carry them around on our back.

Another advantage of revisiting the past with a view of seeing it differently is that we may discover that we interpreted events completely incorrectly. We can be completely wrong about our judgments of people – why go around with negativity based on wrong information?

The second exercise helps us try to look at a situation from a totally different angle. This can be done by pretending we are the other person. Imagine if we could take off our head, place it on the ground and then pick up the head of the other person and place that on our shoulders. Then we would look at the world in a completely different way. If we are able to do this we would be able to come up with many rationalizations, excuses or good reasons for the person who hurt us acting the way they acted. This technique involves being able to imagine we think like the other person, understand all the facts from his/her point of view, have had a similar background, upbringing, mentality etc.... and then from their mindset, understanding why they felt they had to behave in the way they did. In some cases, we may discover that if we were them and in their situation we may have behaved the SAME way (or even worse).

By revisiting the past we are willing to admit that we could have got it all wrong. When we develop the humility to realize we make mistakes or don't understand things 100% then we start feeling more positive towards others. Also, when we see that we can make mistakes, then we are more forgiving of others who also make mistakes. There is no such thing as a perfect person, we all make mistakes – isn't that liberating to know? If we think people have to be perfect then we're going to feel pressured to always perform and we may get really down on ourselves when we don't behave so perfectly. However, if we know we're not perfect (but we're just trying to improve) then we can be happy with our progress and forgiving of our faults. Once we have learned how to forgive our own imperfections we will know how to forgive others also.

Just see life as it really is – people are imperfect – and that's great because now we don't have to try and live up to unrealistic expectations of perfection ourselves!

Doing this exercise will help us develop a more loving and objective view of our past. It will help us drop that emotional baggage and recognize that the baggage we were carrying was picked up by mistake and didn't really belong to us in the first place. This exercise will help us jump for joy, leap with laughter and fly with freedom away from old past problems.

Go on – Unburden yourself from old baggage - Give it a Go!

Day 15

I'm Fine

"I'm ok, I'm really fine," she said as you watched her bleeding all over the footpath. She started to limp off down the street. "Come on," I said as I ran after her with a bandage, "stop for a while. I'll bandage you up and then you can go on." "No, I'm really fine, nothing is wrong with me".

If we aren't willing to recognise that we are bleeding, then we are more likely to keep going in life until we fall down and pass out. There are signs that a person is in pain, they wince, they bleed, and they shake. There are signs that a person has been emotionally hurt, they get depressed, enter unhealthy relationships, and engage in self-destructive behaviour. Emotional hurts can only be bandaged if the person is big enough to admit – "Yes I hurt."

'I'm tough, nobody can get to me – I just don't let anyone close enough to do me damage."

Not letting others close is a sign that we are hurting. When a person has a broken hand, they won't let anyone hold their hand because it hurts. If we are avoiding having close friendships or relationships, we need to know it's time to recognise that we were hurt and to bandage the wound, so we can move on.

"My mother gave me up for adoption when I was a baby. My adoptive parents were loving and giving. I'm so lucky. However, I have problems with feeling lovable. Even though my biological parents never really knew me, they didn't know what I like, what I don't like and all of my kind and good qualities - I still feel that they abandoned me because I must be unlovable. I know this doesn't really make sense but I'm secretly scared that anyone I love will find something they don't like about me and leave me. I'm often trying to get others to prove they love me because of this fear."

When we recognise we have been hurt, and that we are carrying around the hurt, then we have taken the first step towards starting to heal the hurt. Once we know that we say or do things because we are afraid of being hurt again, then we can start challenging those unlovable and unworthy feelings we have.

"I have always been scared that I'll be abandoned. So when my daughter moved overseas, I thought, "Oh no, I've been abandoned again." I knew this fear was coming from a past hurt, so I knew that it was not a real fear. By recognising my hurt, I was able to tell the hurt voice that I wasn't going to let it rule my life and my relationship with my daughter. I make a big effort to ring and write to her regularly and I frequently tell myself that she loves me and hasn't abandoned me. By doing this I've managed to maintain a relationship that I would have severed had I not recognised my hurt and chosen to move on."

Give it a Go!

It's time to take a quick health check and see if we are fit and healthy or if we have some wounds that need to be dressed.
1. Do you find that you pull away from relationships, suffer from depression, self-destructive behaviour, putting up a front – being scared to be or show the real you? If the answer to this question is yes then you must be bleeding from an old wound.

Now let's bandage the wound, and the best way to do that is to be determined to turn the hurtful situation into a springboard for growth and positive change. Why suffer the pain of the past for no reason? Instead use the situation to your advantage and be determined to grow from it.
2. Ask yourself 'How can I use the difficulty or hurt I've suffered to help me become a better person?' Or 'What can I learn or how can I grow from the situation?'

I tried this exercise _____ times.
I would rate this exercise as:

1	2	3	4	5	6	7	8	9	10
(not so good)				(Average)					(Spot on)

Why Should I?

It's going to get us whether we like it or not. No matter where we run we cannot hide. We can pretend it doesn't exist, but deep down we know it's there. When we're lying in our bed we can just sense it. In fact we're so scared that we can't sleep, so we run for the cupboard and try to sleep there but it's so uncomfortable. So when we think the coast is clear we take a dive for the door to run away but we trip on our shoes and fall flat on our face. Someone hears us fall and they come running in and turn on the light. Only then do we see, there was no boogie monster – it was just a shadow of the night, it was nothing, it was all our imagination.

Refusing to recognise that we were hurt is like sitting in a darkroom thinking there is a boogie monster there with us – we will do really weird, uncomfortable or dangerous things just to avoid something that hurt in the past but right now it is NOT REAL. What has happened in our past has now gone, it is NOT likely to happen again (unless the SAME PERSON is likely to do it again – however this is not the situation we are discussing). We need to turn on the light, look at what we fear and see that it's no longer there, it's just a shadow, there is nothing to be worried about.

This exercise will free us from the bonds of destruction we have tied ourselves into. We are able to live lives of close relationships, trust, love, forgiveness and happiness. We just need to recognise that we are reacting to a painful situation in the past. Once we have that recognition we can take positive steps towards freeing ourselves from that pain.

The best way of reacting to a past hurt is to proactively decide to make the most of the situation. When we are working on growing and utilizing the hurt we've suffered to become a better person our fears of this painful situation recurring will fade away. If we can make the most of our challenges from the past we will be less afraid of challenges that may occur in the future.

This second exercise has two benefits. Firstly we become more optimistic and happy about what the future holds and secondly, we are not likely to engage in behaviours that lead to self-fulfilling cycles of pain and hurt. For example, we could use a past relationship hurt as a springboard to become a better person. We might try to brush up on our communication techniques, interpersonal skills or character traits or we might learn how to judge a potential partner's character more accurately. If we do this we will be more optimistic that the next relationship will work out – and it is more likely that the relationship will in fact be successful. However, if we have been hurt in the past and refuse to grow from it, instead we become fearful that it will happen again. If we become afraid to enter a close relationship because we might get hurt, then we are 100% guaranteed to get hurt, because we will pull away anytime things get too close (and pulling away hurts.) Our reaction to past pain - the pulling away from relationships in fact CAUSES us future pain. Running away from the boogie monster of past hurts only causes us to trip and fall (and really hurt ourselves.)

How we deal with our past hurts will decide how well we will be able to live in happiness in the future. If we can take every past hurtful experience and turn it into an opportunity to become a better person then we may even get to a point where we can look at that painful time in our lives and say: "That was the point in my life where everything changed and now I'm a much better person because of it."

Go on – Bandage up the old wounds - Give it a Go!

Day 16

Acceptance

It shouldn't be. That's not right. You can't do that. It's criminal I'm sure
It's not fair. That's not the way life's supposed to be - I shout & throw myself on the floor
I fight it, become bitter and full of anger and hate
I refuse to go forward, to start anew, to open another gate

But then I see that holding on tight to the pain that's locked inside
Doesn't help me get on with life and bid this unpleasant memory goodbye
I look to the future to gain my strength and to know that I can win
I can let go, move on, accept my pain and let my new life begin

I chose to accept the situation, and I know from it I shall grow
I'll use it to become more kind, compassionate and share with others what I know
I'll use the experience I've had to bring out the best in me
I'll use this hurdle in life to help push me higher than I ever thought I could be

I trust that this situation was sent here for my good
I trust that it was engineered to be just the way it should
I trust that in the future I'll be able to see and say
Without that hardship in my life I wouldn't be the person I am today

Regardless of the pain we have felt, and how completely wrong the perpetrator was, we need to let go. Let go of our previously held views of how life is supposed to be. Let go of all the hate, anger, guilt or other negative emotions. We need to let go - not so the other person 'gets away with it' - but because we need to let go of our hurt in order to begin to live, love and laugh again. If we refuse to let go, not only are we allowing this person to have damaged us in the past, but we are giving them the power to keep damaging us now and in our future. We don't want to be puppets and give our strings to another person. We need to take our strings back and choose to use them to make us dance! From now on we can choose to accept a painful situation, let go of the victim mentality and start to live.

Give it a Go!

1. Verbally accept and let go of a hurtful situation.
E.g. I accept that I was beaten up, I refuse to be a victim anymore. I know their behaviour is no reflection on me as a person; I'm a good, loveable and wonderful person. I accept that life doesn't appear fair, but that's ok, I'll still be able to become a great person not despite my pain, but because of it.
Or
'I accept that my best friend didn't make it to my birthday party, I'm hurt, but it's ok, I won't let it ruin our friendship.'
Or
'I accept that life doesn't have to be the way I want it to be. And I'm willing to go along with it and look for the positive side of a situation that I initially didn't want to accept'
2. Look for the good that lies within a situation that you want to reject and **take some action** to make the most of the moment. *E.g.' I wanted to sleep in this morning but the council were doing road works outside my home and they woke me up at 5am. I resolved not only to accept the situation but to make the most of it, so I went for a lovely, brisk morning walk, which I loved – it made me feel so invigorated.'*

I tried this exercise _____ times.
I would rate this exercise as:

1	2	3	4	5	6	7	8	9	10
(not so good)				(Average)					(Spot on)

Why Should I?

If we want to fly like a bird, feel light and free, have high levels of vitality and energy, then we need to learn how to let go of the past. When things in life happen to us and we think 'It shouldn't be like this', then we become stuck and weighed down in the situation. Let's challenge ourselves with questions like; 'Why shouldn't life be like this?' or 'Who said life has to be the way I imagined it should be?'

Not one person in this world is 100% in control of their lives. We may make certain decisions that will lead us down a certain path, but where we end up is never certain. It's like taking a bus. We might make all the right efforts to get on the right bus, at the right time etc. expecting to be at a certain destination by a certain time – but things don't always go as planned. There can be delays, breakdowns, miscommunications, emergencies – millions of things could 'go wrong'. Life is like getting on a bus, all we can do is try our hardest to be at the right bus stop at the right time, but the results of all our efforts are never guaranteed.

Imagine a man sitting on a bus that has broken down and there is no way he can get to his destination. He just has to wait until the repair department fix up the bus or give him an alternative one. He has two choices before him, either refuse to accept the situation or to whole heartedly accept the situation. If he doesn't accept the situation, he is likely to feel uptight, angry and impatient – these negative feeling will not help him reach his destination quicker. In fact, by the time he finally does get to his destination he will feel exhausted by the experience and he probably would not only have upset himself but also spread his anger and negativity to others. If however he chose to accept the situation and thought 'What can I do to make the best of the situation?', he would feel more calm, have clearer thinking and by the time he had reached his destination he probably would have made a few new friends or enjoyed the extra time to himself.

Refusing to accept the unpleasant things in our lives is a block to moving forward and is a huge obstacle in the way of our happiness. When we are able to walk through life with a high level of acceptance then we are usually happy. We can work on increasing our levels of acceptance and affirm to ourselves that the situation we are in is OK. In fact it is better than OK – it couldn't be better. Yes the unpleasant situation that we just experienced couldn't have been better for us. You may be laughing at such a statement, but it is true. Every situation we have in life is a chance to bring out something good, or some dormant talent we have.

Challenges and unpleasant situations are often where we can discover things about ourselves that we didn't know existed, or they can nurture good parts of us that make us grow into great people. An easy life isn't necessarily a good one.

A person who is plugged into a life support system has no pain of moving around, no pressure to go out to work or to perform well on any exams, popularity polls or beauty competitions. We could say in some respects he has a really easy life. He just lies there and everything is done for him.

But nobody thinks his life is a good life. Everybody would say it is a tragedy. It's not a lack of pain that makes life good. Pain is sometimes needed in order to achieve pleasurable things. For example it's painful to run around a basketball court with a small ball, jumping, huffing, puffing and working up a sweat – but it's so pleasurable to play a good game. So therefore if we have pain in our lives we can't erroneously conclude that it is bad.

Since we have such little control over our lives, all we can do is try to enjoy the ride as much as possible. We can try to use those painful moments as springboards to help us grow into better people and use them as opportunities for greatness. The only way we can utilize those painful moments well is to firstly ACCEPT the situation. Accept that it happened. Accept that we're not in control and life doesn't have to be the way we think it should be. Accept that it's not reflection of our self worth and accept that there is something that we can learn or gain from it. Acceptance doesn't mean lying on the ground and giving up. It's the opposite. It means getting up and doing something. Acceptance is understanding that the situation is given as an opportunity to take up the challenge.   Will we choose to grow from this challenge or will we choose to destroy ourselves with anger, hate, guilt, worry or bitterness?

Life is like a bus ride with lots of breakdowns on the way. How are we going to choose to react to those breakdowns?

This exercise releases all tension, anger and built-up frustration. It will enable us to move on and really enjoy life. The more we can utilize the exercise the happier we will become. If we become experts at acceptance, we will discover that so many things in life that used to bother us now don't. We will become more positive, loveable and inspiring people to be around.

Go on - Do yourself a favour – Give it a Go!

Day 17
Jail Break
You've got the power

We don't have to be prisoners of the past. We don't have to define ourselves the way others defined us. We also don't have to react in a way that is self-destructive, unproductive or shows we are expecting to be hurt again – we can break free of old habits, judgements and negative thinking.

We can work on loosening other people's holds on us. By allowing other people's definitions of who we are to determine our self definition is giving them power over us. We can take back control of our own lives and define ourselves according to who we really are and not by who others have told us we are.

"I was told that I was lazy and wouldn't achieve anything with my life. I believed the person who told me this, so I never followed through on things and I didn't set myself any goals that were a bit ambitious. I would excuse my failures by saying, 'I was just a born loser, no point trying too hard'. Then one day a friend of mine really needed some help, she had to have an emergency operation, and she needed someone to pack her bags, organise the health insurance claims and heaps of other things. I stepped in to help, I knew she had no one else that could do it for her. It required a lot of work and a lot of persistence especially dealing with the doctors and health care funds, but I did it. After the whole incident was over my friend said to me, 'You know you're a born organiser; you've got the drive, persistence and orderliness to handle the most daunting tasks.' This comment caused me to see myself in a different light. I wasn't lazy, hopeless or a complete failure, I just needed to learn to believe in myself and that I could make great things happen."

Every person has talents and abilities that can be used to become great. If we can't see the special gifts we have, it is because we haven't looked hard and honestly enough. We may have believed what someone said about us – but who said they're right? We don't have to be imprisoned by what other people think we can or can't do; we can break out of old self- definitions and start to see the real us.

"I once heard that when a circus comes to town, they don't cage the elephants, instead they anchor a large pole into the ground and then tie the elephant to a pole. It seems strange that a large pole would keep an elephant tied to the spot, after all an elephant could just wrap its trunk around the pole, uproot it and walk off. However, the elephant doesn't do this because when the elephant was very little, the circus trainers tied the baby elephant to a large pole that was cemented into the ground, it pulled, pushed and tried with all of its might to uproot the pole, but it had no success. The elephant concluded it just wasn't able to uproot the pole. As the elephant got bigger it still held on to the belief that it couldn't move the pole, so even though a grown elephant could easily uproot a large pole – it doesn't even try."

How often are we like the grown elephant, mistakenly believing that we don't have the strength, intelligence or other abilities to achieve things that we really could – if we weren't being held prisoner by our previously held views about our abilities?

Give it a Go!

From today onwards, try and look out for things you do or say that will prove to you that you are good at some things you previously thought you weren't good at. It is a great idea to buy yourself a notebook and write these small discoveries inside.

I tried this exercise _____ times.
I would rate this exercise as:

1	2	3	4	5	6	7	8	9	10
(not so good)				(Average)					(Spot on)

Why Should I?

We are not the people we think we are. We have so many talents and abilities that we don't even know exist. We are human beings, the most intelligent, enlightened and gifted creation on earth. Not only that, but each one of us is a unique individual – there is no other person in the world like us, who has our set of talents and can do all of the things we can do. We were all born with so much going right for us, with so many treasures and resources hidden inside. How much of our lives have we spent discovering these talents?

When we were children we were too immature to discover what we are good at. We based our entire self perception on the feedback of others. As we get older we may start to define ourselves a little bit beyond the input of others, but for the majority of people they stick to the old self definitions they were told as children. But we are not children any more, we have grown up, developed and changed. We should never stick with the same self identity that we had when we were children because it is guaranteed to be wrong.   As we grow we need to update our self definitions.

If someone said the word 'computer' in the 1970's what sort of image would pop to mind? Probably a huge building with many rooms full of enormous machines. If we were to say the word 'computer' today a totally different image pops to mind – maybe a small laptop, or a handheld device. Our self definitions also need to be updated. When we say our name and envision ourselves, what sort of images pop to mind? Are they the same images that we've had for the last 10 years? If so it's definitely time to update.

People are in a constant state of change. A one year old is beautiful, but if we come back to see him 10 years later and he is still doing the same things he was doing when he was one, we would say it is a tragedy. A 10 year old is beautiful, but if we come back in another 10 years when he is 20 years old and he is still doing the same things he was doing when he was 10 yrs old it would be a tragedy. What about if we know a 50 year old and don't see him for another 10 years when he's 60 years old and he's still doing exactly the same things he was doing 10 years ago, is it a tragedy? It might not appear so at first but it is a tragedy, because we are here in this world to grow, and life, with all of its experiences provides us with many opportunities to grow. If we don't use the experiences of life to grow – it's a tragedy.

The fact is that we all grow – we may not notice our growth because it is so incremental, but we are growing and changing just like a baby grows and changes. So if we are defining ourselves by who we used to be, our definition is going to be incorrect, because we are not factoring in our growth. We are different people compared to the person we were 5 years ago. We just need to look closely enough and we will see.

This exercise will help us keep updated on who we really are (and that will change constantly throughout our lifetime.)

If we can persist in writing down our previously unnoticed talents in a notebook, we will discover powers and talents within ourselves that we never knew existed. We'll have a totally different, updated and more positive self definition. We are powerful, we can do many things that we didn't know we could. We just need to believe we can do it. Once we believe we can do it, nothing can stand in the way of us achieving our goals.

Go on – Update your self definition- Give it a Go!

Day 18
Work it Out!

"I've tried to work it all out, to see it from their point of view, to forgive and to move on, but I really have a huge amount of hatred and resentment towards the person who hurt me."

Most people in this world are not mean horrible bullies who go out of their way to make another person's life miserable. Most of the time the people who have hurt or offended us don't even realize they have crushed us. One great way of removing resentment and hatred towards a person is to TELL THEM they hurt us and ask them to apologise. When we tell a person they have hurt us we need to do it in a way that gives them a chance to explain themselves and apologise.

When we've really tried our best to see the situation or other person in a better light but we just can't get past our hurt, resentment or anger, then this tool is very helpful. However, if we are just hormonal, uptight or always getting annoyed with people then we really need to work on ourselves more than we need to let everyone else know how miserable they make our lives. So assuming we have a generally positive attitude towards people and life, and we don't expect everyone we know to change in order to make us happy, then keep reading as this is a great way to remove emotional blocks.

There are five steps to take when approaching a person who has hurt us. These steps are designed to help achieve inner peace and peace with the person who hurt us.

5 steps to Lasting Peace:
Firstly, to get their defences down, explain that we like them (or care for them) and how we can see that they are basically a good and kind person. E.g. "You know I love you and I know you wouldn't purposely try to hurt my feelings."

Secondly, try to come up with a reasonable explanation or rationalization for their behaviour. Judge what they did in a favourable way. E.g. "I know you have been under a lot of stress lately."

Thirdly, say how YOU felt or interpreted what happened. Although the way the other person saw it may be different, that's not important. What we are trying to convey is how the situation affected us. They can't argue or persuade us that we didn't really feel that way. Also we need to try to use soft words and avoid an accusing tone of voice. For example a good way of doing this might be saying, "I felt so embarrassed and incompetent, when I thought you called me 'stupid' in front of my friends."

Fourthly apologise for any part we played in the situation (if any) e.g. "I'm sorry I called you a horrible name." (We don't need to get into details, or defend ourselves saying we were justified in what we said.)

Fifthly, offer a solution that what they can do now, e.g. a way they can save face, fix up the problem or just apologise. We should make sure our suggestion is SPECIFIC, reasonable and realistic e.g. We DON'T say, "I want you to prostrate yourself on the floor, crying copious tears and beg me for forgiveness." (even though that is what we really might want.) But we could say, "I would appreciate it if you would apologise" or "Let's just forget about the whole incident, but please promise me that you will never try to wilfully hurt me like that again" or "Could you please make an effort to compliment me at least once in front of my friends next time." We must always keep our eyes focused on the future by asking ourselves: 'What do we want the person to do NOW to fix up the problem?' It is no use moaning about the past, but it is very helpful to give clear, fair and reasonable requests that can be done now or sometime in the future.

"I don't need to get someone to apologise to me, it doesn't really affect me. I've got nothing against him, it's just that I can't be bothered with him anymore and I'm not going to talk to him again."

We shouldn't fool ourselves. We only cut off communication with another person if we have been hurt by them. If the person that hurt us is a close family member, or close friend, then it is normally much healthier for us to make up with them rather than ignore them.

Pretending that we aren't bothered, doesn't change the reality that we are truly upset. If we are merely pretending it doesn't bother us when it does, then it is eating us up inside and doing a lot of emotional damage to us, and this zaps our zest for living. It is better to face our problems and solve them, than to erroneously claim they don't affect us.

If however, we cut off a relationship because that person is likely IN THE FUTURE to continue hurting us and we can't do anything to change them or the situation – then that is different, and it might be best to avoid them. However in most cases before we cut anyone out of our lives we should first be kind and give them a chance to make amends.

Give it a Go!

Is there anybody that you are no longer on talking terms with, or who you harbour some resentment towards?

Ring/visit or talk to the person TODAY and try to re-establish the relationship (you may want to use the 5 steps to lasting peace mentioned above, if relevant.)

I tried this exercise _____ times.
I would rate this exercise as:

1	2	3	4	5	6	7	8	9	10
(not so good)				(Average)					(Spot on)

Why Should I?

Asking for forgiveness helps us let go of the hurt, it will take the sting out of our pain. Imagine a person who was humiliated by a teacher and 40 years later the memory still brings feelings of pain, anger and hurt. Then, all of a sudden they meet the teacher and explain to him/her that they still feel pain from the incident. In most cases the teacher will not remember the incident, but once being told about it will apologise. Once the person hears that apology, he/she will find that the pain is so much less. Getting an apology from the person who hurt us is a great way of freeing ourselves from the pain of the past. We can also use this tool to help free us from hurts we recently felt, by dealing with them straight away, speaking with the person and not letting a little thing blow up into a major resentment.

PART 2 – SEEING THE GOOD IN OUR PAST

There is another advantage to asking someone for forgiveness (or to fix up a wrong). Which is that we will hear their side of the story. In most cases when we hear them out, we will discover they aren't the embodiment of evil we thought they were. They just made a mistake. By hearing how this person interpreted the event, it becomes easier to see the situation more objectively.

Yet another advantage of approaching the person who hurt us is, we give them a chance to free themselves from their tendency to make that type of mistake again and from the guilt they may be feeling. Sometimes when people hurt us they are fully aware that they inflicted this suffering upon us, but they feel too uncomfortable or embarrassed to approach us to apologise. By approaching the person we give them the chance to make amends. And if the person didn't realize that they have hurt us they will become aware of how their actions affect others. This may help them become a more sensitive and better person.

If we approach others who have wronged us, we are giving them a positive message of 'you are a valuable and important person. I have faith in you and I will not give up on you. I see your goodness and I believe in you and your ability to make amends and grow from this situation.' In fact, when done with sensitivity and love, informing another person of their faults can be a great act of compassion and love to our fellow human being. Conversely when we refuse to approach a person who hurt us we are really believing and giving them the message of 'You are so hopeless, beyond help and unlovable, that I don't care enough to even let you know you hurt me. I'm going to take revenge against you by remaining coldly aloof.' Thinking and behaving in this fashion doesn't make us into elevated, happy individuals, instead it brings out the negative, resentful and lowly side of our personalities.

Doing this exercise will free us from our past hurts, remove built-up hatred, resentment or anger and help us develop into caring, forgiving, loving, self confident and assertive people.

Go on - enrich your life – Give it a Go!

Day 19

I Admit

"I was hurt terribly by my step-mother as I was growing up. Her constant criticism and unreasonable demands made me feel worthless. I know that she didn't really mean to hurt me, and I can see the good in her. In fact I've worked things out so well that it shouldn't bother me anymore."

Sometimes we can recognise that we've been hurt, and we can take steps not to let that hurt wreck our lives, we can even get to a stage that we can forgive the person who hurt us. But then we think that we shouldn't feel the hurt anymore. It's not true; it's ok to still feel the hurt.

"I just got off the phone with my cousin. I had told her that she caused me so much pain as we were growing up, but I wasn't going to let her poor behaviour towards me determine how I value myself. I wasn't going to let her control my future. I also told her that I forgive her even though what she did was wrong. She was shocked that I called, but I didn't feel intimidated. I spoke up and said what I had planned to say - I felt great, as though a burden had been taken off my shoulders. From now on I was never going to feel bad about what she did to me."

If we hide the hurt under a blanket of "I've worked it out and have forgiven them", when we really still feel the pain this can actually slow down our emotional healing process. It is ok to say, "I've worked it out, and have forgiven them. It was a really painful situation and now I'm moving on". However, forgiving a person doesn't necessarily make the past hurt disappear in a puff of smoke. The hurt may still be there, but now it's dealt with, the intensity of the pain will slowly dissipate. It is fantastic to get to a place where we can forgive and forget, however, this may take time. We need to be patient and loving with ourselves, accept the feelings we have as real and keep going knowing we will feel better and more positive as time goes on.

PART 2 – SEEING THE GOOD IN OUR PAST

Working out a problem and forgiving the other person is like putting a plaster cast on a broken bone. The bone doesn't heal automatically, it takes a little while.   The same applies to emotional injuries, sometimes the treatment just needs time to show results.

Give it a Go!

It's time to get quiet again. After you have forgiven a person for hurting you, feel the pain, don't tell yourself that it shouldn't hurt anymore, just relax and let yourself feel it. This will help you let go.

(Warning: this exercise may make you feel really down for a few days, but longer term you will find that you've reached heights of self-acceptance, self-love and happiness that you've never felt before.)

I tried this exercise _____ times.
I would rate this exercise as:

1	2	3	4	5	6	7	8	9	10
(not so good)				(Average)					(Spot on)

Why Should I?

This is the last active stage of letting go of emotional pain of the past. It is cleansing and revitalizing to get to a stage where we know in our heart that we have forgiven all those who have hurt us in the past. This last exercise helps us from blocking and halting the final healing stage. Forgiving hurts is not denying that it hurts or thinking it shouldn't hurt anymore. When we fight against hurt feelings that we have, rather than accepting that is the way we feel, it takes longer for the feeling to pass.

We are like policeman directing traffic down a one way street. If we stop the huge, smelly truck from passing through because we don't want it polluting our atmosphere, then we in effect cause the atmosphere to be polluted longer than if we had quickly accepted the fact there was a smelly truck there and waved it on as quickly as possible. Accepting our uncomfortable feelings and then moving on, rather than insisting they shouldn't exist, will cause the atmosphere of our mind to be more pleasant in a shorter amount of time.

Go on – speed up the healing process, forgive, don't deny the pain, and move on - Give it a Go!

Day 20

Forget It!

Once we have moved on from a hurtful situation it is very important not to go back and re-live the painful memories again and again. Re-living painful memories just zaps us of all our vitality, we don't have to live in the past we can live TODAY.

Our minds are a very powerful tool. We can use them to think about whatever we choose to think about. It is natural that unwanted thoughts will pop up into our heads, but the best way of dealing with them is to just move on and think of something different. It is counter-productive to re-hash old problems to try and work out why or how it happened etc... It is also counter-productive to 'fight' the negative thought by telling it 'you shouldn't be here, go away' because that just makes us think about it more.

If somebody told us not to think about green doors, what would be the first thing we would think about? Green doors, right? So trying NOT to think about something never works. The way we remain positive in our minds when negative thoughts come is to be very casual about it. Don't think 'I'm not going to think about that', but instead think 'What would I like to think about that makes me feel good?' and then re-direct our thinking to what we enjoy thinking about.

If a painful memory pops up, the best way of dealing with it is not to deny that it didn't hurt (or say it shouldn't hurt anymore), but instead say 'Yes, that was a painful moment in my life, but I have moved on now', and then think about the fantastic life we are living now. If we focus on bad memories we feel sad. We can choose to be happy by choosing to focus on all the good things in our life NOW!

When we first start learning to re-direct our thoughts to happy ones we may need to re-direct our negative thinking many times a day (or even many times an hour), but as we get used to thinking positively and not re-living sad memories we will find that we need to re-direct our thinking less and less.

Give it a Go!

This exercise is a life changer when done after all the previous exercises mentioned in this section.

1. Write down a list of happy thoughts, experiences or topics you enjoy thinking about.
2. From TODAY onwards (for the rest of your life), when sad/painful, worrisome or drag-me-down memories/thoughts pop up, gently and lovingly move your thoughts onto something more positive. *E.g. 'Yes that was painful, but now I'm going to think happy thoughts and think about the wonderful people that I love and who love me – I'll think about all the good qualities in my sister... she's kind, only just last week she..."*

I tried this exercise _____ times.
I would rate this exercise as:

1	2	3	4	5	6	7	8	9	10
(not so good)				(Average)					(Spot on)

Why Should I?

This is an exercise, which once mastered will enable us to be a master of happiness. Feelings of happiness and joy come from the thoughts we are currently thinking. If we master the ability to direct our minds away from negative thinking and into positive thinking then we can choose to be happy at any moment of the day.

Negative thoughts about the past, or unproductive worrying thoughts about the future are the main cause of needless misery. The past has gone, the future is an unknown illusion, the only time that matters is now, and now we can choose to make life a wonderful experience. Learning to redirect our thoughts will give us upgraded levels of happiness every day.

We might find this exercise really challenging to start with, but it will get much easier (even second nature) with practice. Initially however, in order to be able to do this exercise easily it's a good idea to write down a list of happy things we would like to think about. We could do this when we are in a good mood. Once we have an appealing, detailed list of happy topics we are armed and ready for action. The next time an attack of negative thinking comes, grab the list and start thinking about some of the happy things on the list. If the negative thoughts are too loud and are blasting out the happy ones, then we should try verbalizing (i.e. talking it out loudly) all the happy memories, dreams, experiences etc. that we want to think about.

Go on – Give yourself the gift of Happiness – Give it a Go!

SMELL EVERY ROSE

KEY #1- SEE THE GOOD
(THE SKELETON KEY THAT OPENS ALL DOORS)

PART 3 - SEEING THE GOOD IN PEOPLE

Day 21

Alternative Reality

"We fixed up the old wound that became infected, swollen and very painful. But what do we do about the little scratches that we receive today. How can we see them through the prism of goodness?"

Fixing up emotional wounds we suffer today is much easier to fix than the emotional wounds we suffered in the past. Firstly because the new painful incident hasn't had time to affect us and the way we view ourselves. Secondly, we can learn some quick 'first aid' tools that help us quickly deal with the emotional blow we've had and move on more quickly.

The first tool we can learn is to re-interpret the incident.

Imagine someone picks up a red block and stacks it on top of a blue block. How does that make us feel? Most people would say it makes no difference to how they are feeling. What if prior to placing the red block down the person says, "I'll give you $1million dollars if I put the red block on the blue block?" Now how do we feel? – Terrific! What if prior to putting the red block on the person says, "if the red block goes on the blue block it's proof that you are a valueless nobody?" How do we feel? – Possibly irritated or angry.

The actual act of placing the red block on the blue block was neutral, however, the way we FEEL about this neutral event depends on how we interpret what the event means to us. We are constantly interpreting the world around us, and judging how it affects us. Read carefully because this is a very important principle to know. We can challenge and change the way we interpret events and live a life filled with bliss.

"When someone dropped a cup on the floor I initially interpreted that meaning the person was a clumsy, irresponsible moron. Then I chose to re-interpret things in a more positive light. I thought – the person made a mistake, I also make mistakes, and they must feel embarrassed. When I

changed my interpretation of the event my emotions changed from being annoyed with her and wanting to scream at her, to feeling sorry for her and wanting to help her."

If we ask ourselves, "How can I view this (neutral) event in a way that makes me feel less negative"?

This may be by:
- Seeing it from the other person's perspective.
- See the other person is in pain, and their unkind treatment of us is actually just a symptom of their pain.
- Understand that another person's disapproval doesn't affect our value and worth
- Assume we don't have all of the facts, and there must be some good reason why this person did/said something we didn't like
- Possibly there was a communication problem, whereby we or they misunderstood what was trying to be conveyed
- Finding the humorous side to this whole incident.
- Putting it in perspective – how will we feel about this in 10 years time, or if the person died tomorrow.

Give it a Go!

Take one incident that happened to you today (e.g. someone stepped on your foot, you dropped a glass or someone bumped you etc.), and try and re-interpret the incident in a positive way. (If that's too hard, at least try and re-interpret it as neutral e.g. a person's foot was accidently stood on.) We can practice regularly saying to ourselves: 'I would like a more positive interpretation of that incident please.'

This is a great tool to practice and re-practice. The more we can practice it the better we will get, the quicker we will be able to re-interpret and the quicker we will heal from everyday emotional hurts.

I tried this exercise _____ times.
I would rate this exercise as:

1	2	3	4	5	6	7	8	9	10
(not so good)				(Average)				(Spot on)	

Why Should I?

Imagine all of the little things that we find annoying now eliciting a response of laughter. Imagine going from being uptight and grumpy to easy going and quick to smile. We can do it.

Our minds are the most powerful tool at our disposal, they helps us generate feelings of happiness or of sadness. When we learn how to use our minds to think laterally or think outside of the box of negativity that we are used to thinking in, then we start to enjoy almost all experiences in life.

Life happens! It's how we interpret what is happening around us that determines the emotional feelings we will have to those happenings. Nobody is forcing us to stick with the first thought or interpretation of events that pops into our minds. We are the master of our minds. We can choose to say to our mind "I would like a more positive interpretation of that one please!" It may require a little bit of creativity – but we are all creative. If we were creative enough to put a negative interpretation on a neutral event, then we are guaranteed to be creative enough to put a positive interpretation on it.

Sometimes our negative interpretations of events are purely born out of habit. For example if someone spilt water on the floor (a neutral event) and a person who grew up in a household where water being spilt on the floor meant being yelled at or given an angry glare, then they would initially interpret the spilling of the water negatively – because that's the way they were bought up. The fact is however, regardless of upbringing and habits we can choose to stop ourselves and say 'No, spilt water is not a negative event – I would like a more positive interpretation of that one please'. Making a conscious choice to think positively helps us retrain old bad habits and start to form some new good habits. It may be that with time the same person may see water being spilt on the floor and automatically think 'Great this is a good opportunity for me to clean that part of the kitchen floor.'

You have the power in your mind to turn your life into one big party. Start by learning the ability to re-interpret things.

Go on, you will love yourself for persisting in learning this tool – Give it a Go!

Day 22
Understanding Gobbly-gook

Have you ever noticed that people don't say what they really mean? We all do it. We might say something like, "Go away, get out of my face, I never want to see you again." But what we really mean is that we had a hard day and would like to have a little bit of time to ourselves. Or we might say, "This is the best ice-cream I've ever tasted", but what we mean is that we are really enjoying the ice-cream. The more emotionally charged we are the less likely that our words actually reflect what we mean. In fact the words said and the meaning expressed can be so different that it can be like we start speaking another language. A language where the words "You're obnoxious" needs to be translated into English to mean "I wish you could speak in a more refined way." Or "I hate you" could be translated to mean "my feelings were hurt."

If we were to look at every person that speaks to us as an alien from outer space, and in our mind we had to decode the real meaning of their words, we would actually have many more positive interactions with people. When a person criticises or condemns us we need to learn to translate their emotional outburst. Once we have translated it, we can respond to what they are REALLY trying to say, rather than reacting to their verbal onslaught.

"I've told you a thousand times, call me if you are running late. You're so irresponsible and you're grounded!"

We might hear the above statement as, "You're hopeless and irresponsible." And then we may feel unloved, misunderstood, persecuted and unfairly treated. But if we can remember to turn on our internal language translator and try and work out what the person is really trying to say. We may translate the statement to mean, "I was really worried about you, I love you and I was scared something bad happened to you."

Once we have translated the sentence our response would automatically be more productive. We might say, "I'm sorry Mum, I didn't mean to worry you so much. I know you were so worried because you love me. If I had known that it would have caused you so much distress I wouldn't have done it."

Sometimes the person that is firing verbal abuse at us doesn't even know what they are really trying to say. If we can learn the art of translating, then we can also help that person identify what is bothering them. Once the true problem is identified it is much easier to come up with a real solution to their gripe.

"You're always on the phone, and if you're not on the phone you're out."
(Translate: I feel unloved)

"Do you mean to say that you feel I don't make any time in my day to have a relationship with you."

"You're dead right; you don't care two hoots about me."
(Translate: I feel unloved and uncared for)

"It's not true that I don't care about you. What would you like me to do to show I care?"

"I want you to stay home every moment of the day and never talk on the phone."
(Translate: I really love you)

"You know I love you so much, and enjoy spending time with you, but that request is not reasonable. What about if I block out half an hour a day just to be with you. We can try it out for a few months to see if that'll help you feel the love I feel for you. Does that sound good?"

"I don't know, but I suppose it'll have to do; what other choice do I have?"
(Translate: sceptical but Yes)

(We don't need to worry if our translations are wrong – We will be able to tell from the other person's reaction if we are really off the mark, and we can re-translate to what might be correct. We just need to keep translating and not get sidetracked by the emotional language used.)

Give it a Go!

Ask a friend to tell you something in emotional language, and practice interpreting it into what he/she really means. Take turns.
Alternatively, you might try to replay and review in your mind a conversation you had with an emotional person, and then try and work out what they were really saying.

I tried this exercise _____ times.
I would rate this exercise as:

1	2	3	4	5	6	7	8	9	10
(not so good)				(Average)					(Spot on)

Why Should I?

Do you want to upgrade your relationships, have more friends and feel less drained by other people's emotional outbursts? If yes, then this is an exercise for you.

When we learn the skill to successfully translate what others are saying we learn how to be a composed, in-charge, level headed caring person. Translating helps us keep our emotions, sensitivities and self-esteem out of the picture, and instead concentrate on solving the problem, understanding the other person and acting in the most effective way possible for the situation.

If we find that we are often drained, exhausted and down after having to deal with emotional people, then we should take hold of this exercise and run with it until we feel we've mastered it. It's time to turn the tables on those who use emotionalism to try and influence us. We can take control of the interaction and our lives by becoming a master translator. Our lives will be more stress free and those that we interact with will love us more, because they will feel that we really care about them and can truly understand them. Everyone loves a person whom they feel understands and cares about them.

Go on - Turn a person whom you've previously had a hard time getting along with into a loving admirer - Give it a Go!

Day 23
Totally Unreasonable

"I tried translating what my friend wants from me, and she always wants things that are totally unreasonable. She wants me to be everything for her all of the time, I can't satisfy her needs – even if I had a thousand years."

After we have learned to translate what others are saying to us, we may discover that what they really want is not realistic, or is not what we are prepared or capable of giving. Recognising our own limitations, and accepting that we cannot ever make another person happy, we can only try to be kind and accommodating to the best of our abilities, helps us not feel resentful to those people who have unrealistic expectations of us.

"I have a brother who is never happy. I do his homework for him, I take him to the park, I play with him when he says he's bored, no matter how much time I give him he always wants me to do more. I used to get so frustrated with him, that I would spend weeks ignoring him because I couldn't handle the pressure I felt to be there for him. I knew this wasn't the best way to solve this problem so lately instead of trying to bend over backward to satisfy him, I thought I'll do whatever I can to a point that I don't feel resentful, and before I reached that resentful point I would say 'no' (nicely.) I would reassure him that I love him, but that I am not responsible for his happiness, I'm just here to help him when I can and at this moment I need to do something else, and I will help him again later. When I first said this I was expecting him to throw a big tantrum and he did, but over time, he has learned to trust that I do come back to him and that I really do love him. I think that by me taking a stand and setting limitations it has helped him much more than when I was stuck in the cycle of doing more, resenting and burning out."

Sometimes we have unreasonable expectations of ourselves. We expect ourselves to be perfect. We may not expect that we are perfect at everything but we might be striving to be perfect in certain areas of our lives.

"I knew I was capable of getting 100% on a maths exam, but when I got 89% I felt worthless. How could I do so badly? I had studied so much; I knew the work, what a failure I am in life."

It is very important to set goals. It is also important to have confidence that we can achieve our goals. But when we fall short of achieving our goals, we can still take pleasure in the bit that we did achieve. We can aim for perfection, and be pleased with whatever result we get. The key to being able to do this is to **value our effort, and take pleasure in the results**. If we only value results then we are setting ourselves up for misery. Nobody achieves perfect results all of the time. If we value that we tried our best, and feel satisfied that we gave it our all, then the results don't really matter. We couldn't have done better because we did our best; we need to accept that limitation. It doesn't mean that we shouldn't plan how we can do better in the future, or if we could have tried harder to try harder next time, we should. Being happy with where we are now, doesn't mean not going forward in the future. We need to pat ourselves on the back and say we tried out best and then just enjoy whatever results come our way. It's not results that really matter - it is the ability to consistently give it our best that makes us into a champion.

Give it a Go!

1. Ask yourself 'Do I feel disappointed with myself, because I am trying to live up to somebody else's unrealistic expectations of me?' If so, then refocus and appreciate who you are and what you do, even when it's not what others expect of you.

Even if you don't have anyone else making unrealistic expectations of you, try the next exercise – It'll help you tune into appreciating yourself - even when you're not perfect.

2. Set yourself a small task to do today then try to enjoy achieving even a small part of the goal - even if the results were not as great as you expected. (E.g. If you wanted to clean the whole house, but you only got to clean one room, then enjoy that room.)

I tried this exercise _____ times.
I would rate this exercise as:

1	2	3	4	5	6	7	8	9	10
(not so good)				(Average)				(Spot on)	

Why Should I?

Why be weighed down by our own, or other people's unrealistic demands? Let's appreciate ourselves for whom we are. We can learn to love ourselves, accept our limitations and see the good in everything that we do. There is a silver lining to every cloud, so even when we fail to achieve our goals there is always something good that we have done – we can feel pleasure from that small bit of success.

If we learn to concentrate on all the good things that we have done, we will have more energy to keep going and we will eventually achieve more, have more successful relationships and stop beating ourselves up for not being perfect. Accepting our limitations doesn't mean settling for second best or resigning ourselves to failure. It means accepting that we are not perfect, that we have limitations and working with who we really are. It also means not trying to be as perfect as somebody else we know who might easily be able to do what we struggle to do.

This exercise helps turn us around from enjoying the few seconds of achievement to learning to enjoy the whole process. Wouldn't it be great if we could enjoy working towards our goals as much as we enjoy that momentary pleasure that comes when we finally achieve them? When we learn to enjoy the process, see everything we do as a major achievement, see every step along the way as significant and good, then we will have a joyous life – even if we fail to reach our goal.

Life is a process, not a goal. A person is a work in progress not a finished product. So we can enjoy life – every day, and love ourselves even when we don't measure up to those unrealistic demands of others (or ourselves.)

This exercise will show us how we can be happy, accepting and successful when we may have previously thought we were a failure.

Go on – Feel like a success every day - Give it a Go!

Day 24
All Good

Have you ever asked a group of people, "Do you think you are basically a good person or a wicked person?" All jokes aside, almost everyone in this world will say they are good.

If we'd asked one of the 9/11 bombers before his death if he was a good person he would have answered, "Sure. I'm such a good person, I would even give up my life to fight for my cause and rid the world of Western decadence."

If we'd asked a murderer if he was basically a good person he would say something like, "I've done some bad things, but deep down I'm a good person; when I murdered the person he really deserved it."

How can it be that people who are the worst of all humanity think they are good?

There is a basic human need for a person to look at themselves as good or ok. People will do all kinds of things that damage others and justify their behaviour, because they need to maintain this feeling of being good. It is healthy to think we are good, because if we give up on ourselves we plummet into the depths of despair. So we need to be good, but the question to ask is, "Are we really going to be good or just fool ourselves that we are good?"

When we are calling ourselves good – how do we know for sure we're right? If we just do whatever we feel like, without thinking whether it is objectively a good way to behave, then we will naturally think we are doing well and that we are good, when in fact we are causing others a lot of hurt and pain.

If the 9/11 bomber stopped to ask himself, "Is this really the best way to bring goodness into the world?", if he was really honest and had listened to his quiet voice, not the rationalizing noisy voice, then he would have heard the answer, "no."

To make sure that we are good and kind we need to run things past our deep inner wisdom – especially when we think we are justified in hurting another person (for their own good of course).

Give it a Go!

1. Think about a time when you hurt another person's feelings and you thought, "It's not my fault, they deserved it or it had to be done that way."
2. Then ask yourself, "How could I do it better next time?"

I tried this exercise _____ times.
I would rate this exercise as:

1	2	3	4	5	6	7	8	9	10
(not so good)				(Average)					(Spot on)

Why Should I?

We all want to be good in our own eyes, the need is so deep and ingrained that we are even willing to deceive ourselves into thinking we are good. However, this self deception eats away at our inner happiness and distorts our ability to truly see what is good. We also all have a quiet reflective part of us that knows the truth, it knows whether we are fooling ourselves or not. In order to get the most out of life we need to believe without any self-deceptions that we are good. We have to be able to tangibly see our goodness, and work on increasing that part of us.

This exercise is designed to help us take a look in the mirror, with honest eyes. We don't need to be afraid that we'll see something that we don't like, because being able to see our self-delusions is fantastic. Imagine we have a super-fast computer that all of a sudden started processing things at a snail's pace. We do a systems check and we're thrilled to find a virus. Now we have a quick and easy solution to our computer problem – we delete the virus. Our computer is now running like a slick, brand new machine. Finding a self-delusion is like finally finding a virus. Once we've found it we'll be able to get rid of it and once it's gone we'll feel the energy and vitality return to our whole being. Finding out that we have made mistakes gives us an opportunity to make amends, resolve not to do it again and move on to a better life. There's no need to get down on ourselves even if we find out that most of our life was a mistake. Be happy, because it means the rest of our life will not be.

There are two types of guilt. Disempowering guilt which is where a person feels that he is bad, hopeless or incorrigible and that his actions were so disgusting and unforgivable that he is completely paralysed and depressed. A person who feels this type of guilt will repeat his mistake over and over and over again because he views himself as so bad that there is no way he could behave better. This type of guilt takes away our ability to get back up and keep going. The second type of guilt is empowering and we call this 'regret'. Regret is the feeling that 'I'm such a good person, yet what I did was so stupid. How could have I acted that way, I wish I never lowered myself like that'. A person who feels regret is more likely not to repeat his mistakes because he sees that he's too good to make such foolish mistakes.

The second part of this exercise helps us not to wallow in the guilt of making a mistake. It helps us learn how to move on. The exercise suggests visualizing ourselves doing better next time. By doing this, it is like we are re-writing history because we are thinking of how we wished we could have acted and that visualization is stored in our memory, as if we had really done it. The next time we are faced with a similar situation we will think about our positive and successful visualization and those thoughts will give us the power to act the way we want to act.

Thinking positively leads to doing positive things. So too, thinking how we wished we would have behaved lead to actually behaving that way in the future. The power of this type of visualization is enormous. The more we can practise visualizing ourselves doing things right – the more often we'll do it the way we planned. The amazing power of this tool will only be felt by giving it a go.

Self-delusions drain our ability to see the good in ourselves. By opening our eyes to our self-delusions we will find it to be invigorating, energizing, and it will help us to be the type of person we really want to be. Once we are living our lives as the person we want to be, we will see endless amounts of good in ourselves and others. In order to see the beauty in an old silver goblet we need to polish it and remove the impurities. In order to see the beauty in ourselves, all we need to do is look in the mirror, wipe off the rationalizations and self delusions, and we will shine like we've never shone before.

Don't be afraid, you are really beautiful and good- just wipe off the cobwebs and take a good look.

Go on –See your rationalizations for what they are - Give it a Go!

Day 25

Judging Good People

We like to view ourselves as basically good, although we make mistakes. In fact everybody likes to see themselves as basically good although they make some mistakes. However, when we bear the brunt of the other person's mistake, it's very hard for us to see that he's basically good and that he only made a mistake. When someone else hurts us, we can be quite sure the person actually felt justified – and the painful effect it had on us wasn't even taken into account or the person thought their goal was worth our pain.

Daughter: *"I was running a bit late for school this morning and when Mum saw me. I knew she was in a foul mood. She called me names, screamed and yelled and then locked herself in her room so no one could talk to her. She's always screaming at me, I've had enough, so I packed my bags and walked out to stay at my friends for a night. She's never treated me well, she doesn't treat anyone well, I hate her. I'm never going to treat my kids like that."*

Mother: *"I was feeling so depressed this morning, my husband left me, I was fired from my job two months ago and I can't find another one. My daughter has been so disrespectful and unsupportive. This morning I got up in a particularly bad mood and I saw her eating breakfast at the computer when she should have already left for school. I told her in no uncertain terms that she needs to pull up her socks and be more responsible. She's such a brat - she screamed at me, packed her bags and said she can't stand being in the same house as me – now she's abandoned me too. I know I've got a bit of temper, but if people treated me better they would see I'm actually a nice person."*

If we try and look past the pain that the other person caused us and see them as basically good but with some blemished parts it helps us remain calm in the face of insults.

Daughter: *"Mum was in a bad mood this morning. Sure I've been a bit temperamental myself lately. I know she had a really hard time recently and her self-esteem has taken such a beating – that's enough to make anyone depressed. When she yelled at me this morning she only wanted to teach me to be more responsible, she just had a very bad way of teaching me. I know she was yelled at as a child, so she's probably never learned to express her feelings of frustration in a nicer way. Mum probably thinks it's her motherly duty to yell at me – she probably thinks that's the way to teach her children to be more responsible. Although I don't like the way my mother treats me, and at times I find it too much to take, (I really should ask her permission to go and stay somewhere else) – I still love her and I see she's doing the best job as a mother that she knows how."*

Mother *"My daughter's going through adolescence and it's not easy. She's got hormones all over the place, giving her mood swings. She's trying to work out who she really is and who she isn't and she's probably having some problems on the social scene – as almost all teenagers do. I know I shouldn't take it out on her, but she's the only one I've got in the whole world. I love my daughter, I know she'll calm down and come back. I might ring up the school to see if she's ok."*

Give it a Go!

Think of someone who annoyed you today (or hurt your feelings.) Now try to;
1. see things from the other person's point of view,
2. see them as basically a good person who made a mistake; and
3. focus on their virtues

I tried this exercise _____ times.
I would rate this exercise as:

1	2	3	4	5	6	7	8	9	10
(not so good)				(Average)					(Spot on)

Why Should I?

We have learned in a previous exercise how to go back into our past and re-interpret what happened (Day 14). This exercise is similar except it is a tool for us to use now and today. We can take away our feelings of anger or hurt, and replace them with understanding and love.

This exercise will help us sail through our day. We will always be on the lookout for some positive spin on why someone did/didn't do something that we didn't like. When we train our mind to lovingly accept other people and all their foibles we'll have joyous interpersonal interactions with all the people in our life.

This exercise is particularly good for those who are married or living with others. Often when we live in close proximity to others we get annoyed with them about minor things. Maybe they throw their clothes on the floor, maybe they squeeze the toothpaste from the top, maybe they burp really loudly, whatever it is, there are some things that just get on our nerves. However, if we can develop the ability to see things from the other person's point of view, love them despite their faults and focus on their virtues, we will find that our annoyance or anger quickly disappears. Developing our ability to do this is the beginning to actually feeling unconditional love for others.

Everybody has faults but everybody's essence is good and loveable. Looking past the annoying parts of a person and concentrating on those good, likeable things will bring more positivity and joy into our lives.

This exercise will help us improve our frustration tolerance levels, learn to love unconditionally, see everyone in a positive light, and feel more relaxed and loving towards others

Go on – Feel more loving and accepting - Give it a Go!

Day 26

Speak it Out

Once we have started to train ourselves to see the good things in life, then it's time to start speaking about them. There is an expression, "You are what you eat." A greater truism is that "You are what you speak." A person naturally speaks about topics that interest them. For example if you are involved in a theatrical performance and you are excited about it then you talk about it to everyone you meet.

Speaking something out also helps internalise it. If we wanted to try and remember our times tables in primary school then we recited them out loud. If we want to psyche ourselves up before competing in a competition we might say, "I'm going to win, I'm the best, etc". So if we want to really start to feel all the wonderful things in our life that we have just started noticing – then we need to talk about it. And if nobody is willing to listen – then we can tell ourselves.

"I walked inside after a day at school and Mum asked the usual question, "How was your day?" I was just about to give my usual answer "good", but I chose to use the moment as an opportunity to express some of the good things that happened to me. I told her "Fantastic! I got an "A" on my exam. Most of my friends liked my new hairstyle. Molly shared her chips with me at lunch-time, and I saw the most beautiful bird in a tree on the way home."

"I was sitting down enjoying my lunch, and I commented to my best friend, "This sandwich is great, look the bread is so soft, it looks like it came fresh out of the oven 1 hour ago, and the salad inside is so delicious and crisp."

———

"If I talked like that everyone will think I'm weird, they will make fun of me and they will avoid me"

When we start speaking positively maybe some of our friends may poke fun at us –to start with. But that's okay; they will still like us, in fact they will like us even more than before and they will get used to our new ways. When we speak positively about things, and we are genuine about it, then people will appreciate it, and they will actually appreciate us. We will find that we will start attracting people to ourselves, because people are attracted to positive people. The trick is that it has to be genuine. We have to use our own words, and express things that we notice and emotionally feel are positive. If we say in a dreary voice, "Oh isn't it a nice day", then it will come across as fake, and it won't have the desired effect of lifting our mood (and the side benefit of lifting the mood of others). So let's try to focus all our powers of concentration on the great things in our lives and we will find naturally that we will want to share our life and positivity with others.

Give it a Go!

Try and have an ALL positive conversation with your friend. This is a conversation where you don't say anything negative, where you don't run anybody down, complain about anything, or even express a mild level of dislike either in speech or in your facial expression. Get out a timer and see how long you can do it for, or if you prefer, make it a competition - whoever can last the longest wins.

I tried this exercise _____ times.
I would rate this exercise as:

1	2	3	4	5	6	7	8	9	10
(not so good)				(Average)					(Spot on)

Why Should I?

There is a great power in this world that is often underutilized if not ignored by most people, and that is the power of verbalization. Speech is a gift given to mankind and it is a major factor that differentiates a human being from an animal. A bird can fly, a fish can swim and the unique power of the human is to speak. Speech turns potential into actuality, a thought into a word, an abstract thing into a concrete reality.

When we speak about something our emotions are affected. If we speak inspiring words we inspire ourselves and others, if we speak encouraging words we encourage ourselves and others. Conversely, if we speak negative, destructive, hateful or angry words we affect ourselves and others to be more negative, destructive etc...

Are we serious about upgrading our lives, reaching our goals or changing our character traits? If so we need to talk about it and keep talking about it until we see it done.

The power of speech is so great, that the little we have written so far is just the tip of the iceberg. We can harness this power, we can use it for our own good. We can use the power of speech to make ourselves feel great, to motivate ourselves to achieve our goals or to influence others to share our visions.

This exercise helps us use positive speech to feel more positive, happy and joyful. But the power of speech is much more far ranging than just this exercise.

We can use the power of verbalization to;
- gain clarity on issues by asking ourselves questions and verbally giving answers to them,
- achieve our dreams by speaking about what we wished we could do and how we plan to do it,
- give ourselves a pep talk before a job interview or major client appointment etc.
  (We don't even need to have someone to listen to us – but it is more effective if we do).

So let's learn to harness the power of positive verbalization. This exercise ALONE will make us into positive people and it'll make us and anyone we interact with feel great! Some people have found this exercise so powerful that they have made it a way of life – they never speak negatively (unless there is a positive reason to do so).

Go on – see how you can transform your life – Give it a Go!

Day 27

You're doing a great job!

"You did it," "Your picture is so creative," "You've got a great hairstyle," "You got an "A"," "You're so smart," "I love your smile." These are great ways to give someone a compliment.

People need praise and compliments just like a flower needs sunlight. Without sunlight a flower will wither and die rather than bud and bloom. Everybody we know likes to be told when they are looking good or doing things well.

"I don't like it when people compliment me – I just wish they would be quiet!"

If a person doesn't like to be complimented it is usually because they feel they don't deserve it. If we tell someone who gave us five cents that he is the most generous and philanthropic person in this whole world, the compliment wouldn't be received well. Both of us know that it's not true.

If we want a person to accept our compliment it must be specific and honest enough for them to say, 'Yeah, you're right.' So if we say to the person who gave us five cents , "You saw I was short five cents and you took the trouble to help me out, you're kind. Thank you." In this example we simply stated what the person did, and gave it a positive label. That type of compliment is more likely to be accepted because it was specific, pointing out what was done and showing the other person how what they did was good.

"I know someone, who whenever I compliment her, no matter how honestly I do it, she says it's not true."

Some people don't see themselves as very good or loveable. When we meet people with such low self-esteem, it is a great kindness for us to compliment them and help them see the good points in them, especially since they don't see them. When complimenting a person with low self-esteem, we need to start off small and eventually as they see themselves in a better light we can compliment them more. The same principle applies: be very specific. However instead of labelling we can say how it made us feel – then she can't argue with it. E.g. "I liked how you shared your lunch with the girl who forgot hers, it makes me feel so happy when I see people being kind to each other."

When we notice something good in another person, if we can turn it into a compliment we are reinforcing our own happy upbeat way of living, and we are often helping the person we are complimenting to see beautiful parts of their personality that they never knew existed.

Give it a Go!

Think of someone who would really benefit from an honest compliment. Plan in advance what you could say that will hit the spot and make them think, "Yeah, I am good."

I tried this exercise _____ times.
I would rate this exercise as:

1	2	3	4	5	6	7	8	9	10
(not so good)				(Average)					(Spot on)

Why Should I?

We can turn ourselves into positive, up-beat and encouraging people overnight. Our friends, family and co-workers will love us for it. People will go out of their way to please us because they are just dying for honest compliments. We will make friends wherever we go and everyone will enjoy our company. We will be invited to more parties and we'll have more people wanting to shop at our shop, help us in business or do whatever they can to bring us success.

Honest compliments point out something that is good in another person and then we can praise them for that. Flattery, which is a despicable trait, can often be confused with compliments. Flattery however, is where we compliment another person because we want to get something out of them. Flattery is embedded in an attitude of taking, it is the thought 'I will tell you good things, so you will like me and then you will buy my merchandise – I don't really care about you, only what you can do for me.' Honest compliments are when the main thought behind the compliments is 'I want to highlight what's good in you, because I want to bring to the forefront of your consciousness the great things in you. I want to make you feel good and I want to bring more goodness into the world.' This type of thinking means that the compliment is an act of giving – wanting to enrich the other person. So although honest compliments may lead to other positive fringe benefits such as that person buying our merchandise, the purpose of giving the complement is to GIVE not to TAKE.

This exercise will help us develop a more positive way of looking at people, because when we are trying to see what we can compliment a person about, we are focusing on the loveable, successful and good parts of the person. Focusing our mind on the good in others makes us into positive people, and this in turn makes us happy people. Also when we learn to enjoy the pleasure of giving, encouraging and uplifting another person our levels of self-fulfilment and joy increase enormously.

This exercise is guaranteed to make us feel great. The more we can practice doing it the more natural and effective it will become and the happier we (and others) will feel.

Go on – You only live once – make it a good life – Give it a Go!

Day 28

Helping Others

"Nothing ever goes right for me. Nobody loves me. Nothing good has ever happened to me."

"Do you know what he did to me? Oh I'm so angry, how could someone treat me in such a way?"

"Life's a big disappointment."

We can help other people out of their misery. When we share our insights on how to enjoy life, we can actually increase the level of joy others have.

If someone tells us how angry or disappointed they are with another person we can help them by offering reasonable explanations as to why that person acted the way he/she did.

The more we can help others see the good in their lives, the more proficient we will become at seeing the good in our own lives.

"I have a friend who is my study partner for exams. We study in an unusual way; we take turns in pretending to be the lecturer and giving over the information to our 'student'. When I teach my friend, I'm forced to explain it in a clear and concise way and as a result I actually understand the subject matter much better."

Whenever we teach anything, it enhances our ability to understand and utilize the information we've taught. The more we can show others how to have a life filled with happiness, the more our life will be full of happiness.

To teach another to look up high
Is to learn for ourselves how to fly
To show others how to open their eyes and see
Will give us deep insights and endless clarity

Because to help another is to be a friend
With rewards and surprises that never end
To be good, kind and give to all
Is our guarantee that we will never fall.

Give it a Go!

Today try and help another person see something in their life in a better light.

I tried this exercise _____ times.
I would rate this exercise as:

1	2	3	4	5	6	7	8	9	10
(not so good)				(Average)					(Spot on)

Why Should I?

Are you serious about being happy? Do you really understand how to do it? If we want to gain a greater clarity on how to be happy and if we want to fully integrate feelings of constant happiness then we need to teach it. When we teach others we have to clarify in our own mind what we are teaching. We also have to experiment with the ideas before advising others how to apply what we know. When we are teaching others to see the good in their lives we have to think about being happy and seeing the good in life. We have to talk about it, write about it, answer questions on it... We are constantly being preoccupied with seeing the good in life and being happy. This preoccupation will make us reach levels of happiness that we've never touched before.

Also when we teach another to be happy we are giving them a skill they can use for the rest of their lives. This skill will enhance their lives and the lives of everyone they come into contact with. A person who has learned to see the good in their lives will smile more frequently, get annoyed or angry less often, have fewer disagreements and fights, and have more stable and fulfilling relationships. A happy person by osmosis makes others around them feel good. When we teach another the skills of being happy we are giving them the gift of life – a good, rewarding, successful and happy life.

Imagine if we could all teach one person how to see all the good in their lives and this person teaches one or two more people the skills. The impact on the world over time would be huge. Now imagine most of the people in this world feeling happy. There would be so much more kindness, less depression, crime, addictions etc. Did we ever imagine that we were so powerful and influential that we could change the world for good? By teaching others how to see things in a positive light we have the power to affect the lives of millions.

Go on – Be seriously Happy - help others! It will enrich your life and the lives of those you help - Give it a Go!

Day 29
Yay for YOU!

"I have had a tough life: trouble with my parents, trouble with school, and trouble with the police - just trouble, trouble and more trouble. However, I'm now a successful business man, with a thriving business, a great wife and two kids. If you'd asked me how I got out of all my troubles, it's because I had someone who believed in me. My best friend at school was a really positive guy, and whenever I would get into trouble, he would tell me things like, "You're going to get out of this, you're doing really well, you've come so far, I'm proud of you and I'm cheering you on." His encouragement and belief in me gave me the strength to get past my troubles and move on to a great part of my life."

Encouragement is being able to tell another person that we believe in them, we have faith in them, we'll stick by them and we won't give up on them. In order to have this attitude we need to develop our ability to see the potential of another person, even when it doesn't look like it is being actualized. Seeing the potential in a person is a highly developed form of seeing the good in a person, because it's seeing what is not apparent but what is really hidden under the surface.

We can also encourage ourselves and see our own potential. Look at what you've done well in the past. Try and see what major talent or character trait lies underneath that success. One person may be good at maths, so they are logical. What other things that require logical thinking could this person be successful at? Maybe it could be: Chess, Bridge, Computer programming, or private investigations. Another person may have been good at running fast, so they are athletic. What other things could an athletic person be successful at? Maybe a personal trainer, sports teacher, or any running based sports. We all have talents and things we are good at. What areas/careers/activities etc. have you never tried out, but would be really in-line with the inherent abilities you have?

"I had never performed in a major production, but I knew I was good at acting and singing. When auditions came up for a famous musical, I thought to myself, 'What do I have to lose; I'll give it a go – who knows I might just land a leading role.' To my surprise I did get a leading part. I think the only reason I had the inner strength to audition was because I knew I had talents and abilities that could make me succeed."

We need to encourage and believe in ourselves. We have to look at what we could potentially do, or who we could potentially be and then chase our dreams, knowing we can succeed. We need to develop the ability to see the good in ourselves and others – even if it's not actualized yet.

Give it a Go!

1. If you know someone who is struggling with life – call him/her up and tell them you believe in them and point out some things they are good at - offer them words of encouragement. And/or
2. Sit down and ask yourself "What is good about me that I've never brought out and expressed properly?" (Don't listen to that loud voice that says 'nothing'.) Wait for a quiet answer. Sometimes it takes time (even days or weeks) to receive your answer.

I tried this exercise _____ times.
I would rate this exercise as:

1	2	3	4	5	6	7	8	9	10
(not so good)				(Average)				(Spot on)	

Why Should I?

There is so much hidden talent and untapped potential out there. Imagine if everybody, everywhere in the world utilized his/her potential for the good. What a great world we would live in. A major obstacle in bringing forth talents, abilities and success is being blind to the inherent potential that is within. How are we supposed to recognize the potential we have? The only way we can start to see our potential (and the potential of others) is if we look deeply, dig down hard and uncover all the wonderful talents lying within.

Imagine everybody was given a tool box. A handyman has nails, hammers, screwdrivers etc in his tool box. A surgeon has a mask, scalpel, injections and bandages in his tool box. . Each professional has what he/she needs in their tool box to do their job. What about if we were handed a tool box and it had seeds, soil, a shovel and a watering can? Would we guess that we were supposed to be a gardener? What if we look in our tool box and noticed that we had some freeze dried food, some weird looking tools and a big cumbersome coverall suit? Would we be able to guess what we're supposed to be? Probably not without taking a really good look, investigating further or doing a bit of research. Finally we may discover we were supposed to be an astronaut.

In life we are given a tool box. It's not visible but it consists of our temperament, talents, abilities and life circumstances. We need to look at our tools – all those good things about us and try and work out how we can use them to bring out the best in us. Although life is a process of understanding ourselves, growing and maximizing our potential, the start of self-fulfilment is to start to open up our tool box and see what great things we've been blessed with.

Another side advantage of looking honestly in our tool box is that we will appreciate our tools more and we will no longer want what others have in their tool box. It would be pointless for a handyman to have a scalpel in his tool box as he couldn't fix things with it, and it is dangerous for the surgeon to have a hammer in his tool box. So too when we see our tools and appreciate all the good things we possess we won't want to be like other people, or want all their talents or blessings. Being happy with who we are, is a great feeling.

When we take time to notice or identify tools that others possess in their tool box, it is a great kindness for us to point it out to them and to explain how they can use them. Believing in another person gives them a belief in themselves. Showing another person how to use the gifts they have been given is helping them reach their potential.

This exercise will help us give expression to some of the many hidden talents that lie within. It will also develop our ability to see talents in others and encourage those talents until they are realized. Focusing on the potential good in ourselves and others makes us into positive and happy people. We will become like a miner, digging deeper and deeper into the ground uncovering priceless jewels. As we dig deeper and deeper into our tool box and help others dig into their tool box we will uncover many priceless jewels (talents/tools). There are so many hidden jewels in this world – this exercise will help us find them and become rich with happiness.

Go on – Open your tool box – Give it a Go!

Day 30

Seeing Others

"We're used to it so it doesn't seem too harmful, in fact it's just the way everyone behaves, no one means anything by it, we're only joking and it's really true."

When we run another person down, make a joke at their expense, talk about a foolish thing they said or did, we are concentrating on the not so positive side of the person. This makes us a more negative person, and on some level it makes them feel slightly less good about themselves. Calling others names, even in jest, is not the way to lift ourselves up and become more positive and happy people.

"But it's ok, I don't mind when people knock me – it's just part of the fun of social bantering."

If the social bantering we are doing is all about taking away our focus from what is good in other people, then it's not good for us to do it. And really when we are honest with ourselves we would prefer it much more if people complimented us as part of the fun of social bantering. Ask your quiet voice if this is really true.

"I stopped making smart wise cracks, I refused to tell others the local 'hot gossip' which really means mean nasty information about other people, I even stopped going from one friend to the another to say 'do you know what she said about you...' I didn't want any part of it. As a result of restraining myself a tiny bit in this area I have become such a positive, happy and friendly person. I know people respect me for my attitude, and more importantly I respect myself."

We all know the expression, "what goes around comes around." When we are good to others, we will ultimately reap the reward for our goodness. When we try hard not to laugh and poke fun at somebody else doing something really foolish, then when we do something embarrassing people will look the other way. When we are kind and friendly, we will meet more kind and friendly people. When we treat others better than we expect others to treat us – we will have many pleasant surprises in life, and others will treat us better than we could have imagined.

"I was in a parking lot and discovered that the local city council had recently made it a fee paying parking lot; previously it had cost me nothing to park there. I didn't have the $2 required, I only had a $50 note, so I pulled up next to the ticket machine, where some people were waiting. I asked if anyone could break a $50 note. One kind person said, `I'll give you $2', to which I replied 'No it's ok, I just want change'. He just turned back to the ticket meter, put in $2 and handed me a ticket with a smile. I was amazed how kind he was. Not only did I not have to pay for the ticket, I didn't even have to park my car, walk to the meter, get the ticket and walk back to my car to put the ticket on the car. Then I had a strange feeling of de já vu: I remembered that I had once bought a $2 ticket for someone else. It took a few years between the two incidents, but I was sure they were connected."

Another benefit of speaking well about others is we will be a better friend, a happier person and people will like us more. They will come to trust us because they will notice that we don't speak badly about other people behind their backs, and therefore they will correctly assume that we won't speak badly about them behind their backs.

Give it a Go!

Try for half a day not to say or imply anything negative about the people in your life today. After you've successfully done this, get in touch with yourself and ask, "Did that feel good?"

I tried this exercise _____ times.
I would rate this exercise as:

1	2	3	4	5	6	7	8	9	10
(not so good)				(Average)					(Spot on)

Why Should I?

Do you want to know the secret to success with people? It's quite simple to say (harder to do). Look for the good in each person, concentrate on that good, identify that person with that good and you will love them – they will feel your genuine love and concern and they will in turn have fond feelings towards you. Simple! Did you know, people who like us will do amazing things for us? They will defend us when we're attacked, support us when we're down, rescue us when we're in trouble or encourage us when we need it.

Verbalization/Speaking affects our emotions. If we speak negatively about another person, we feel negatively about that person and there is NO WAY we are going to be able to concentrate on that person's virtues. Loving other people entails concentrating on their good and speaking about it. We can't fully love someone if we are concentrating on what we don't like and commenting on it.

A person may say 'I love him, warts and all – what's wrong with talking about the warts?' We could answer him by saying we can love a person warts and all, but if we concentrate on the warts we are not loving him to the best of our capacity. We can actually deepen our levels of love, help the person also love themselves and bring more happiness to the world by ignoring the warts and commenting on the loveable qualities.

Relationships can be of different qualities. For example if we buy potatoes, we don't care if there is a bit of dirt on the potato, because the dirt doesn't affect the price of the potato significantly. However, if we are buying diamonds the scales are dusted, the diamond is blown, so as to make sure not a tiny speck of dust is on it because the speck of dust is significant to the transaction. The same principle applies to relationships, we can choose to have 'potato' relationships where the amount of dirt we dig up on the person doesn't matter to us – the relationship is not that precious. Or we can choose to make our relationships diamond relationships, in which case we blow away the dirt, and concentrate ONLY on the good in the other person. If we want to elevate our interpersonal relationships to the level of diamond – don't speak badly about people.

This exercise will make us into a 'diamond' friend, spouse or person.

Go on – Uplift the way you express yourself – Give it a Go!

SMELL EVERY ROSE

KEY #1- SEE THE GOOD
(THE SKELETON KEY THAT OPENS ALL DOORS)

PART 4 - RIGHT NOW AND IN THE FUTURE

Day 31
It'll be good

"It's going to be great, we're going to go out there and sell more than we've ever done before. We're the greatest team, and today is going to be the best ever. We'll smash every sales record since the beginning of the company....."

After a pep talk like this the sales team is likely to come out onto the shop floor, full of life, enthusiasm, joy and is really more likely to sell more. Why? Because they anticipated something good; that gave them more energy and zest for life as a result of which they steamrolled towards their goal. Anticipating that things will be great – actually can make great things happen.

"If I anticipate something fantastic happening and it doesn't happen, then I'll be really miserable, because I'll feel let down."

Protecting ourselves against the unpleasant feeling of failure, defeat or disappointment doesn't actually give us a more joyful life. If we imagined that things will work out well (and they normally do work out well), but in this rare case it didn't work out well, then what did we lose? The time that we were anticipating good things we were happy, when we get the blow of disappointment, then we feel sad for a short time, maybe 10 minutes. But then we can cheer up thinking, "It's okay, something good is bound to come out of this", or we can just move on to some other goal, and look forward to achieving that. This way 95% of the time we are happy.

What if we do it the other way around, but we achieve our goal (which is less likely because when we are pessimistic, then we are more likely to fail)? Imagine the whole time whilst we are pursuing what we want, we are miserably expecting the worst. And what if surprise, surprise it works out really well. Then we may feel happy for 10 minutes, and then we slip back into pessimistic mode and think about other negative things that might, possibly, remotely, could happen to ruin our current happiness – which means we're unhappy again.

In the first example the person who was optimistic was happy for the whole day, except for the 10 minutes of disappointment. In the second example the person was miserable the whole day, except for the 10 minutes of excitement when something unexpected happened. Which type of day would you have preferred to have?

"I was going on holiday. I thought maybe the weather will be cold and rainy. Maybe the hotel will be small and unclean. The attractions won't probably be as good as the brochure makes them out to be. The plane will probably be delayed... I thought I was preparing myself for the worst – maybe that way I might be pleasantly surprised when things weren't so bad. My sister was coming on the holiday with me, she was such an optimist. She said she thinks the weather will be great it might even snow and she could make a snow man. She was looking forward to meeting new people and seeing new places, trying new food etc... She worked herself up into such a frenzy, that the day before the trip she could hardly sleep, she was so excited."

Who do you think had a better holiday?

Who was more likely to enjoy the attractions?

Reflect and access your inner wisdom by asking yourself: Why?

Give it a Go!

Think about tomorrow and how it is going to be a great day. Anticipate with joy the start of tomorrow.

I tried this exercise _____ times.
I would rate this exercise as:

1	2	3	4	5	6	7	8	9	10
(not so good)				(Average)				(Spot on)	

Why Should I?

Every day is the start of the rest of our lives. Have you ever watched a sun rise, the sky is black and the stars are vibrant and then slowly in the east a haze of blue begins appearing? As we watch the sky gradually change colours, there are many different shades of blue, yellow and red. The air in the morning is crisp and the whole experience is one of renewal and newness. Every day we start afresh. We can choose to begin our lives again from that moment.

New beginnings are vitalizing. We can drop the old bad habits, thinking and unproductive worrying and say 'That was me before, but the new me is beginning now.' (We can actually do this 100s of times during the day whenever we want to refresh ourselves.) When we start each day with the anticipation of a new start and anticipating good things happening, we will enjoy our day immensely.

Looking forward to a new day gives a person a sense of serenity, joy and happiness. This exercise will help us look forward to the future. Once we've taught ourselves to look forward to great things coming our way, we will actually notice them more when they do eventually come. Enjoy life, every moment, every day and every possible future pleasure. Life's great, why shouldn't it continue to be great forever?

Optimists have more fun. Go on – become an optimist – Give it a Go!

Day 32
I'll be back

"How could I say the future's going to be better? Look at me - I'm a complete failure. Whatever I do I manage to mess up. I'm a walking disaster. I've tried and I've failed over and over again – it's only realistic to expect that I'll muck things up again."

Life is full of ups and downs. Which means, yes we fall down, but we will rise again. Sometimes the dips of the down may seem very long and very low, but the rise will come. We need to remember during the times that we are down, that we can get back up and that we have had some successes in doing this in the past.

If we fail to train ourselves to see the good in what we have done in the past, then when we are down we will forget that we've done anything worthwhile. After all, when we have a down time we can sometimes feel totally worthless. We can help ourselves through our downtimes by keeping a notebook of all the good things we have done. We can also keep a notebook of all the good things that we want to do in the future. When we are feeling down, it's a good idea to take out that notebook and read it over and over.

Setting ourselves small, easy to do goals is another great way of helping us appreciate who we are and also a great way of seeing ourselves progress. When we can see that we have progressed then we can start to predict that we will progress even more in the future. This ability to set meaningful and reachable goals is a great way of looking forward to an even greater future. When we can appreciate the current "ME" whilst simultaneously envisioning an even better "ME", then we can take pleasure in that vision.

"On New Year's Eve last year, we had a great party. One of the fun activities that a friend decided to get us all to do was to write out a description of how our year was - pretending we were writing it a year from today. So we had to pretend that we did whatever we could imagine was possible , and wrote it down as though the year was over and we were

looking back on our incredible year. I wrote (on 31 Dec 2010), "The year 2011 was just the best I've ever had. I got straight A's in my midyear exams. After exams Kate and I went on a fantastic holiday to the Bahamas where I tried scuba diving and ...." By the time I'd finished writing about my year to come as if it had already happened I felt so happy. I was actually really excited to start out such a fantastic fun-filled year. Although it was completely from my imagination it really helped me focus on having a great future. But the most AMAZING thing about it all was just before New Year's this year I got out the piece of paper that I wrote on last year and I was floored – I had actually done most of the things that I had fantasized about. My friend who introduced me to this idea said that most people actually do most of the things they wrote on their list. Just writing down in a solid and concrete form what good things I want to anticipate to happen – actually caused them to happen. This is completely amazing."

Give it a Go!

It is time to look forward to the future.
Imagine you have been time-warped a year into the future. Write from there how your year was. Write down anything that you would find enjoyable. However, write it as though you have already done it. When choosing what to write you must only write down what is possible for you to do (e.g. not "went to Pluto" or "went deep sea diving" – when you are scared of water and don't want to learn how to swim). Try and make it as detailed as possible, including which month you did it in, who went with you etc. You don't actually have to do what you write down – it's just a fantasy, so dare to dream. Then put the paper away and make a note in your diary to read it in a year. Then sit back and feel how good your year is going to be. In retrospect you will be surprised about how wonderful your year was.

I tried this exercise _____ times.
I would rate this exercise as:

1	2	3	4	5	6	7	8	9	10
(not so good)				(Average)					(Spot on)

Why Should I?

We have to try this exercise to believe its power. It is phenomenal!
When we write down our fantasy year, we'll find that there will be times

in the year that we'll make tiny decisions that lead us towards our dreams, even when we don't consciously remember what we wrote. This exercise works on our deep sub-conscious level and it ignites a desire within us to pursue our dreams.

Have you noticed what used to be science fiction fantasy is now becoming modern reality? Imaginary shoe or watch phones are now real mobile/cell phones. Imaginary space stations are now a reality. Whatever man can dream eventually becomes a reality. We are only limited by the limitations we place upon ourselves.

This exercise will free us from narrow minded vision. It will open up a new world of pleasure, excitement and achievement.

How does it work? For the analytical type it could be explained as the power of willpower or power of the mind and the subconscious. For the spiritual type it could be explained as a way of sending out a message or desire to the Universe, which then creates a response or power that causes things to happen so that our vision becomes a reality. Any way we wish to explain it, the fact is this exercise is powerful and IT WORKS.

Go on – Have the best year you've ever had – Give it a Go!

Day 33

Never say Never

"He's never going to change. He'll be like that until the day he dies. He'll never admit that he's wrong and he'll never apologise."

We can look to the future with hope. We hope that we will be better people, life will be better, and we should also hope that others will also become better with age. We shouldn't write off any human being.

 If we have a child that is going through a difficulty we can think about how in the future he/she would have got over whatever was holding them back.

If we are fighting with our parents, we can look to the future and hope that in 10-20 years time we will have a peaceful and loving relationship.

If we see a glint of what is good in another person, then we can use our imagination to extrapolate that out, and imagine if the person developed that good thing how amazing that person would be.

It's important to try and see the potential of another person. It is great if we can share our vision with that person and encourage them to develop what they can. It is kind to help another not to give up on themselves and tell them we still believe in them.

"I'm a little artistic. I like to draw cartoons and make funny jokes with my characters. When I was growing up my mother always encouraged me saying, "Son, you are going to have a leading cartoon strip in a major newspaper one day because you are so talented." My mother saw something in me, and she encouraged that to grow. Now, I do have a cartoon strip in a major newspaper. If it wasn't for my mother seeing the talent I had and seeing me in the future utilizing it, then I think my talent may have been relegated to a back drawer, never to be used to its full potential."

Seeing a good future for others helps them aim for a good future.

"I see my brother has potential, but he never uses it."

As long as we can see the potential in another person that is great and positive, they don't actually have to use their potential. We can view people in a more loving and positive way when we see something admirable about them. Admiring potential makes us positive, encouraging and joyful people. What others do with our encouragement is completely up to them. We can enjoy a person not only for who they are now, but for who they have the potential to become. This is another way to increase joy and love for others that we have in our lives.

Give it a Go!

Think of a person who you would like to appreciate more. Try and see that person's strengths and imagine that they used those strengths to do great things. Now picture the person having achieved all of the greatness they are capable of. Enjoy this person.

I tried this exercise _____ times.
I would rate this exercise as:

1	2	3	4	5	6	7	8	9	10
(not so good)				(Average)				(Spot on)	

Why Should I?

Learn to love people, all of them. We have said the key to happiness is to focus on the good in life. The key to loving people is to see the good in them and identifying them with their good. The key to maintaining this positive loving outlook is to become a connoisseur of life. This exercise will help us become a connoisseur of people – even those who on the outside don't look that wonderful. The more often we can see the good in other people the happier we will be. When we are able to see the good in people we'll find that our interactions with others will be positive and more fulfilling.

Also when we see the good in others they will sense this, and will react to us in a more positive way than they do with most other people. If we've had strained relationships with people, then seeing them as a polished finished product or as a person who has realized his/her potential will open up our hearts and enhance our relationships. This exercise is a good mental trick to do on ourselves to make us positive and focused on seeing the good in people, even in the most trying of circumstances.

Go on- Turn every interaction with people into a pleasurable, positive experience – Give it a Go!

Day 34

Living in the Present

"I've got so much to do. Today I have to go to the dentist, pick up the package at the mail box, attend 5 meetings, join in an after-work office party and then take my Grandmother out to dinner for her birthday. Tomorrow, I have to pack and catch the 9am flight to New Zealand, where I've got meetings and conferences all lined up. But I can't stop worrying about what happened yesterday, and whether my boss said what he said because he's thinking of firing me."

We live so much of our lives thinking about what we have to do or what happened in the past. If we can learn to live in the present, to be right now totally focused on what we are doing, we feel less stressed and we enjoy the here and now more.

"Everybody lives in the present, that's where we all are, what are you talking about?"

Sometime we can physically be here but our minds are so far away it is like we are really on another planet. Somebody could be speaking with us and we don't even notice, or we might hear what they're saying, but we are not focused on what they are saying and we mightn't respond in the best way, because we only half heard them.

"I have to go, or I'll be late for the bus. Ahh I forgot to pack lunch, quick I need to make something. Oh Mum just arrived home from an overseas trip; I'll quickly say, "Hi Mum, nice to see you. I hope you had a great trip. I've got to go, I'll catch up with you tonight, bye." Phew I made the bus. Now I can calm down. Ohh I should have really given Mum a big hug and asked her how she was feeling, I should have been more focused on her and then she would have felt more loved and cared for."

When we are on fast forward we miss out on a lot of the joy of life. We may recognise this at some later date and spend ages feeling bad about how we should have been more caring/loving etc. Yet while we are thinking like this we are missing out on THAT moment as well, which we could enjoy. The trick is to try and bring our minds back to where we are at, that very second.

"I try to live in the present by pretending nothing exists in the future and nothing has happened in the past. I look around the room and really look at where I am. I think about how I'm feeling at that very moment and I relax. When I learned to do this, I tried to develop the ability to being fully present when talking to someone. I try to concentrate fully on what they are saying, their facial movements and body language, and I try to just enjoy their very presence. Every time my mind wanders off to something else, I bring it back to the here and now. I've found that by living in the present my levels of calmness and joy have increased dramatically, and my interpersonal relationships have improved out of sight."

Give it a Go!

Stop and pause for a moment. Don't think about what you need to do or what you've done - just enjoy the moment. Listen to the sound of your breathing; are there any other noises you can hear? Don't get distracted thinking about where they come from or what the noises mean. Is there a breeze on your skin? How do you feel? Try viewing yourself, as if you are looking down from the ceiling at yourself. Now notice all the sensations that you enjoy e.g. the soft cushions on the sofa you are sitting on, the comfortable shoes you are wearing, etc.

I tried this exercise _____ times.
I would rate this exercise as:

1	2	3	4	5	6	7	8	9	10
(not so good)				(Average)				(Spot on)	

Why Should I?

The only way we can be fully alert, alive and vibrant is to be fully present. Have you ever had a conversation with somebody who you knew was only half listening to you? If you have, you would be able to understand that when a person is only half listening they are not really hearing you, feeling your feelings or relating to you. It's more like interacting with a zombie – the lights are on but nobody's home. This is what we are like when we don't live in the present. We interact with the world in a half hearted fashion. We are incapable of fully enjoying the pleasures around us and the saddest part about it is we don't even realize how much we are missing out on life.

This exercise is another life changer - it is our wake up call. Let's teach our mind to live in the present, to see, feel and experience life fully. When we escape into past worries or future plans we become desensitised to the wondrous world of NOW. In order to enjoy life to the fullest we need to be fully awake, fully alive and fully present. This exercise will teach us how to train our mind to enjoy the here and now.

The more often we can practice living life NOW the more we will savour every moment of our existence. Those who have mastered this technique, have mastered the ability to be serenely empowered. People who are able to live in the present are able to enjoy each moment while simultaneously using that moment for maximum achievement. If we can learn to master the ability to live in the present, we don't walk around with regrets, wishing we had used our time better. We operate at peak performance all day!

Live your life fully charged, fully aware and fully present – You'll be amazed at how great life is and how productive you can be when you're fully engaged in the present.

Go on – Make the most of the moment - Give it a Go!

Day 35

Awesome!

"I had a taste of mind-altering reality. It happened when I went to the mountains; I sat in on a rock and looked at an apple on a tree. I just stared at it for a while, and then it hit me. It was a feeling of Wow! Here was an apple – a small red juicy ball hanging off a branch of wood. Imagine how amazed I'd be if my kitchen table, which is also made from wood, would have an apple hanging off it. I thought about how a flower had come on the branch, blossomed and then slowly turned into an apple. First it was green and sour, but when it was juicy and ready to be picked it turned bright red – as if to advertise, 'Look at me, and eat me!' When I looked at the apple I felt like I was looking at a miracle that happened before my very own eyes. It was a phenomenal feeling, like I was above reality."

Have we ever stopped, really stopped to look at the world around us? It's awesome. Just look at how our hands move. We are made up of atoms, and when we think that we want to move our hand, our brain sends a signal to the arm which is another bunch of atoms, which then makes the arm move. And what about how complicated our eyes are – we see life through jelly!

If we put on our awesome glasses and walk around, we would be so taken back that we would find it hard to just get to the end of the street.

By plugging into awe, we will be able to see phenomenal levels of goodness that we just didn't notice were there. The more we can plug into this, the more we can fly, in feelings of happiness, excitement and bliss.

"Why is it that we don't all live with this feeling of awe?"

When we were little babies and first saw an apple, our minds were not mature enough to comprehend how amazing it was, however, we probably were awed to a small degree by the apple. If we were to give a young child a tissue box, we would notice they very excitedly take one tissue out, then another, then another – it's fascinating to them, they may throw the tissues in the air, wipe their face, toes or arms. We adults just get annoyed with their mess making, but really we could use the opportunity to re-experience the marvel of tissues.

Young children, to a small degree, look at the world with awe, but as they get older they also get used to all the amazing sights, sounds and sensations. Now that we have matured and our minds are capable of noticing so much more detail, we can revisit all those things we discovered as a child and re-discover them through the eyes of an adult. When we re-discover the world, we will be seeing life in an entirely different way and this will heighten our appreciation of the world we live in. The more we can appreciate life - the more we will enjoy it.

Give it a Go!

1. Pretend you met somebody who had never seen a butterfly before. Describe how it looks, grows, reproduces etc. Try and do this with your 'Awesome' glasses on.

2. Look around the room you are currently in, focus your attention on one object. Now look at it as if you've never seen it before – experience the awesomeness of the object. (Some people who know how to meditate, may decide to meditate on that item)

I tried this exercise _____ times.
I would rate this exercise as:

1	2	3	4	5	6	7	8	9	10
(not so good)				(Average)				(Spot on)	

Why Should I?

Let's re-sensitize ourselves to the joy of living. Have you ever noticed how a one or two year old child is always smiling and laughing? They may fall over and hurt themselves but then they get back up and within minutes they are laughing and running around again. How is it that they can be so happy all of the time? How is it that they have so much energy to run, jump and laugh all day? The secret to the happiness of children can be explained by their ability to live in the present and see the awesomeness of life. Everything they see, feel, taste etc is new and exciting. Even running around in circles or playing "catchy" with a friend is exhilarating.

We were once children, so we have within us the ability to run, laugh, jump and interact with our friends in carefree happy ways. We can enjoy the excitement of finding an ant on the street, or a worm in the garden. We can giggle when the wind blows our hair into our ears – tickling us. We can enthusiastically enjoy the beauty of flowers as we pass a florist. We can choose to see the awesomeness of living. It's a conscious decision on our part. And if we decide to re-sensitize ourselves to the awesome world we live in, we will re-gain our youthful exuberance, joy and energy.

When doing this exercise we may not feel any different straight away, but if we manage to enter the state of viewing something even ONCE in our lives with awe, we'll never be the same. Some describe the experience of seeing something through awesome glasses as 'euphoric, mind-altering, prophetic etc...' So keep trying until you can do it.

Go on – Invigorate yourself – Give it a Go!

Day 36
Trace it back

In order to cultivate the most amount of seeing the good in our lives we can learn the skill of tracing it back to its source. For example if we enjoy the shoes we are wearing we can trace it back to feeling grateful to the shoe shop, or our mother for buying them for us, or the cow that died so we have leather, or to the grass that sustained the cow so it could grow, or the farmer who reared the cow etc - as far as we can go.

The more we can trace it back, the more pleasure we will be experiencing because it helps us appreciate the things we have in a more detailed way, and it also helps us see how many people have helped us. Tracing back our pleasures helps cultivate a feeling of 'I'm so important and cared for'.

There are many types of pleasures we may experience.

Some types of pleasures we may experience are:

Physical Pleasures
All the things we own, or body parts that allow for the ability to see, smell, hear, feel, taste. Basically anything that brings us pleasure by seeing (e.g. a waterfall), touching (e.g. a soft blanket), hearing (e.g. uplifting music), tasting (e.g. a delicious meal) or smelling (e.g. a Jasmine plant in bloom), etc.

Emotional Pleasures
Such as the feeling of being loved, loving others, belonging, meaning, friendship, etc

Achievement Pleasures
Such as: winning, being the best at something, overcoming an obstacle, finishing something meaningful, being in control or having power, etc.

Awareness/Intellectual Pleasures
Such as: understanding something deep or profound, having clarity on an issue or having direction in life, etc.

In order to feel these pleasures more, it's great to trace it back to how we got to that pleasure, who helped us on the way, or what was the original trigger that lead us on the path culminating in this pleasure. For example, we could trace back a feeling of being loved. What makes you feel loved? Or, who makes you feel loved? Who helped them learn to love others so that they knew how to convey that they love you? (etc.)

Give it a Go!

Take one pleasure from each category and see how far you can trace it back. The further you can trace it back - the bigger is your awareness of the pleasures you are experiencing, and the deeper will be your appreciation for your own pleasures. The more we appreciate the pleasures we are having the happier, more energized and more dynamic we will be.

I tried this exercise _____ times.
I would rate this exercise as:

1	2	3	4	5	6	7	8	9	10
(not so good)				(Average)					(Spot on)

Why Should I?

We have to give this exercise a go. It's a must! If we want to be happy and really enjoy life, then we have to be aware of all the pleasures we have. But if we only half-heartedly appreciate our pleasures, then we're only going to be half-heartedly happy. Tracing our pleasures back, gives us the big picture and the full view of how pleasurable our life really is. When we are able to trace our pleasures back, we will have a feeling of being so loved, appreciated or cared for. We will look at life as one big pleasure palace rotating on its axle just to serve us and our wants.

Our levels of appreciation and gratitude will soar the more often we can do this exercise. The exercise will make us feel happy like we've never felt before.

So Go on – Open your eyes to reality – Give it a Go!

BEWARE! There are times that this exercise may make our mind spin... Sometimes when we start tracing things back, we get bogged down in detail, and then the exercise might appear to be futile. There are two ways of dealing with this problem:

For the analytically inclined:

We can keep tracing things back as far as we can find meaning. For example when tracing our shoes back, some people may find it's only meaningful to trace them back to the shop they bought them from, others may stop at the manufacturing plant, others may find it meaningful to think about the cows that were used in producing the shoes, for others that's just going too far. Once we hit a spot in tracing things back where we start feeling 'this is ridiculous', then stop. We would have already gained a greater appreciation of the pleasures in our life by just starting to look at tracing things back.

However, we may find that the more we do this exercise the more meaningful it will become to trace things back further and further. The more good we feel in our lives, the more we actually search deeper and deeper for every bit of pleasure. But the main point of the exercise is to make it meaningful enough to tangibly feel the overwhelming volume of pleasure we have in our lives. So remember – if it's getting ridiculous, stop and move onto a different pleasure.

For the spiritually inclined:

Sometimes when we trace things back we might get stuck in all the detail, and that's fine. We might find that we trace all pleasures back to sub-atomic particles or some unknown power. Eventually, as we get really good at doing this we will see that EVERYTHING in this world has its origin in an unknown power. This is the power that keeps sub-atomic particles flying around, the power that initiated the big bang of creation and is still constantly maintaining our universe. The whole universe and all life that is found within it is constantly being kept in motion, guided and controlled by some kind of power. Recognising this power and knowing it is everywhere, at all times, and it is this power that is the Ultimate Source of all good, will heighten our ability to appreciate everything.

"If this power is the ultimate source of all good, then it must also be the ultimate source of all bad too, right?"

This power is the ultimate source of everything! However, as we learn to see to good in everything, we will learn to see that even in bad there is good and behind ALL bad there is eventually good. Thus we will also learn to see that this power is only good (not good and bad) and it is THE

Ultimate Source of all good. Life is good - very good, for those who learn to appreciate it. So for those of us who are spiritually inclined, we should keep tracing things back until their Ultimate Source, because this will give us the ultimate amount of pleasure we could ever experience.

Day 37

Seeing the patterns

When we get good at seeing the good things in life and noticing all those wonderful details that we've previously been oblivious to, we will start noticing patterns. We will notice various people will pop up in our minds that have always been there for us when we needed it. Or we will notice who of our friends gives us the most pleasure. Or we may notice that we enjoy the day more when we get up earlier. By opening our eyes to see the patterns, we become sensitized to how much good other's do for us, what gives us the most pleasure and who we should appreciate more.

"Whenever I keep tracing back where all the good in my life comes from, certain people keep popping up."

This is a great step for us, because it shows us who we really should be valuing in our lives. If we know who gives us the most, then we know who we really should feel grateful to.

"I kept tracing so much of the good in my life back to my mother. She gave me life, she cared for me, she taught me how to be a good person, she taught me how to love, to laugh, to believe in myself, and she paid for my education. The more I thought about how much she has done for me, the more I felt my levels of love and appreciation for her grow and grow."

Seeing the patterns of who gives us the most brings us a feeling of appreciation so great that it brims over, and we feel we just have to express it to the people who have done so much for us.

There is another reason we should look for patterns in our life and that is so we can identify where we are getting most of our pleasures from and then we can go and get more.

Every wise company tries to identify who it is that is buying their products. They want to know who gives them the most profit. Why? Because if they can determine who their best customers are, they can then market to them better, start loyalty programs to keep them coming back, attract similar types of customer etc... Basically they need to know where they are getting all their sales/profit from in order to plan how to keep it coming in or increase it.

We are like a business (the biggest and most important business that we could ever run). Except in our business we don't want just profits, we want more – we want pleasure. If we want to increase our pleasure in life then we'd best start learning about where we get most of our pleasure from. Once we've recognised the sources of our pleasure we can work out how to get more pleasure. Seeing the patterns in our life and noticing what/who gives us the most pleasure, helps us know where to turn, or what to do to get real, lasting and continuous pleasure.

Give it a Go!

1. Trace back where you got the 5 most important life wisdoms (e.g. A good work ethic or always speak truthfully etc), or other life gifts. Are there any patterns? Acknowledge the source of your gifts.
2. At the end of the day, before you go to sleep, mentally review your day and make a note of what were the 3 most pleasurable things about your day. Do this for a while, until you start noticing patterns in what you find most enjoyable. Once you've noticed a pattern, then plan your life so that you can incorporate these pleasurable things in your day, every day.

I tried this exercise _____ times.
I would rate this exercise as:

1	2	3	4	5	6	7	8	9	10
(not so good)				(Average)					(Spot on)

Why Should I?

Do you want to appreciate life on a higher level than you've done before? We all want to see who in our lives is really worth knowing, who has really helped us and who has done so much for us. We can be a pro-active go-getter of pleasure. These exercises will help us enjoy and appreciate life and achieve our goals.

When we are astute enough to see the patterns of good in our life, we will be able to tap into that good whenever we desire. Happiness is not a product of random happenings, it can be worked at and planned for. When planning for a happy and successful life it's crucially important to see where we've previously found the most happiness and success. When we recognise the source of our pleasure then we will easily be able to go back to those sources to get more.

It's time to be like those successful companies – identify where we are getting most of our pleasures from, zoom in on the source, see how it enhances our lives and then go back and get more pleasure. The best way to go back and get more pleasure is to make opportunities to revisit the source. So if we get pleasure from a certain person, plan to see that person more often. If we get pleasure from doing a certain activity, plan to do that activity more often. We need to plan our day, plan our week and plan our life, making sure to always make time for those things or people that give us the most pleasure.

Only happiness and success can be gained from doing this exercise. It will enrich your life immensely.

Go on - Discover your patterns for success – Give it a Go!

Day 38
Ohhh Ta!

We were taught from a young age to say thank you - but how many of us remember to mean it?

"I woke up one morning and thought, "Today is going to be `Thank you Day'. I'm going to try and thank everybody who does something for me – even if it is something small. I thanked my Mum for greeting me with such a cheery "Good Morning". I thanked my Dad for going out to work and earning the money to buy me a delicious breakfast. I thanked my teacher for the fascinating class she gave and the extension she allowed me for my assignment. I thanked my best friend for always being there for me when I need her. I even thanked my sister for being cute and making funny wisecracks. I really brightened up everybody's day, but even more so I was in such a good mood - saying thank you is one way to get a real buzz!"

"I try and think of a new person every day that I've never thanked for something. The first few days were really easy – I rang up my first employer, and thanked him for giving me my first break. After a week or so it got a bit harder, so I thanked the shop keeper, the milk delivery man, and the farmer, and even the cow!"

"The more I notice good things in my life the more I realise I have a lot to thank a lot of people for. Most of all I've realized how much I've got to thank my parents for. They gave me life, fed me as a baby, got up and comforted me when I screamed at night, gave me great holidays, nice clothes, an education, tried to instil in me some good manners and even told me they love me. I know others will say they really did it for themselves – but the fact is I benefited from it. This reminds me of the time that I shopped around for a whole week finding the perfect present for my friend's birthday, and I was really excited to give it to her. When the day finally arrived I was bubbling with excitement, when she opened the present she was thrilled. I felt so good being able to give to her. In fact I looked happier than she did, and she noticed this and said, "You just gave me the present to make yourself feel good". Yes I felt good, but her

accusation wasn't true - I really did it for her. So although my parents wanted to have me and enjoyed giving me all they have – I still have a heap to be thankful for."

"I found the best way to really feel grateful to others for all the good they have given me was to remember that EVERYTHING I am given is a gift. I don't deserve anything. As long as I don't feel that I'm owed anything by anyone or the world at large I find I live a much more appreciative and grateful existence."

We were born with nothing, and when we die we will not have anything. Anything we receive along the way is really just a gift. Even the 'gift of life' is a gift. Happiness comes from appreciating the gifts we have. There is a simple slogan which if we were to keep it in mind would increase our happiness incredibly. It is:

Expect everything = Appreciating nothing, but,
Expect nothing = Appreciating everything.

Happiness is often dependent upon our expectations. If we change our expectations of life, to not expect anything, then we will have immense appreciation whenever we are given anything. This feeling of appreciation brings us true happiness. If we integrated the thought, 'everything in life is a gift', we would be exceptionally grateful and happy people.

"But don't happy people expect good things to happen in the future?"

Happy people ANTICIPATE good things happening, but they don't think they have a "right" for these things to happen. Having an expectation that life owes us something leads to misery. Having an upbeat outlook that good things will happen, leads to happiness.

Give it a Go!

Try and thank three people today. This can be done by speaking/writing/calling/gesticulating or any other way you can think of.

I tried this exercise _____ times.
I would rate this exercise as:

1	2	3	4	5	6	7	8	9	10
(not so good)				(Average)					(Spot on)

Why Should I?

Happy people are grateful people, and grateful people are happy people. When a person enters the mindset of gratitude, automatically his/her mental focus is positive. The attitude of gratitude requires that a person look outside of their own selfish 'I want, I need...' and instead focus on 'I have, I'm fulfilled...' Gratitude also enables us to see others – those that give to us. When we see the kindnesses other people do for us and we express this, we actually start to feel that others care for us or love us.

Gratitude helps integrate the knowledge that others love us, into an emotion of actually feeling loved and cared for. The more we express our thanks to another, the more WE FEEL good. Saying thank you is good for our emotional wellbeing. It's not just a social nicety or a polite thing to do.

People who are good at noticing all the good others do for them and commenting on it, are not only happier people, they are also more popular and appreciated by the givers. When we express our thanks to another we are strengthening their ability and desire to give again. People are happy to do favours for those whom they believe will appreciate their efforts. The more we appreciate the gift and thank the giver of the gift, the more likely the giver is to bless us with more gifts. So we can see that gratitude leads to receiving more gifts. However although one of the benefits of developing a grateful outlook is to receive more, the purpose of expressing gratitude should never be to get more. (We want to be givers not takers.) Instead we should express our gratitude to help us realize how much others love and care for us and to give them the pleasure of a thank you.

If we could do this exercise everyday for at least 3 months, we will notice how much more we'll appreciate life and how more loved we'll feel. This exercise is a great technique to help remould our entire personality. It'll bring about amazing results that we will be so pleased with. In the end we will even begin to thank ourselves for persisting in acquiring this ability.

Go on – Start to feel the love and care that surrounds you – Give it a Go!

Day 39
Nobody Home

What do you do if you're home alone and you're feeling blue?
You've looked all around for something fun to do
And you've tried all the tricks that usually work for you
Then try this one; it's fun and it's new
Walk around the home saying Thank you.

Thank you for the blue sky, the green grass and the shady tree
Thank you for my computer, my cell phone and for ME!
Thank you for chocolate cake, strawberries and apple pie
Thank you for every year, every day and every moment that goes by.

We are surrounded with so many good things. Walking around and expressing thanks for all that we see, hear, smell, touch, or feel is guaranteed to uplift our spirits. There isn't one day that goes by without something to be grateful for.

"I like to pause before I eat anything, I look at my food, appreciate its beauty, marvel at how many ingredients went into making such a scrumptious meal, and I say, "Thank you, this looks great." And when I've finished I say, "Thanks - that was terrific – it just hit the spot." I say this even if nobody else is home."

When we notice the myriads of wonderful things we have in our lives, then we start to feel happy. But there is a way of making us feel a deeper sense of happiness and that is by, not only noticing the good we have, but saying 'thank you' for all that good. The more we notice the good in our lives the happier we will be, and the more we **appreciate** the good in our lives the more we are able to reach exulted levels of happiness and bliss. When we hear ourselves say 'Thank you' our appreciation levels increase. Saying thank you is a practical tool to help us work on increasing our ability to appreciate everything.

Give it a Go!

1. If you live at home with others, try this game – at dinner tonight see who can come up with the most number of ingredients, people, packaging and processes that were needed to get the main course on the table – the person with the most on their list gets a double dessert! Then say a big "Thank you".

2. If you're alone, then walk around your home for 2 minutes saying "thank you" for everything you see and appreciate. (It's helpful to set a timer that will beep when your 2 minutes are up. That way you don't get distracted by the time and lose your train of 'thankyou' thoughts.)

I tried this exercise _____ times.
I would rate this exercise as:

1	2	3	4	5	6	7	8	9	10
(not so good)				(Average)					(Spot on)

Why Should I?

We don't need to wait around for somebody to come along and do us a favour in order to tune into the benefits of feeling grateful. We can look around and see all of the wonderful things in our life and say 'Thank you'. As mentioned in the previous exercise, the expression of gratitude causes us to feel beloved and cared for. Why not walk around with this feeling, even when nobody's home?

The first exercise is great fun, it gets everybody into the spirit of seeing the good in their lives and feeling grateful. It creates an atmosphere of positivity, love and happiness. Children will want to play it again and again (especially if they win and get the double dessert.)

The second exercise is a marvellous pick-me-up when we feel down and somewhat uncared for. Just walk around our home and say out loud 'Thank you for the.......'' and within a few minutes we'll feel happy, loved and peaceful.

There is so much we have in our lives that we can be grateful for. The more we tune into the goodness that we already possess, the happier we will be. Some people have made it their daily practice to do this second

KEY #1 – SEE THE GOOD

exercise for approximately half and hour to an hour a day, and they have reached heights of happiness that most people don't realize exist.

If we decide to do this exercise regularly, we don't have to think of new, exciting or different things every day. We can 'go back to the basics' and just appreciate the small things. We could look in the mirror and appreciate every part of our bodies that works smoothly, painlessly and effortlessly. We could look in our wardrobe at each item and re-live the appreciation we felt when we first bought it. We can think of all the good things that happened yesterday. We could look at the sky, clouds or stars. There are an infinite amount of things we have in our lives that we can feel appreciative about.

It may sound like a very simple exercise and it is, but don't let that fool you because it is very powerful.

Go on – Feel the power of gratitude – Give it a Go!

SMELL EVERY ROSE / [149]

Day 40
It's so hard

"It's easy to say thank you for the little things like thanks for the ride, passing me my bag etc. But it's embarrassing to say thanks for being given something big that I couldn't have accomplished on my own. Like last week when I broke my leg and I couldn't walk, my brother carried me to the ambulance. I said to him, "You're the greatest." Because he really helped me, but actually saying thank you felt too embarrassing."

When someone does us a favour, deep down we know we owe them something. If we find it too embarrassing to say thank you it's because we really want to avoid admitting that we owe this person something that honestly we can't repay. The closest we can come to repaying the favour is by paying our debt of gratitude. The bigger the favour a person did for us, the bigger the debt we have. With big debts, sometimes we would prefer to pretend they just don't exist.

"I find it easy to say thank you to people. I even sometimes buy them little gifts, as a token of my appreciation. However, recently I found out that an acquaintance that I don't like very much saved me from being fired from my job. I didn't want to go and thank her, I wanted to pretend it didn't happen, because I didn't want to be two faced. I don't like her, I don't want to lower myself and grovel – why should I say thank you."

When someone we don't like does us a favour it is a great opportunity to upgrade our happiness. It can be a catalyst for us to start to see them in a better light than we previously saw them. If they have done something kind for us then they MUST have some good or redeemable qualities. When we are strong enough to admit we may have been wrong about how we perceived another person we are on the road to upgrading our levels of joy immensely. The more people we can see in a good and positive light the more humanity looks good in our eyes and the happier we will be. Saying thank you is not lowering ourselves, it's in fact being big, admitting our debts and repaying them – we are making ourselves higher and better people when we do this.

"I was on the verge of filing for a divorce, when someone recommended that I dedicate some time each day to thanking my husband for all the good things he has done for me. When I contemplated what benefits I've gained from my husband I realized that he had paid for over 1000 meals I've eaten, bought 80% of the clothes I have in my wardrobe, helped me wash the dishes over 500 times, gave me a break and looked after the children over 200 times and even complimented, smiled or encouraged me when I was feeling down. When I started focusing on what he had done for me, rather than what I do for him, our marriage took a turn for the good overnight"

Sometimes we overlook all the good and kind things that those closest to us do for us. The magnitude of what our parents, teachers, siblings, spouse and children do is so great that we actually become desensitised to appreciating it. If we could imagine a complete stranger doing the exact same things for us we would really know how to notice and appreciate all the good our closest ones do for us.

Give it a Go!

Think of the 3 most important gifts you've been given in life – have you adequately thanked the giver for them? If not, thank one of them today. (If the person is no longer alive, you can still verbalize your gratitude and pretend they are standing in front of you.)

I tried this exercise _____ times.
I would rate this exercise as:

1	2	3	4	5	6	7	8	9	10
(not so good)				(Average)					(Spot on)

Why Should I?

If somebody has $10 but owes $8 then they are worth $2. If we are recognising and upgrading our worth as human beings, but we refuse to acknowledge the debts of gratitude we owe, then we are reducing our real worth by the amount of the outstanding debt of gratitude. So increase your overall worth – pay your debts, acknowledge those who you owe so much to and thank them – you'll feel great!

It's a fantastic feeling to go back over our lives and work out who we owe a debt of gratitude to and then to actually pay it by saying thank you. The person who we thank will be so surprised (they'll never expect it) and we make them feel important and happy. We will feel good about ourselves, because we all love the pleasure of making another person happy. We will also have sense of feeling lighter. There will be more bounce in our step, song will pour forth from our lips and we'll smile more readily, because deep down we will actually feel the weighty debt of gratitude gone and instead we will feel our self worth soaring - we will feel like a million dollars (or more.)   Imagine all of this pleasure and elation from just one little 'Thank you'.

Go on – Put more bounce in your step – Give it a Go!

Day 41

Grumbling

The biggest poison to a life of positivity and upbeat goodness is to grumble or complain. Grumbling means looking at what is in our lives from a negative viewpoint. Grumbling is not to be confused with seeing a situation that needs to be fixed, and then doing what we can to rectify what is not to our liking. Instead, it is the useless expression of negativity which has no positive result at all.

"Oh, what horrible weather."

"I can't stand it when she …"

"My life stinks …"

"You can never do anything right."

When we slip into focusing on what is wrong with our life and others' lives we drag ourselves down immensely. When we share our negativity with others by verbalizing it, then we are like a person spitting foul smelling poison around, because we affect others by our negativity.

"I woke up in such a bad mood. You know how it goes … I wanted to be positive but everything seemed to be working against me."

We all have days when we are feeling down; normally it's due to being sick, tired or hormonally unbalanced. On days like that, it's good to recognise how we feel (i.e. that we are grumpy), accept that it's ok to have off days, and then know with 100% clarity that on days like that we tend to blow things out of proportion and forget to see the silver lining in everything. Once we know that it's just one of those days where we aren't seeing reality for what it is, then we can choose to try really hard not to verbalize our grumps and moans (unless we need to as a release, and even then we should only need to release ONCE).

Holding back on the grumps, moans and criticisms is a fantastic way of building our positive attitude. The more we can hold back when we feel down, the higher we can climb when we are feeling up again. It's like going up a flight of stairs: if we can hold on and stand still on the step when we really feel like quitting and climbing down, then when we have enough energy to resume climbing, we will eventually reach the top of the stairs much quicker.

Give it a Go!

Try and squash a moan, groan, criticism or negative comment about something/somebody today. Feel your strength of character being given a work out by being able to muzzle your moan!

I tried this exercise _____ times.
I would rate this exercise as:

1	2	3	4	5	6	7	8	9	10
(not so good)				(Average)					(Spot on)

Why Should I?

If we can't hold back those moans and criticisms we are just not going to make it to that euphoric state of constant happiness. Moaning is concentrating on the negative things in our lives and criticizing is concentrating on the negative things in other people. Happiness is achieved by concentrating on the good things in life and others. Misery is achieved by concentrating on the bad things in life and others. To maximize happiness we need to get rid of what drags us down into misery. We have to learn to muzzle our mouths, hold it firmly shut and keep silent. Once we have learned the art of holding back our negativity, we can then tell our minds to concentrate on the good things. However, there is no way we are going to be able to re-direct our mind to positive thinking whilst we are speaking negatively, moaning or criticising others.

People avoid moaning, miserable people. They can't be bothered with them. They might not say it to our face, but they don't really care about all our aches, pains and worries – they've got enough of their own. So if we want to get along with people and we want people to like us (or at least enjoy our company), then we need to hold back our negativity and keep our conversations positive.

Sometimes we really have something that is bothering us and we need to talk it over. Talking over our worries or problems is very good and cathartic. Everybody needs a good friend that they can confide in and who can help them by hearing out their problems. It's important to have such a friend and it's important to be a good friend and listener that others can confide in. However, there is a difference between sharing our negativity for therapeutic reasons and just dumping our negativity on everybody. The best way to make sure that we are doing it right is to assign ourselves a good friend (or therapist) and make them our confidante who we turn to when we need to let off steam, work out an issue or just get emotional support. Once we have a confidante, then when we are down we can go and speak with them at length about anything. And then once we have talked our hearts out we should just drop it as a topic of conversation. We don't need to tell 2,4,10,20 or 100 people our problems, that's just going to make us concentrate on the negative in our lives for no positive purpose. If we need to tell another 1 or 2 people because we really think they will be able to help us get clarity on what we can do to solve our problem that's fine. But just telling anyone and everyone our worries makes us miserable and makes others want to avoid us. So tell your confidante all your problems and then hold back those moans and grumbles - you'll be a happier person.

Another form of negative speech, moaning or grumbling is criticising. One reason most people criticize others is they think that by criticising, the other person will change and improve. But that's not how people work. People hate being criticised. Telling a person what is wrong with him/her is like dumping an 'I hate you' message on their head and walking away. People who are criticised don't hear the message others are trying to convey they only hear the message of 'I hate you'. Criticism is not correction, criticism is just air pollution and hate spreading. (Later we will be discussing how to deal with other people criticizing us – and that will be handled in a very different manner. This is because when it comes to dishing out criticism we need to know it doesn't work, but when it comes to receiving criticism there are techniques to learn that can turn it around into a positive. Stay tuned!)

If we truly wish to help others, we need to learn not to criticize them but to HELP them. When we help another person we SHOW the person how they can improve and change, and we show them in a way that they will be able to understand and accept. For example if we have a friend who is wheelchair bound, it's not good to show him/her how we can walk, and what we do to walk because he/she just can't do it. If we try to teach our friend who really can't walk how to walk, we are not helping him/her we are aggravating him/her. So when it comes to correcting people, we have to think first – 'will this person be able to apply this information that I am giving them, given who they are, their mind-set etc...' If we don't think we have the right approach that will work for them then we shouldn't say anything, because anything we do say will be criticism and unnecessary negativity.

On the other hand, if we can be smart and say our correction in a way that makes the other person feel good and empowered to change, then this is correction not criticism and it is positive and good. E.g. "You take such good care of your appearance and dress so well and I really like how well your shirt and pants match so well together. I'm not such an expert on fashion like you, but it might be that if you tuck your shirt into your pants it'll be just like the icing on top of the cake – You'll look a million dollars." Isn't this type of correction more likely to work than saying something like 'Tuck your shirt in, you slob.'

If we can learn the art of correction and never criticize we will be more effective with our interpersonal relationships and our ability to influence others. We will also be more positive and happy. A sign of negativity, bitterness and unhappiness is criticism, whereas a sign of positivity, optimism and happiness is to positively motivate others to do what's good for them. So squash those criticisms they are only robbing us of our own happiness.

This exercise will help us not get pulled down by our internal negativity. Once we learn to ignore those moans, groans and criticisms we will fly high on the power of the positive speech that we'll cultivate instead.

Go on – Transform yourself into the person you want to be – Give it a Go!

Day 42
Wishing Well

"Have a great day."

"I hope you succeed."

"I wish you a year full of goodness and much blessing."

When we wish good things to happen to people, this has an enormous impact on the world for good. We become more positive and develop our hearts to be open and giving. The person receiving our good wishes feels loved and cared for; and the vibes or general atmosphere of the world becomes more positive and loving.

We should be able to reach a point that we are able to think or express something positive to anyone we meet. Every shop keeper, security guard, friend, associate or even someone that we don't like THAT much can be the recipient of our good wishes, happy upbeat manner and our smile. A smile is a way of expressing approval and acceptance of another person, so if we wish someone that good fortune comes their way, and we do it with a smile, we are like a person writing a decree, and our smile is the seal of approval to confirm this good wish.

"When I started wishing that good things happen to people, I noticed so many more people have become friendly with me. I think I must be sending out positive vibes and everyone is attracted to that. Some people ask me what my charismatic trick is, I just say, I sincerely (not faking it) wish good things happen to people, and they do. People love my good wishes and come back for more."

When we wish good things to happen to others, we are actually helping the other person focus positively on the future. As we said before, if we think things will work out well, they are more likely to work out well. Sharing our positivity is a great way of making the world a great place to live.

The opposite of wishing good for a person is to wish that bad things happen to him/her. Doing this is really destructive to our own well-being. When we wish that bad things happen to a person we are becoming negative, pessimistic and really petty. Shouting insults such as "I wish you were ..." will undermine our happiness, cause problems with our interpersonal relationships and bring a feeling of negativity into the world, and as we know, what comes around goes around. So just don't do it! If we can't find anything nice to say about or to another person, then in order to be an elevated individual it is best not to say anything at all. Or even better still, try and rack our brains to find some redeeming feature in this person, and express that.

The most destructive type of wishing bad onto other people is when we wish bad things happen to people who have bestowed good upon us. This behaviour is ingratitude par excellence. As we know gratitude is a way to reach higher levels in inner happiness, and so is wishing that good things happen to others. If we do the opposite, then we are dramatically harming our ability to see the good in our lives and we are destroying our upbeat, positive outlook that we are trying hard to build.

Give it a Go!

1. Resolve from today onwards, never to wish bad upon anyone who has ever bestowed any goodness upon us.

Also:

2. Today wish another person well. (It makes a positive difference to us and the world if we verbally express a good wish for another person even if that person can't hear us.)

I tried this exercise _____ times.
I would rate this exercise as:

1	2	3	4	5	6	7	8	9	10
(not so good)				(Average)				(Spot on)	

Why Should I?

Cursing or wishing bad upon one who has blessed us with good is ingratitude par excellence. It is also a result of twisted and negative thinking – it is the opposite of everything we have discussed until now. If we want to be happy we need to see the good, focus on it, appreciate it, express it and be grateful for it. If a person is able to open their mouths with curses and wishes for negative things to happen to others it is proof that they don't see all the good, appreciate it or feel grateful. Instead they probably interpret everything negatively and feel the world and everyone in it owes them something. A person with this mindset is incapable of being happy – even if they won a million dollars they would find something to complain about.

If we want to stay well clear of being dragged down into negativity then we will **never** wish bad upon the one we have received so much good from. Being careful to avoid this will be a good fence or safeguard to stop us falling into a habit of negativity and losing sight of reality. Reality is we are all very, very blessed with much good in our lives and we all have so much to be grateful for.

Doing this first exercise will free us from being dragged down into negativity. If we resolve never to 'bite the hand that feeds us', or 'throw stones into the well from which we drank', we will be forever protected from slipping down that slide of negativity and we will never reach rock bottom again.

The second exercise makes us into a delightful person to be around. When we wish good things upon others, we bring more good feelings into the world, and we also bring more positivity into people's lives. By thinking, speaking and wanting things to go well for other people we generate more goodness in the world – our well wishing is powerful. The power of speech is so great that when we wish something good to happen to another person, it is more likely that good things will happen. Just try it out.

Go on – Make the world a better place to live in – Give it a Go!

Conclusion

The first of the 7 Ancient Keys to Happiness is to see the good. See how good you are, how good your life is, how good other people are and how good everything is. We learned how to recognise the good, appreciate the good and be thankful for the good. When we practise seeing the good and it becomes our new way of viewing the world – we will feel more than happy, we will feel the ecstasy of living, the serenity of every day and a quiet, calm satisfaction with life.

There is however, one poison that will kill our happiness and positivity and that is cursing/wishing bad upon others. If we want to be happy we have to avoid doing this. We have to be 100% clear that cursing others who have done good to us is the fastest way to destroy our own inner joy.

This first key to happiness is based on the first of the seven commandments given to Noah. It is interesting to note that this was 'Do not curse the Ultimate Source of All Goodness.' At first glance it doesn't seem like a key to happiness. But if we analyse it, we see that the first key to happiness is seeing the good, appreciating it and being grateful, and the ONLY way we can achieve this is if we don't slip into negative thinking and habits. We have to open our eyes to the good in our lives, and then we have to be careful to never repay the one who gave us this good with bad (even in our thoughts.) However, if we're not careful to avoid ingratitude and bitterness, we will inevitably spiral into a negative loop and in a split second ruin all our happiness.

If we can rise above our natural downward pull of negativity and avoid cursing, bitterness and hate, and instead strengthen ourselves to see the good, even in the most trying of circumstances, we will make it through the Gate of Happiness dancing and singing with this key.

CLIMB EVERY MOUNTAIN

KEY #2 - OBJECTIVITY

Introduction

Learn to rise above it all, scale the mountain of self absorption, bias and subjective decision making.

Looking at all people and situations objectively is like being on the top of a mountain looking down at the world and seeing clearly where every road leads, every corner turns into etc... Learning the skills of objectivity allows us to render good, fair and honest judgements about the events and people in our life. When we choose a good path, an easy road to travel or a more direct route from the vantage point on top of the mountain of objectivity, then our life will naturally run more smoothly, have less bumps, hiccups or surprises and we will know that we are heading in the right direction towards our goals.

Learning how to be objective is learning how to be a giver. How is that? You might ask. It is because objectivity is giving ourselves and others the gift of a good and fair decision or judgement.

When we learn to judge objectively we are giving ourselves the gift of well thought out, 1st grade, top professional life advice. If we are objectively judging the people that impact on our lives, then we are giving them the gift of love. We are giving them a fair chance, and seeing them as real people whom we may be able to help. As opposed to if we deal with people on a subjective emotional level we may over-react, dramatize, over-extend or engage in any other emotionally charged behaviours that negatively impact on the other person. Objectivity allows us to be a loving, fair and caring person and at the same time not be walked all over, spat on, used or abused. Only through learning the ability to be objective can we find the happy and healthy balance between seeing what's good in everything and protecting our precious positive world against negative influences, which may destroy all the positive and good work that we have tried so hard to nurture.

Day 43

You're the Judge

Until now we have been talking about trying to see the good things that we have in our lives. Through training ourselves to see the good, and by concentrating on that good and even tracing the good back to the source of where the good came from we have learned how to start to lead lives filled with contentment, satisfaction and joy. The next step, in our journey, is to learn some tools to help up protect our ability to continue to think positively and see the good and the best tool to learn is objectivity.

The most important ability we need to learn in life is the ability to judge ourselves objectively. We all need to be able to honestly look at ourselves in the mirror and see us for who we really are. This includes seeing the good things about us and it also includes seeing the 'warts and all'.

Why do we need to do this? Because we are important and we have amazing amounts of potential. We need to see ourselves as important enough to take seriously. Our lives and personal development are serious issues. If we don't want to improve ourselves to be the best we can be – nobody else in the world is going to do it for us. If we don't want to work at maximizing our potential, no fairy is going to come along and wave their magic wand to make it happen.

Another point to remember is we don't have all the time in the world to make the most of our lives. Every single human being is born with a terminal illness – called lifespan. How old do you think you'll be when you die? 80 years, 90 years maybe 120 years if we're lucky. No one knows how long he/she will live, so we need to get up and move now. Time is ticking away. We need to set our goals in life and work towards achieving them now, before time runs out.

The best way to maximize our potential is to do a daily accounting. This means working out what we did with our day and how we can improve. Nobody else can do this for us as nobody could really be bothered doing it for us. We need to take charge of our lives, we need to be the judge of how we are going, and we need to plan and work out how we can do better. Once we can do this we will be soaring towards success.

When we learn how to honestly judge ourselves we are able to direct our lives towards good and avoid all the pitfalls of the past. A little bit of objectively looking in the mirror at ourselves, gives us a lot of self-knowledge and direction in life.

Give it a Go!

It's time to get quiet, be by yourself and introspect again.
At the end of the day, think about your day and ask yourself the following six questions:

1. What were the 3 best parts of my day today?
2. What did I do (say or think) that was good or bought out the elevated side of my nature?
3. What are my goals in life?
4. How did my actions today lead me towards my goals?
5. What's ONE thing I did (said or thought) today that wasn't reflective of the type of person I want to be? (Don't get stuck in negativity, try to stick to only finding ONE thing that you wish you hadn't done that day.) If however, you **honestly** can't think of anything you did wrong that day – then CELEBRATE, pat yourself on the back, dance or sing - you had a great day!
6. How can I do better tomorrow (or next time)?

When answering these last two questions try and tap into your quiet voice answers, because when thinking about a negative incident the noisy voice may shout "blame him/her/me/this/that....never talk to him/her again....." Blaming is not productive, and neither is getting angry, guilty, depressed, despondent, anxious or losing your calm centred feeling. Ask this question in a loving way, looking for positive and constructive answers from your quiet voice, answers that if you implement, will make you feel like a more elevated type of person. Don't be afraid of being honest with yourself, and don't be afraid to admit that you've made a mistake. It's human to make mistakes but it's foolish not to plan ways to avoid making them again in the future.

I tried this exercise _____ times.
I would rate this exercise as:

1	2	3	4	5	6	7	8	9	10
(not so good)				(Average)					(Spot on)

Why Should I?

This exercise is the key to continued, sustained success and growth. It will keep us positive, keep our eye on our goals and help us weed out anything we are doing that is destructive. The essence of this exercise is to be able to look objectively at ourselves and our day and then take action.

Some people have taken this exercise on as a daily before bed-time ritual. People who do this consistently are guaranteed to have successful lives. Why? Because they are reinforcing their successes and boldly facing their failures in order to turn those failures into successes as well. These people have a tangible feeling of success, growth and rejuvenation because they are constantly achieving, becoming better people and reaching their goals.

The process of evaluating our day is something that all highly successful business people also do. They see their sales, analyse their losses and plan ways to avoid making similar mistakes that caused those losses. They focus most of their attention on the positive, that is on the sales, how high they are and how they can make them even higher, but they don't neglect to plan against their losses.

If we want to live a good life, it is extremely important that we learn to honestly evaluate ourselves and every day we live.

When we speak about honestly evaluating oneself, it doesn't mean just looking at what we did wrong. That wouldn't be an honest evaluation, because we also did heaps of good things that day too. An honest evaluation of ourselves is being able to see all the great things in us and our day, as well as seeing where we went astray from our goals. Once we have an honest objective view of ourselves and our day then we can plan for a better future. If however we are not viewing ourselves honestly (by being either too critical of ourselves, or conversely refusing to see our mistakes), then we won't be able to zoom full speed towards our goal and achieve phenomenal success. But if we are honest and objective – we will be like a missile – on target, fast, powerful and unstoppable in achieving our goals.

Go on – Achieve every goal you've ever wanted to – Give it a Go!

Day 44
Live and let Live

Imagine we just invested many hours planning, designing and finally creating a sumptuous meal for a dinner party we were having in the evening. Once we have made the food, we are careful to protect the fine food from maggot laying flies entering our kitchen and spoiling our hard work. So too we should be careful to protect our positivity from negative 'flies' entering our lives.

Our ability to remain positive and focused on the good in our lives and other people is often hampered by various negative influences that we may have in our lives. The influences may be certain people, places or activities that we do. If we want to maintain our positive focus we need to learn to navigate through these negative influences that threaten to tip us off balance.

Imagine we are the ruler and judge of a kingdom. In our kingdom we judge those who come before us fairly. We make criminals return what they stole, we help make peace between bickering neighbours and we try to be good and fair to everybody. The objective of our judgements is not to just punish because the person did something bad, but purely on a case by case basis we try to work out the best way to fix up the situation and guard against it happening again. Sometimes we have a criminal who is really a negative influence on the rest of our happy kingdom. Being a loving and caring ruler and judge we try to teach the criminal how to behave in a way that will not be damaging to the rest of society. However, if a particular criminal is just not capable of listening to our advice and is not able to be integrated into society, what do we do? We lock him away in jail. When we lock him away we feel sad that we can't help him become less destructive, but we know it's for his own good and for society's good.

Every person is really a judge. We judge people, places and events all day long. In order to lead a life full of joy and happiness, we need to learn how to be objective, benevolent, but true and fair judges. We need to know when to distance ourselves from destructive influences, and when to try and rehabilitate those destructive influences and allow them to remain around us. When judging we need to be truthful to ourselves, we need to see the good in others, events and situations, and at the same time we need to be fully cognizant of the negativity that they may introduce.

We can climb the mountain of our own bias and subjectivity and rise above ourselves to see the situation objectively. Once we have done this, it is easier for us to decide what might be the best course of action to follow with respect to these negative influences. Then we need to follow through with our resolve. All the time that we are doing this it is important to keep in mind and know that we are precious and that we need to protect that part of us that is beautiful, pure and good. The more we value ourselves, the more we will realize that we are worth protecting. By learning to climb the mountain of subjectivity, we can then look out objectively onto a beautiful world and decide the best way of protecting our precious selves and dealing with negative influences.

The previous exercise explained how to judge ourselves in order to achieve our goals. But we also need to learn how to judge others and to honestly evaluate them. When we can see others objectively we are in a better position to decide how we should relate to them and interact with them.

"I'm a live and let live type of person, why should I judge others?"

We judge others whether we like it or not; it is a human trait to decode the environment we are living in, and judge how that affects us and act accordingly. Judging others doesn't mean walking around with a condemning mindset – that's a good way to be miserable. Judging others means seeing the good and the not so good, then putting both of these in perspective, and analysing how this person, place or event impacts on us and the other people around us. If we conclude that the person, place or event is having a negative effect on us then we decide what to do. It doesn't mean being mean, nasty or rude, but it does means thinking what's best for us and those we care for, and acting to protect them.

If something is likely to cause us harm, wouldn't we like others to warn us? Of course, we would. What about if we knew that someone would be killed if they were to walk into a certain room – would we warn them? Of course, we would. We instinctively desire to save others from harm, and we want others to help us avoid being hurt. Saying 'live and let live' when people are going to get hurt is not a compassionate doctrine. In general, it's not right to be overbearing and forcing our opinions on others in general, but when it comes to preventing people from being hurt, there is a time to act or at least warn others.

"Okay, you have to stop people hurting others really badly, but some people could take this idea too far. We all should have the freedom to express and be who we want to be."

The way in which we know that we are doing it right is if we maintain the loving perspective – even to those doing what we want to distance ourselves from. If we dislike the harm a person does, but not the actual person, then we can often balance this correctly.

Give it a Go!

Think about a person you don't like very much.

Now ask yourself: 'Why don't I like him/her?'

(Is it because of a 'feeling', 'some bad vibes', or you simply don't like the look of them etc? Or, Is it based on evidence, facts, experience etc?)

Now ask yourself: (Circle Yes or No for the questions below)

Am I being fair and objective in my judgment of this person? Yes/No

Have I honestly looked at this person? Yes/No

Am I able to see the good side of them as well as the bad? Yes/No

Am I distancing myself from this person because they are likely to be a negative influence on me or others? Yes/No

If you answered "No" to any of the questions then you will benefit greatly from learning the skills of being able to objectively judge others.

I tried this exercise _____ times.
I would rate this exercise as:

1	2	3	4	5	6	7	8	9	10
(not so good)				(Average)				(Spot on)	

Why Should I?

We are constantly judging people. This exercise will open our eyes up to see that most of the time when we judge others we are not doing it objectively.

Many people may judge others on a 'feeling' they have about that person. There is nothing wrong with using our intuition, in fact, it's great to be in touch with our intuitive side. However, we need to back up our intuition with objective thought. If we don't engage in objective thought we are likely to feel dislike or hatred towards a person who has never (and may never) done anything bad to us.

We want to learn to judge others objectively and fairly. If we can learn this skill, we will have a more open and loving heart, even towards those people we have to distance ourselves from.

In order to be happy, upbeat and vibrant people we need to know how to deal with drag-me-down types of people in a loving but firm manner. We don't need to let negative influences on us make us into bitter or angry people. We can learn to judge objectively, taking nothing 'personally' and leave our negative emotions out of it.

When we don't judge people objectively we are likely to get ourselves all worked up. We can become aware of when we are judging subjectively by feeling our emotional pulse. Are we letting this person get on our nerve, increase our blood pressure, get us angry, sad, panicky etc? If we are, then we know we have slipped into subjectivity. Objectivity takes the heat and sting out of the situation.

Wouldn't it be great to reach a point where you can smile, feel loving towards a person and yet say "No, I'm sorry, this situation/friendship etc. is just not for me"?

We can be assertive and caring, happy and firm, loving and self-assured all at the same time. This exercise will teach us the first step, and that is getting in touch with how we currently judge people. Over the next few days we will be looking at various ways to become a better judge and hopefully by the end of the section we will be a loving, confident, wise and objective judge.

Go on – See things as they really are – Give it a Go!

CLIMB EVERY MOUNTAIN

KEY #2 - OBJECTIVITY

THE DYNAMICS OF JUDGING OBJECTIVELY

The following sections are some ways to learn how to objectively judge other people. They are guidelines to help us maintain a positive outlook on life and not get dragged down by other's negativity whilst at the same time not living in La-La Land where we are not prepared to protect ourselves against the negative side of humanity.

Until now we have been focusing on seeing the good, but that doesn't mean negative influences don't exist - they do. We just want our mind to focus on what is good in the world because that will make us happy. However, if we bury our heads in the sand to the real potential areas of harm in our lives we are likely to get hurt. It's a fine balance between always looking for the good and avoiding the harmful influences in our lives. This section hopes to provide some guidelines to help walk the tightrope of balancing these two – i.e. to remain positive, upbeat and loving yet street smart, assertive and tough.

Learning how to Judge people/situations has four steps:
1. Hearing the charge
2. Listening to the Prosecutor
3. Hearing the Defence
4. Handing down Judgements

Only once we have mastered these four steps will we be able to confidently say we have climbed the mountain of subjectivity and can now grasp the second Ancient Key to Happiness - 'Objectivity' with both hands. Read on to discover how to master these four steps...

Day 45

Hear the charge

When passing judgment on anybody we really need to start a court case. A court case has many preliminaries before the decision is passed down. The first preliminary is to hear the charge. Before any evidence is given normally a charge is read out. So before we start digging up the dirt on people we need to find out - what is the charge being made against this person? Is it serious enough to warrant a court case?

If someone were to come before a judge and charge the accused with the crime of "She dresses in such outdated ugly clothes", then the case would be thrown out of court, because it's petty and doesn't really warrant wasting the judge's time and attention.

When we are judging others we need to act like a real judge in court. As such, the first thing we need to decide is: "Is this an area serious enough to require me to waste my time or thought space on?" After all, when hearing evidence in a case, a lot of negative information must be processed. If we want to remain positive people, we need to weed out paying attention to negative nonsense. If we keep in mind that we only want to hear negativity solely for the purpose of doing good in the long run, then we will discover there is a lot of information that people want to tell us that we don't need to know.

So what if someone wants to tell us hot gossip about shocking or funny things that other people have said or done, that make the person look foolish or unimportant? If people want to tell us information that runs others down, then we have a choice. We can choose to listen, and let our whole mind-focus become negative, and ignore the good, lovable and honourable side of people. Or we can choose to throw the case out of court and refuse to listen, because the information is irrelevant to our lives.

However, before we proceed, it's important to determine whether we really should be hearing the charge. So how do we know when it's good for us to listen to other's negativity, and when it's good for us to avoid it?

When judging a court case we need to determine a few preliminaries:
1) Does this come under our jurisdiction – that means do I need to know about it so I can take action? i.e. Has this negative comment got anything to do with me or my life?

Situations that come within our jurisdiction can be:
a. When I can change the situation by speaking with the person, educating them, giving a punishment as a deterrent for a future repetition of this behaviour (not because we want to take revenge or 'I'll show them') AND it is likely what I do will have a positive effect,
b. When I can reform the accused – by slowly, over time, helping the person to behave better. This can only be done if we are the one who can influence them. We have to be honest with ourselves and know when we can have a positive effect on a person, or if our meddling will make things worse for those involved.
c. When I can be on guard against a **possible** hurtful situation. Most of us listen to negative information about others, thinking: 'Perhaps I'll need to know this sometime in the distance future – you never know when you need to know.' Having a good grip on reality helps us decide if there is really a possibility of a hurtful situation arising, or if it's just somebody sensationalizing and blowing things totally out of proportion, or feeding us conjecture and making us view the world negatively for no good reason. Any message of "watch out for them" where "them" is a faceless nameless person/people is just going to rob us of our peace of mind for absolutely no constructive purpose.
d. Helping others to avoid being hurt. If we focus on others' shortcomings, or anything else that is not so good and positive in order to help another person from being hurt then we are listening for a constructive purpose and that's great. Like in the above situation, it has to be a situation that is possibly harmful and it's likely that we will know someone who will need to be warned/helped.

If the information is not relevant to our lives – then why do we need to clog our minds with others' negative poison? In order to answer this question we need to focus on what is likely to influence us, and what is so remote and unlikely to make any impact on our lives at all. There is a good rule of thumb to go by to determine what is likely and what is remote that is: If there is a double degree of doubt don't worry. That means if there is a "perhaps this will happen and then if that happens perhaps this other thing will also happen and then the situation will be really bad" type of scenario. e.g. Maybe I'll go overseas (unlikely) and maybe I'll sign a business contract with him (but I'm not even in business). Or 'perhaps the murderer will escape from jail and then perhaps he will come to my neighbourhood 500km away...' Why worry about such unlikely occurrences – information about such things is really not relevant to our lives, it'll only drag us down.

2) Is it important enough to dwell on or is the accusation trivial. Does this really warrant my attention, or is it mindless gossip and negativity? We all know these examples "she said that he said that you said that he has a big nose!" We don't need to pay attention to childish bickering.

3) Is the person reading out the charges a trustworthy person? If we know someone makes up stories or blows things totally out of proportion then we may decide to discount their accusations. It doesn't mean to dismiss anyone's opinion if we don't agree with it. But if we've tried and tested out someone and we know they just don't know what they are talking about, then we shouldn't listen to their negativity because it will only drag us down, and we know it won't be for a positive purpose. We need to learn to know who we can trust to tell us important information and who just likes shooting off their mouth.

In summary ask yourself:
"Do I really NEED to know this information?"
(Or is it just going to drag me down into somebody else's negativity for no good reason.)

Give it a Go!

Make a note (mental note or written down) of how many times someone concentrates your attention (by making a non-positive remark) on something negative, unpleasant or not to their taste, whether it be about another person, place, thing or event. Then at the end of the day add up how many of those comments you really needed to hear, i.e. how many were cases that your internal courtroom needed to judge, and how many cases really should have been thrown out of court. This exercise is quite eye opening and will show you how often you are needlessly pulled down by others' negativity.

I tried this exercise _____ times.
I would rate this exercise as:

1	2	3	4	5	6	7	8	9	10
(not so good)				(Average)					(Spot on)

Why Should I?

Do you want to stay upbeat and positive without having to go off into the hills and become a recluse? Of course you do. We all want to be happy and positive whilst managing the bumpy waters of inter-personal interactions. In order to maintain an elevated mindset, without running for the hills we need to learn the art of filtering. We need to filter out all the negativity and keep only those things we really need to know about.

This exercise will give us insight into the negativity that we are absorbing without even realizing it. We are constantly being bombarded with negativity from other people and the media, and most of the time we don't need to know about it. Not every vice of human kind is going to affect us, we don't need to know every detailed account of how rotten some people are, some companies are or how life is. Often the negative information we receive comes from people who have a hard time seeing the good in life. We don't have to swallow their view of the world.

We need to learn the art of being discerning. Yes, there are times we need to know things, in order to take proper precautions, but as this exercise will show us – most of the negative information we are fed is absolutely irrelevant to us and our lives. Why be bogged down unnecessarily by other peoples negativity and emotional baggage?

Free yourself from the insanity of other's needless negativity. Open your eyes to the times you are just swallowing their pessimism, hate, and negative pills. Only once you have learned to see useless negative information for what it is, will you be empowered to do something to avoid it.

Go on – See when others are needlessly dragging you down – Give it a Go!

Day 46
DEAF

"I don't want to be dragged down by other's negativity, but what can I do – I don't want to be rude or look weird?"

When we are being subjected to others bombardment of needless negativity we can choose to be DEAF.

D – Defend
E – Educate
A – Alter
F – Flee

Defend
We can choose to defend the person being verbally attacked. We can say "It's not that bad", or "I'm sure she had a good reason: maybe it was …" We can down play how bad the speaker said it was e.g. "her clothes are really not that bad, I quite like them." After we have defended the person we should try and change the subject, or else the speaker might try and counter-defend and prove how what they originally said was correct. We don't need to get into a conversation concentrating on others faults. We can change the subject by asking a question such as "What time is it?"

Educate
We can teach the person who is focusing on the negative things in life how to cultivate a positive attitude and look for the good in things. We might be able to do this by explaining how good they will feel if they changed their focus from what's wrong in life and other people, and concentrate on what is good about them. If the person is not open to deep discussions like this we could just simply say something like, "I hope you don't talk like that about me." Saying such a comment however, might embarrass him/her a bit, so again change the subject so they don't feel they need to wallow in their embarrassment.

Alter

Alter the subject. This is a great fun game. You probably never knew you had so much power, but you do. We can actually change the subject of conversation whenever we desire. The more we practice the better we will get at it, and the fact that we are changing the subject will go unnoticed by most people. Some good ways to change the subject are to ask questions e.g. "what did you do on vacation", tell a riddle or a joke e.g. "what's black and white and red all over" or say "that reminds me of"

Flee

If we are stuck with someone who just won't stop dumping their negative garbage on our heads - we can choose to leave. This is quick and simple, and it can be done easily without hurting or offending the person. We can pretend we need the bathroom and leave, or say 'bye, I've got to go now." People will get the hint eventually, and will be happy to have positive conversations with us. After all, everyone really enjoys a good uplifting positive conversation.

Give it a Go!

Try each of these techniques out with your friend (who you are doing this book with). Take it in turns one person saying something negative and then get the other one to defend, educate, alter or flee.
Or if you are doing the book by yourself, try out these techniques over the next few days with people who are trying to dump their negative garbage onto you. Play with the techniques to discover which ones work best for you in which situations and with which people for you.

I tried this exercise _____ times.
I would rate this exercise as:

1	2	3	4	5	6	7	8	9	10
(not so good)				(Average)					(Spot on)

Why Should I?

Take your life into your own hands. We don't have to be a victim of other's negativity. We have the power to turn things around. We can make sure all of our interactions are positive. We don't have to be a passive sufferer of things that drag us down. Take charge and be a pro-active positive person.

LEARNING TO JUDGE

The more skilled we become at these tools the more frequently we will have positive conversations with people. This will make us feel great and it will also make other people want to be around us more. As we have said many times – people love positive people. They don't really enjoy it when they moan and groan, they are dying for someone to take them out of the misery of their own minds and show them an elevated positive way of seeing the world. When we are positive we give others around us a momentary trip into the world of goodness and positivity whilst they are interacting with us . People will love it, and they will come back for more, over and over again.

Most of all however, we will feel great. We will have the skills to fight off attacks of negativity from others. We will be able to easily maintain our happy outlook, and will feel a sense of empowerment and achievement in being able to be upbeat and positive in the face of all adversity.

Go on – Take charge and make every interaction a positive one – Give it a Go!

Day 47

Listen Carefully to the Prosecutor.

What if others are telling us negative things that we need to know. On the one hand we want to stay upbeat and positive so we don't want to hear stuff that drags us down. On the other hand, if they are telling us information that we need to know in order to protect ourselves or others from harm, we would be foolish not to listen.

So if someone starts telling us something negative about another person we have to decide if it's something we really need to know. If we do need to know the low down on the person, then we should listen and listen carefully, so that we can be a good and informed judge. When we listen to the 'prosecutor', we need to keep thinking "Is this true?" "Is this a convincing case?" Just accepting negative information about another person without analysing it doesn't make us a very good judge. Judges need to be smart, turned on and listening fully.

Imagine if someone told us "Shopkeeper X is a thief." This is the charge. If we go to Shopkeeper X's store (or we know someone personally that goes to that store), then we want to hear what the person has to say, to protect ourselves or our friends.

So we encourage the person to tell us more. Imagine they said "I went to his shop yesterday and he overcharged me on the toaster I bought. I saw it advertised in another store's catalogue for $20 cheaper."

We need to then ask ourselves: 'Does the fact that the same toaster can be found on sale at another shop make the shopkeeper a thief?'

Sometimes people will accuse others of terrible things, having wrongly deduced one thing from the other. If we accept blindly other people's conclusions, we may find that we are viewing the world negatively and hating people for absolutely no good reason.

We can ask ourselves, "Is the evidence good quality, sound evidence that is good proof of the charge, or is it mere guesswork?" or "Did I really understand correctly what the 'prosecutor' was saying? Maybe I misheard and need to clarify what I thought she said."

Sometimes we need to have MORE evidence to decide. For example: "Are the rest of the items in shopkeeper X's store also way above market price?" or "Was the other store that advertised the toaster selling below cost, second-hand goods/returns/damaged items etc." We can even ask other people if they have seen or heard similar things (e.g. did you hear anything about shopkeeper X's pricing policy?)

The main point to remember is, if we need to know negative information, it doesn't mean that we should accept what we are told to be 100% true. We can hear the low down on people and take actions to avoid being hurt by them, but we don't have to believe that this person is the embodiment of evil that we are being told they are. We don't even have to believe what we are told to be true. We can act as though it MIGHT be true while we investigate further to find out if the information is true. We don't have to take other people's negative interpretations and information on board. If we can investigate the matter ourselves, it's advisable to do so. If we can't investigate the accusation, we can at least, in our hearts, have some doubt about the accuracy of the report, whilst still taking precautions not to get hurt. It's like driving a car. We put on our seat belts 'just in case' we have an accident, but we don't honestly expect to have an accident. The same goes for taking precautionary action to avoid being hurt by someone – we will take the precaution but we don't have to expect to be hurt, (e.g. if we thought it was wise we could go to Shopkeeper X's shop, but making sure that we only buy what we know is a bargain and not rely on his word.)

If we blindly believe the negative information we are told without analysing it, we might cause ourselves a lot of heart-ache and anger. We might fight with a loved one, break up with a friend or wilfully take revenge on an innocent person – all because we believed another person's false negative report. In order to lead happy lives, we have to be willing to listen to some necessary negative information but not to over-react or believe everything we are told.

"I grew up being told that my grandmother was a mean, nasty, vengeful and wicked person. I have very few childhood memories about her. But as I got older I decided to meet her and fill in this missing piece of my life. I was so surprised when I finally met my grandmother – she was kind, loving, sweet and giving. It seems that she and my parents had a falling out and as a result the grandchildren grew up never really knowing their grandmother. I was glad I made an effort to seek her out, it just proves to me that you can't judge other people based on another person's impression."

Give it a Go!

Think about a time recently when someone told you something negative about another person (that is important for you to know). Now analyse the evidence that person presented. Was the evidence sound and completely conclusive? If the evidence wasn't that solid, then resolve not to believe what you were told but be on guard – just in case they were right. Then try cross-examining the person who told you or do independent investigations, until you have enough facts to enable you to make a good, logical and fair decision.

I tried this exercise _____ times.
I would rate this exercise as:

1	2	3	4	5	6	7	8	9	10
(not so good)				(Average)					(Spot on)

Why Should I?

Why introduce unnecessary hate and negativity into our minds? Why accept other people's pessimistic view of the world as a fact? We can protect ourselves against harm without going overboard and adopting others often overdramatised 'we're all doomed' mindset.

Also, sometimes people are wrong. They might think they have all of the facts but people are human and they make mistakes in judgment. Have you ever been accused of doing something you've never done? Or if you did do it, it was because you had a good reason. If someone had the decency to ask for your side of the story then you wouldn't have looked half as bad as others were saying you were. People misjudge others so often. We shouldn't just gullibly swallow negative verdicts about other people's behaviour.

Only a fool believes everything he/she's told. Don't be a fool, be wise – cautiously evaluate information given to you. On the other hand only an imbecile doesn't guard themselves from a possible danger. So be smart – don't believe all those negative stories but protect yourself anyway.

Go on – Think independently – Give it a Go!

Day 48
You're on trial

"Your sister said that she can't rely upon you for anything. She said that you forgot to buy her the bread and milk she asked for when you went shopping yesterday."

Relating information back to the accused is generally a destructive thing to do, as it's not good for us to meddle into other people's affairs and make others hate each other for no good reason.   Positive people try and make people feel good about themselves and others. Negative people try and drag up the dirt on anyone and anything.

Although it's not good for us to relate negativity for nothing, if someone else tells us something that makes us aware that others are unhappy about our behaviour , then we need to begin a 'new case' and be a good judge of ourselves. We need to listen to the charge and the evidence that the person is relaying and then judge what we should do. I.e." what can I do right now to bring about a positive result from this accusation?" We may have our excuses/defences etc, but the offended party probably doesn't know about them. The best course of action is to not really believe in our heart the statement that we were told - we can choose to reserve the right to decide until a later date. Then we could approach the person who may be upset with us and see firsthand if we have hurt their feelings. This can be done in a non-confrontational way, by casual conversation or by gently bringing up the topic and explaining our side of the story. We should find out if their grievance is real then if it's true, try and find a solution - e.g. apologise.

The other option of going back and forth via a mudslinging messenger (e.g. "What! Did she say that about me? You tell her she is a selfish, self-centred ingrate...."), is more likely to result in lots of ill feeling - so don't do it. If we remember that most people in this world are really good people – but sometimes they act poorly out of hurt feelings, then we will feel confident that we have the ability to sort out whatever problem another person has with us. We don't have to go on the defensive to protect our feelings of self-worth when we know we are good and so is the other person. Together we will be able to work out most problems. We can have confidence in our ability to have peaceful relationships, and have belief in the other person's goodwill.

After we have sorted out the grievance we could take action so this "he said, she said ..." scenario doesn't happen again. If the person who spoke against us is open to it (i.e. it's not going to cause a fight by mentioning it), we could ask her to speak directly to us about her gripes next time. This can be done nicely without anger, explaining that we really care about her, and want to sort things out with her, but it hurts our feelings when people speak out their grievances to others who cannot help. One great tip to remember about trying to change other's behaviour is: **Don't focus on the past - always try and rectify things for the future.** However, if it's not likely that the situation will ever occur again or the person is incapable of changing, then there's no point discussing it.

Give it a Go!

Think whether today or recently someone has said something negative about you "e.g. you're a scatterbrain." Ask yourself: "What's the evidence?" "Is it true?" (e.g. that I am forgetful.) If the answer is "yes" then pass judgement on yourself by asking: "What should I do now to make up with anyone I've hurt?" and "What can I do today to help prevent this harming myself or others in the future?" (e.g. buy a diary and write things in it).

I tried this exercise _____ times.
I would rate this exercise as:

1	2	3	4	5	6	7	8	9	10
(not so good)				(Average)					(Spot on)

Why Should I?

Earlier we wrote about how important it was to evaluate ourselves every day. In this scenario however, it's somebody else evaluating us. If we want to be the best person we can be, we'll want to know how we can improve. When we've stepped on other's toes, it's great that they yelp 'Ouch', then we can apologise and fix up the damage that we have done.

We don't mean to hurt other people, but because we are not perfect and human beings are such complicated creatures we often end up hurting people. When we are told about it, we should jump for joy as we have been given an opportunity to clear up a misunderstanding or hurt before things really turned sour.

We can be brave, strong and confident. We can face our imperfections and say 'Yes, I'm not perfect – I'm sorry.' Only somebody who is truly strong can do such a thing. If we shy away from fixing up our mistakes, then it doesn't make the situation better and in the long run it will rob us of our vitality and happiness.   Being pro-active in patching up little hurts and interpersonal relationship blunders will make us feel great. We will feel in charge of our lives, we will feel strong and victorious. And those that we approach to appease will be impressed with our honesty, integrity and self confidence. Not many people are brave enough to face their problems. Doing this exercise will train us in the art of self mastery, integrity and inner strength.

Go on – Build up those 'hero' muscles – Give it a Go!

Day 49
Confidently Criticized

We don't always 'find out' that someone is upset with us from a third party sometimes the person who is hurt tells us directly. Or sometimes a person is not really hurt by us, but tells us what's not good about us. We all get it from time to time. It's not pleasant, it's a blow to our self-confidence and sometimes it's even true – it's called criticism. When we get doses of criticism we again can put on our objective judge hat and try to see the situation for what it really is.

"I asked you to do this for me and you forgot. You let me down again."

"How could you get such a low mark?"

"I hate you, you're a worthless good-for-nothing."

So how does a person with self confidence handle criticism?
1. Hear what the other person is really saying (we learnt how to do this in "Understanding Gobbly Gook".)
2. Ask ourselves: "Is what the person saying true?" This means doing some self-introspection. We may find that there is an element of truth to what they are saying. E.g. we did let somebody down. Or we may find that the person is completely wrong and just reflecting on to us some of their faults e.g. someone who is obsessed with her weight is likely to falsely accuse us of being obsessed with our weight or will make an untrue comment about our weight. The only way to get this right is to take the other person's comment seriously enough to fully consider it, and yet have a strong enough knowledge of ourselves to know when someone else is completely wrong.
3. Admit to ourselves that we are not perfect. Having a realistic picture of ourselves, including our imperfections, is a great way to have self-esteem. We can still love ourselves even when we stare our faults right in the face. When we stop running away from our imperfections or sweeping them under the carpet, and

actually admit them and love ourselves anyway, then we are not so upset when others notice our faults.

4. Admit any fault of our own to the other person, and apologise. E.g. I know I didn't do well on my test, but I tried hard, and that's the best I could do. I'm sorry I disappointed you.

5. Positively affirm ourselves. After we've been dealt a blow of disapproval, we need to applaud ourselves for handling the situation so well, for becoming a more elevated person, for all the other good qualities that we do possess, and have confidence that with time we will be able to overcome this current flaw of ours.

Look at criticism as a tool which can be used to become a better person. The more we love criticism, because it opens our eyes to our hidden faults, the happier we will be when others criticize us. Yes, we can actually reach a level where we are HAPPY to receive honest criticism. After all, we want to be the best person that we can be. Other people's criticism can help us in our quest for perfection.

If we don't feel self-confident enough to handle criticism in the way mentioned above, the second best way to deal with the situation is to admit to the other person that we can't handle their criticism. E.g. *"Dad, you know when you say things like that to me, I feel really bad about myself. It throws me into a depression for 5 days, I can't eat or sleep. Please help me, I want to please you, but this criticism just gets to me."* We can say this type of statement over and over again to the person who really loves us but criticizes us. They don't want to hurt us, so they will try and find a way to help us without hurting us.

Give it a Go!

Go and ask 3 people for 5 areas you need to improve on. (The first one is usually the person warming up to see if you really want to hear, so bite your tongue and keep listening). If you find anything that the 3 people say in common, then that may be an area you need to work on. Be strong and be proud of yourself for having the courage to want to hear what you need to work on.

I tried this exercise _____ times.
I would rate this exercise as:

1	2	3	4	5	6	7	8	9	10
(not so good)				(Average)					(Spot on)

Why Should I?

Make the most of yourself and your life – learn to see other people's criticisms as free expert advice on how to become the best you.

Many companies pay thousands of dollars for experts to come into their businesses and tell them what they are doing wrong. The more problems the expert can find the happier the company's directors are. Why? Because they want their business to be the best and most profitable it can be. By having someone come and show them how they can improve, they know they will eventually be making huge profits.

We need to treat ourselves like a business. We are in the business of pleasure and happiness. The more we can improve and become better people the happier we will become. We should pay other people to criticise us and show us where we can improve!

This exercise will help us overcome the fear of being criticised and will enable us to develop a positive mindset to criticism. Not all criticism we get is helpful or true, but we can learn to discard the unhelpful advice and tune in and make the most of that insightful advice we just know we can benefit from.

Don't be afraid of disapproval – look at it as a gift from a business guru whose expertise is helping you make the most of your life.

Go on – Show them you're not afraid to be the best – Give it a Go!

Day 50
Hear the Defence

Once we have heard the charge against the accused and we have decided that the charge is important enough to listen to and it falls within our jurisdiction then it's time to start the case. First we listen to the evidence and then in order for a trial to be fair, it's important that we have somebody to defend the accused against the charge.

"Why should we defend her if she's done something really wrong? After all, we only listened to the low down on her because we needed to protect ourselves or others."

None of us would like to be put on trial without a chance to stand up and explain our behaviour. Everybody in this world does things for a reason. The reason may not justify the act, but the person doing it **feels** justified. It is important to be able to see things from another's perspective in order to get a full picture on the situation. After all there may be some mitigating circumstances, misinterpreted information, or a perfectly good explanation for the thing that seems so wrong in our eyes.

E.g. Mr X. was brought up in a home where his mother taught him from an early age how to steal. He went to a school with other children who were brought up stealing and he really didn't have much chance in life to learn how to do better. However one day he decided that he wasn't going to steal anymore. His resolve was strong, and for about 6 months he didn't raise a finger to take what wasn't his. Then one day temptation was too much, and he was caught stealing a car stereo system.

If we were to be judging the case, it would be important for us to know his background and his current frame of mind to decide what we should do with him to help him not steal and to help society not be victimized by him. Although, we still need to be wary of him, or take action to make sure he can't steal from others, we are more likely to hand down a fair judgement if we know all the facts.

If we can apply this to our lives it might go something like this: "My mother/father/Step-mother/Step-father/sibling was a ..., but I suppose s/he couldn't really help it. The home environment s/he grew up in was enough to make anybody a ... In fact if I grew up the way s/he did, I don't think I would have acted any better. My poor relative, must have been messed up from a very early age." Once we have defended the person, it doesn't mean we should expose ourselves to being hurt by them. Defending someone just helps us understand them and judge more objectively and with less anger. However the judgement may still be: avoid or minimize contact with the person – if they are likely to harm us in the future. We will discuss judgements more later.

Give it a Go!

Think of somebody who has done something wrong to you recently (e.g. maybe someone 'stole' the car parking place you were just about to park in). Now try and see if there were any mitigating circumstances. Try to defend them.

I tried this exercise _____ times.
I would rate this exercise as:

1	2	3	4	5	6	7	8	9	10
(not so good)				(Average)				(Spot on)	

Why Should I?

The more we can learn the art of defending people who have hurt us, the less angry we will be. Also the more we are able to defend wrong doers the more we are able to judge objectively. If we can only see a person as all bad or all wicked or all wrong then it is 100% guaranteed that we are not an objective judge. To be objective we must be able to see BOTH sides of the equation – the good and the bad in the person.

Defending people will help us develop our positive imagination and our skills to see the whole picture. If someone bumps into us and we drop all our shopping on the ground we could choose to be angry thinking 'how dare someone be so careless and thoughtless' or we can use our positive imagination and think 'they must have been in a hurry, they mustn't have noticed me, maybe they were born with a poor sense of body space/sight/judgement etc.' If we can develop this skill we will not only be happier, less angry people, but it will be more likely that we are correct when passing judgments against others.

A lot of the interpersonal misery that we have in our lives is due to us erroneously thinking others are purposely hurting us, scorning us or making our lives miserable. But the truth is most of the time, most people in this world are not purposely doing anything to hurt us, in fact most of the time they are totally oblivious to the effect they have on us. Most people are too self absorbed to realize the impact they really make on others. So if we want to live in reality and see people for who they are we MUST defend their actions because that is the only way to see the situation truthfully without our personal bias.

Once we have learned the art of defending people we will find that our lives are full of more joy, happiness and better relationships. We will also discover that we are capable, effective and objective judges. We will be able to judge each person/situation based on knowing all the facts and then we will make good decisions that we will be confident are correct.

Go on – Turn your back on self inflicted misery – Give it a Go!

Day 51

Talk it out

One of the best ways to hear a good and true defence to another person's accusation and evidence is to actually go and talk to the person being accused. If we can approach the seemingly guilty person, that's great. For example imagine we were the judge of a court case, the 'criminal' is bought before us. Wouldn't the most intelligent thing be to ask the 'criminal' what his side of the story was, or how he pleads to the charges against him. It's such a waste of time to run a full on court case and investigation if a simple five minute talk with the 'criminal' will clear up the whole matter.

Some people may find it really hard to approach another and ask them for their side of the story. They may say "Oh that's too embarrassing! They might think that I think they are no good." They don't want to face the person because they don't honestly believe the person is innocent or could have anything redeeming to say. This can't be true, because every person has something good about them, and every person has reasons for doing what they do. Being too embarrassed to approach someone because of what they will think of us is ludicrous. The only reason a person is embarrassed to approach the other is because deep down they don't think they are good and they can't see anything redeemable in them. Let's see how ridiculous this is. We're too embarrassed to ask them for their side of the story because we don't want them to know what we really think about them. This means we're more embarrassed about being 'caught' possibly thinking badly about others than actually thinking terrible untruths about this person.

We all want to be givers, so deep down we want to give the other person a chance to clear their name or explain themselves (rather than being condemned as 'guilty' in the courtrooms of our minds). If we think another person is incorrigible, no good etc. then it's better for us to sort out our grievance with the other person than to secretly dislike them in our hearts. If we were accused of doing something pretty drastic, and we noticed that people were avoiding us because of the rumour, we would like to be told about the rumour and be given the chance to explain and defend ourselves. Let's be kind to others as well. When we approach another person in a loving way, we are really showing them that we believe in them and their goodness. E.g. imagine we heard a rumour that a close relative of ours said they were going to disinherit us. The loving and kind thing to do is to find out why they are upset with us. We could approach them and ask "I heard from someone that you were upset with me, is that true?" If the rumour was true, then we have a chance to fix up the misunderstanding or grievance, and if it's not true then imagine all that anger, resentment and negativity we've saved ourselves by speaking up.

By speaking with the 'defendant', we give him/her a chance to explain the situation, or to fix up the situation on their own. We might find that the information we received was misheard, misinterpreted or that the 'defendant' was all heated up when they said it. Now they have cooled down and are not really planning to do what they said they would.

When speaking with a person who may harm us or others we need to know an important tool, and that is the art of listening to what they are saying. Most of the time, if a person is all uptight and really wants others to hear their defence, they won't be satisfied with just saying their side of the story. They will want the listener's feedback to assure them that they have been heard. In order for a person to know that we are really hearing what they are saying it is a good idea to repeat back or rephrase what he/she has said. When they hear their defence repeated back to them, they not only feel heard but they feel understood. (e.g. "so what you are saying is 'you think I'm selfish and self-centred. You're angry with me and you feel that I'm partially to blame for the problem...your proof for this is ... etc.")

 Another benefit of letting another person defend themselves is, that when a person is given the time to vent all of their feelings, they become more open to finding a solution to the problem, because they feel we are on their side. A final benefit is; when we do finally make a decision (or hand down our judgment) this person is more able to accept our decision because they know it was carefully weighed and well-considered. e.g. 'You've stayed out way past your curfew, and I understand that many factors contributed to this, but I think for your best interests we need to ground you for the next week.' This is more likely to be accepted than an angrily shouted 'you're grounded'. Or "I understand how hard it is for you to kick this drug habit, but you committed yourself to try out the rehabilitation program and you didn't try it out. I know it's a real struggle for you, but I'm sorry I can't go on living with you like this and I'm leaving." This will be more accepted than 'I've had enough – Goodbye.'

There are some cases however, that we shouldn't ask the other person for their side of the story, and that is if we think they will hurt us (e.g. hit, abuse, shout, insult), hurt others, or become even more sneaky about their bad behaviour if they know we know about their misdeed. If this is the case then, we can't use this person to defend themselves, and we instead have to try and think of defences for their behaviour on our own. E.g. We WOULDN'T say "Is it true that you have a terrible violent temper and that people are only safe from physical attack if they avoid you?" Or "I heard you are a con-artist and that you trick little old ladies out of their homes by selling non-existent retirement bonds." When dealing with people like this we can't give them a chance to defend themselves, but we can think of possible defences for them (e.g. 'He's probably got a chemical imbalance in his brain and should really be on medication to help him control his temper' or 'He might be feeling over his head in debt and may be engaging in some shady business practices, or maybe he's running a legitimate business but has some really dumb clients that don't understand the contracts they enter.')

Give it a Go!

1. Think of a person who was accused of something that you believed. Example 1. A friend said 'Kate said she hates you and never wants to see you again.' Or Example 2. 'Shopkeeper X. Is a thief' or even if YOU accused the person of something in your mind. Or Example 3. 'He's a selfish in-grate who never helps me do anything'

2. Try and approach the person in an accepting loving way, and ask with genuine interest and belief in their goodness, why they did/said what they did/said (or if they really did/said it at all). Try and really understand it from their point of view. Example 1 "Kate, when I came over to your house you ignored my existence. Was something bothering you?" or Example 2. 'Mr Shopkeeper, I see your toasters are $20 more expensive here than they are at Store Y. Why is that?' or Example 3. 'Why didn't you pick me up in the car from the train station when it was raining yesterday?'

   You may find the person will answer surprisingly differently than you thought Example 1. "Oh! I didn't notice that you came over. Maybe I wasn't wearing my glasses - I can't see anything without them. I'm sorry I didn't notice, I really love it when you pop over to visit me." Or Example 2. 'My toasters are last year's stock. The exchange rate was much higher then, so it cost me more to buy my toasters, I'm actually selling them at cost price. Store Y. bought theirs recently at a really great exchange rate, so even though their price is lower they are still making a profit." Example 3. 'The car was at the mechanics for repairs.'

I tried this exercise _____ times.
I would rate this exercise as:

1	2	3	4	5	6	7	8	9	10
(not so good)				(Average)				(Spot on)	

Why Should I?

Try this exercise out even once to see how mind blowing it is to actually hear the other person's defence. It'll restore your faith in the goodness of mankind. In order to see the good in life we have to be strong enough to stare seeming evil in the face and say 'So what's your side of the story.'

This technique will help us make informed decisions. Whatever our decision ends up being we will always have more confidence in our decision making abilities if we have heard all the evidence and all the defence.

Hearing another person's defence also shows us with solid proof how wrong other people can be when they judge their fellow human beings. We are all aware of the newspaper articles that have headlines shouting how corrupt/immoral or unlikeable someone is. These grab our attention and we believe to some degree what they say. But a few weeks later, when more information comes to light and the person who was in the headlines is found innocent, all we see then is a small apology from the editor. Most people don't even notice it, and not all falsely accused people are even given the apology. We know the newspapers get it wrong, but we keep swallowing their nonsense. The same goes for other people's negative interpretations of events and people – they get it wrong so often.

Sometimes we are the ones that accuse somebody of something negative. We might be angry, disappointed or annoyed with someone in our lives. But if we don't go and ask them for their defence we will continue to eat ourselves up with our self made negative accusations. Once we ask the other person for their side of the story, often the incident is explained and we find that there really was nothing to be upset about in the first place.

We need to hear another person's defences for our own sanity. We need to know that the charge and prosecutor's evidence is faulty MOST of the time. By doing this exercise we will be strengthened in our resolve not to believe every negative thing we hear (or think). We will also learn the valuable skill of listening to another person, understanding them and seeing the good and redeemable aspects of their nature (even if they are guilty).

Go On – Reawaken your belief in the goodness of people – Give it a Go!

LEARNING TO JUDGE
4TH STEP – HANDING DOWN JUDGEMENTS

Introduction

We've learned how to Hear the charge, Listen to the Prosecutor and Hear the Defence, so we are ready to start to hand down a judgement. However, before we can do that we have to make sure that we are doing it right. We don't want our judgement to be biased, based on emotional idealism or for the process to be unfairly dragged on.

In the next section we will be discussing how to render a good decision. We will also discuss some common types of situations in which we need to use our ability to objectively judge others.

Day 52

Bribes blind the eyes
of the Wise

Before we can hand down a verdict whereby we judge other people or circumstances we have to ensure that we are going to be judging things fairly. One of the biggest hindrances to making an objective decision is personal involvement, or a 'bribe.'

"I was standing up in court defending myself, and I looked over and saw the judge smiling and interacting pleasantly with the prosecutor. The prosecutor happened to be his grandson."

How would you feel if the prosecutor in your case was the grandson of the judge? Doomed – right? Why? Because we all know that when people are biased they don't judge properly. We need to recognise when we are biased.

Things that can make us not really see the situation objectively and truthfully may be when:
- Money is involved (i.e. when we stand to win or lose money as a result of making the decision);
- Our feelings have been hurt (we are definitely not objective when we are still emotionally worked up);
- One person involved is a relative of ours (favouritism will naturally result);
- When one person is more likeable or honourable in our eyes than the other person (e.g. if we respect our friend more than our parents, we will more likely favour the argument of our friends over that of our parents without fully considering the facts); or
- We've been "bribed" (figuratively speaking) (e.g. someone in the past gave us a present, money or did us a favour etc that makes us feel favourably inclined to listening to this person).

In a court case the judge would have to excuse him/herself from judging. However, since we can't excuse ourselves from judging situations in our everyday lives, then we need to have tools to help us judge fairly.

Tool 1 - Objectivity.
We need to pretend we are not personally involved and it is somebody else's problem that we are judging. The more objectively we see a situation the better we will be able to deal with the problem.

Tool 2 - Ask Others for Advice.
When we know that we are so involved in a situation that there is no way we could even pretend to be objective, then it's best to discuss the issue with a good friend, a mentor or an objective outsider who's opinion we find is sound and reasonable.

"I wasn't sure what to do. I wanted to write my brother a letter saying how he had hurt me so much that from now on I would never speak with him again. I knew all of my good friends would just tell me to do whatever I wanted to do, so I didn't ask them. I couldn't ask my parents because they are too involved. So in desperation I thought - who can I discuss this with?"

When we are not sure who we can ask, we can turn to our quiet voice for an answer. Most questions don't require on the spot answers.   If we can wait for a calm moment, when we can be completely relaxed, we can ask our quiet voice to point us in the right direction.

"I didn't know what to do ... so I asked myself 'what should I do?' to try and access my inner wisdom. My quiet voice told me to ask Mrs. King. Without having reflected deeply on this issue I don't think I would have thought to ask her. She's such a quiet but sensible woman that I haven't talked to for years. Mrs. King gave me such wonderful advice. I gave her all the facts. She asked further questions and happily helped me come to a good decision."

When we access our inner wisdom we will discover that the quiet voice is like an advisor. It may not have all of the information at hand, but it will advise us how to go about getting the information we need.

Give it a Go!

1. Reflect and ask yourself: "Who would be a good objective person to help me with my problems?"
2. If your quiet voice doesn't know, then ask "Please help me find a mentor/guide/friend that I can trust and consult" and keep your eyes open for someone who may enter into your life, or someone you already know but hadn't thought of.

I tried this exercise _____ times.
I would rate this exercise as:

1	2	3	4	5	6	7	8	9	10
(not so good)				(Average)					(Spot on)

Why Should I?

We all need someone we can ask for unbiased advice. Anybody who succeeds at anything in life has only done so by asking others for advice. Top medical doctors ask lesser colleagues their opinion on medical cases they find perplexing. Successful business people ask others for advice on how to maximize their profits. World renowned sports stars all have coaches.

We all have personal bias, blind spots of desire or weaknesses in objectivity when it comes to some people and circumstances in our lives. The only way to steer through the bumpy waters of life is to have a friend, mentor or guide who can help us. The guide we choose doesn't even have to be as smart or as worldly as we are. The coaches that help Olympic athletes certainly don't know how to run as fast, jump as high or endure as much as the person they are coaching. But the athlete listens to his/her coach anyway. Why? Because the athlete wants to win.

If we want to win at the game of life we need to have someone who will help us. We have to choose our guide carefully and intelligently, making sure we get a top notch, experienced, highly informed individual. We may already know someone who we feel fits the description, or we may wish to ask around to get a recommendation. Some people will choose a therapist, councillor, spiritual leader or guide. Whoever we choose we have to be willing to trust them and listen to their advice if we think it's for our good. And if we don't trust our advisor or we think they aren't an expert in the area that we need them for – we can look for one that we can rely on for good advice.

The second part of this exercise is to ask our quiet voice for help in finding a guide (if we can't think of one.) This is a great exercise as it will amaze you when you see that you'll actually get answers. A person's name or a 'lead' of where to go might just pop into your mind or into your life from seemingly nowhere. This is actually a common phenomenon we can use. Some people use the expression 'to sleep on it', which means they have a question and in the morning they wake up with clarity. If we can get into the habit of asking ourselves seemingly impossible questions we will start to feel the power in our ability to receive answers. Why is this so?

The analytical approach

Our mind is an unbelievable data bank of knowledge, wisdom and intuition. We know more things than we realize. From the day we were born our mind has been gathering data and storing it away in hidden chambers. There are foreign languages, mathematical equations, philosophical theories and endless amounts of information that we have stored away, but we just don't know how to access it. When we ask ourselves a question and calmly wait for an answer our minds, like a high tech computer it starts running a program to come up with a solution to the question, and then when it finds it - BOOM or FLASH - the answer just appears in our heads.

The spiritual approach

When we ask ourselves a seemingly impossible question we are in fact addressing that deep wisdom within us which is connected to the infinite wisdom of the universe. We are really asking the question to this infinite wisdom and then we wait for a response. The response often comes through an intuitive feeling, a hunch or a flash of inspiration. In many cultures this phenomenon is called prayer. It is our way of having a relationship with the Infinite Wisdom and Ultimate Source of all Goodness. It is an awesomely amazing and powerful experience.

This technique works. So if we ever have an 'unanswerable' question, just throw the question out and wait for an answer to come. If we can master this part of the exercise, we will have opened the gates of infinite wisdom and blessing.

Go on – Get a guide and enhance your life – Give it a Go!

Day 53
Misplaced idealism

"She shouldn't have stolen from him, but he is so wealthy and she is so poor, so what's the problem?"

Sometimes when someone does something wrong, but it doesn't seem to harm the victim too badly or we feel the victim deserved it, we justify the wrong behaviour. Trying to even up the score or partaking in social equalisation is not the place of the courtroom, and we need to make sure we don't use it as such.

"He only stole so he could give it to the starving children in the orphanage."

It is great to be compassionate to the poor, and to try and help out those less fortunate than us, but letting these ideals cloud our judgment is likely to lead to very poor decisions. It is better to set up two departments, one as the Judgement section (or Justice System) and one as the Social Kindness section. If a judgement that is harsh needs to be handed out, then it should still be handed down, because that is the correct judgment. But then the Social kindness section can come along and loan whoever needs the money some funds, or help them in whichever way they need. For example if the judge decides that the person should have a fine of $50 for the crime, but feels bad that the person has to pay such a hefty fine. Then the judge should pass judgment and fine $50. Then he/she should refer the person to the Social kindness section who can lend/give them $50, give them paid community work or find them a job. This way the justice system is just and it is not being distorted with other good agendas.

Do you think Robin Hood was a hero or a thief? To Robin Hood the wealthy were the oppressors causing pain and suffering to the masses. To the wealthy he was a highway robber.

Here is a more extreme example, to help really clarify the point.

Do you think the 9/11 bombers are heroes or murderers? The bombers believed they were heroes fighting against western decadence. To the west they are cold blooded murderers.

Justifying wrong behaviour because the person hurting us has good motives (or they think they have good motives) can bring A LOT of harm to society and ourselves. The ends do not justify the means.

So when we are judging things in our lives, how can we apply this? For example, if we see a friend of ours shoplift because her parents refused to give her money to buy a new outfit for the upcoming social event, then we need to judge and say that what our friend did is wrong and that she is not justified. If we can get her to return the stolen outfit - great. Then we can refer it to our kindness department and maybe we could lend her some money or an outfit, go and buy her an outfit, or get a few friends together to get her an outfit. This way the lines between doing what is good and right for all involved are never blurred.

Give it a Go!

Think of a situation in your life where you need to be tough because something wrong was done, but you find it hard to be tough because you have pity on the person. E.g. Do you have somebody in your life that treats you abusively, but you feel they are justified i.e. they might have been having a bad day, or you think you really deserved the poor treatment? Or do you have an employee that is costing your company lots of money but you don't have the heart to fire him/her? Or do you have a child who does things that are wrong (e.g. stealing, hitting you etc.), but you can't bear to correct them? If yes, now try and put on two hats.

The first hat is to be a good and true judge, so ask yourself:
1. "Should this person behave like this?" (Regardless of the justifications).
   Then ask yourself:
2. "What should be done to/for this person to help this not to happen again."

Continued on next page...

You may want to ask someone to guide you in reaching an answer to these questions. Then once you have passed judgement (and that may be to seek professional advice, disassociate from the person temporarily, fire the employee or send them on a employee retraining course etc), put on your kindness hat.

With your second hat on (the kindness hat) you can ask:
"What can I do, or get other's to do to help this person with their problem now and in the future?"

I tried this exercise _____ times.
I would rate this exercise as:

1	2	3	4	5	6	7	8	9	10
(not so good)				(Average)					(Spot on)

Why Should I?

Let's empower ourselves to never feel like we are in a Catch 22 situation again. We can be strong, courageous, stand up for what is good and right whilst simultaneously being loving, compassionate, giving and kind. This exercise shows us how we can have the best of both worlds. When we are good objective judges we create an environment that is safe and happy for ourselves and others. We don't have to associate being an objective judge with being a heartless tyrant. We can do what's good for everyone. It just means handling the judging process in two parts.

Imagine if all the court systems in the world were run according to this two phase system. There would be true justice and safety for all members of society, whilst at the same time there would also be true kindness and compassion for everyone. The world would be a much better place to live in.

It is actually a fine balance that we all need to work at in order to maintain objective judgement on the one hand and compassion and kindness on the other. However, using this two hat process we'll find a method that helps us become a master balancer, and when we are able to master this we will feel the satisfaction of being tough as well as the contentment of being kind – a double dose of pleasure.

4th STEP – HANDING DOWN JUDGEMENTS

When we learn to judge others with the two hats on we will be able to transform our current environment into one that is perfect for happiness to take root, grow and flourish.

Go on – the power of objectivity and the euphoria of kindness are at your fingertips – Give it a Go!

Day 54
50/50

"The evidence is in (she lied to me). The defendant has given a pretty good defence (she said she didn't really say it, and that I misunderstood) but really nothing is conclusive, how am I supposed to judge this one?"

If we are in doubt, then the best thing to do is to give the other person the benefit of the doubt. There are many times that we lack total clarity on a situation. In that case it is good to be a fair judge and dismiss the case. If however, further facts come to light in the future (e.g. she lied to us again, and this time we confirmed our understanding of what she said), we can always re-judge the case. The main part of this point is to learn to let go, not hold on to maybe, maybe not, and continue to live a loving happy life.

"I'm so annoyed that she stole my handbag, I'm going to take her to court for years. I'll hire the most expensive lawyers and I'll get the judge to make her pay for all of my legal and court charges."

Dragging things on for a long time, or getting the person who did the wrong thing to have to fork out incredible amounts of money for a small wrongdoing is not being a fair judge. A good and fair judge wants to work things out as quickly and cheaply as possible for all involved, because the object of judging is to render a decision, not to indulge in some 'fiefdom' or power play.

 In our personal lives this could be like saying to a friend who hurt us "I don't know if I trust you. I'll be half your friend", and leaving this quasi-friend status to go on for weeks or months or years, without really deciding if we fully want to commit to the friendship. Making our friend pay too much could mean bringing up the incident regularly and saying many times over 'I don't know if I can trust you again'. Both these tactics are unfair on the person who did the wrong thing. We need to judge our cases swiftly (not on a whim, but thoughtfully). It is unfair to leave people hanging around whilst we judge whether they are really a good influence on us or not. Once we have decided, we should just let it go. If we choose to remain friends, then commit fully to it, and if we choose to distance ourselves, then we should do that (lovingly) and not send mixed signals.

Give it a Go

Is there any unfulfilling relationship/friendship or difficult situation you are currently involved in? E.g. Are you still trying to decide if you want a certain person in your life? Or Are you mulling on a punishment you MIGHT give a child? Or, have you 'half' fired an employee? If so, make a decision – get all the facts, give them a chance to defend and make a well thought-out decision, but do it Today (or at least by the end of this week).

I tried this exercise _____ times.
I would rate this exercise as:

1	2	3	4	5	6	7	8	9	10
(not so good)				(Average)				(Spot on)	

Why Should I?

People deserve the decency of being treated fairly and lovingly. Even when we need to make tough decisions, we don't have to drag others 'over hot coals' whilst we sit around and do nothing. Most decisions DO NOT require weeks or months to think about. Most of the time, the reason we put off the decision isn't because we are contemplating the best course of action to take. The biggest reason we put off decision making is because we are engaging in power play, revenge or plain procrastination, not wanting to make an uncomfortable decision – secretly wishing the whole matter would disappear in a puff of smoke.

However, we want to be givers and kind, happy people. In order to become the type of person we are proud of we need to learn how to judge objectively and move on quickly. Nobody likes to be strung along, not knowing what will be with their future, especially if they suspect something ominous on the horizon. So let's be kind and act in an elevated way. We can make our well thought out judgements timely and efficiently – and we'll be proud of ourselves.

Go on – Make your environment a happy one TODAY – Give it a Go!

Day 55
The Verdict

We've heard the charge (e.g. she's mentally unbalanced). We've seen the evidence (e.g. she screamed insults at a person who accidently bumped into her). We've tried to understand it from her point of view and find a reason for it (e.g. We've read up on various mental illnesses and understand that a person with her clinical condition has little control over their levels of frustration. We also realize she has never been taught the tools to deal with the frustration etc.) And now what are we going to do? We need to make a decision about what we are going to DO with the information we have.

 When deciding what should be done, we need to consider what is for the good of ALL involved, and balance out the effect on the individual (i.e. the person who did the wrong thing), and the effect on others (e.g. society at large or us individually).

For example, with the case of the person who is mentally ill: if she is someone we don't know very well, we may decide the best thing to do is to avoid her and have nothing to do with her. If, however, she is our mother, then cutting off all ties would hurt her feelings incredibly, and we would also miss out on all the opportunities to do things for our mother that a child might do e.g. shopping, cooking, household chores etc. Here we need to balance the discomfort she causes us versus our duties as a child, and our obligation to show her gratitude for bringing us into the world. Sometimes if she's only a little verbally abusive, we can put up with it and say to ourselves, "I'm sad she's like that. I wish I could cure her of her illness." If, however, we find that her abuse affects us very negatively e.g. we are depressed for one week after talking to her, then we may choose to limit our contact with her to once a month. If her abuse is very bad, then we may have to say 'Sadly, my mother is incapable of having a relationship with me." We may also need to distance ourselves from her completely, until such a time comes that she/circumstances change. If that happens, it will be time to re-evaluate our decision.

There are a lot of factors we need to take into account in order to decide correctly. Just doing what we feel like doing – on a whim, is bound to bring unwanted consequences. Well thought out decisions are lasting, constructive and in the long run move us towards a more beautiful life and a more beautiful world.

Judging a case takes a lot of wisdom. It's not fair to punish the perpetrator too much, e.g. if a person stole $5 it's not 'justice', to fine her $5000. Or if a person was a little nasty to us, it's not 'justice' to sabotage her whole business. Revenge is not justice. When we are judging a case to decide what to do, we must keep far away from feelings of revenge and hatred. Instead we must try and keep our problem solving hat on, and come up with a decision that is good for everyone.

Each verdict must be handed down on an individual basis, making sure that we take all the evidence, the defence and the personality of the people involved into account.

To re-cap: the purpose of learning to judge what we see and hear is to be able to make informed decisions about what we can do to protect ourselves and others from harm (present or future). Passing an incorrect, thoughtless, unfavourable judgement on anyone or anything is likely to lead to pulling away when it is unnecessary or even good to draw close. If the judgment is too favourable this may result in drawing something harmful close, when it really should be pushed away.

"Didn't you say everyone and everything has good in it? So if we just focus on the good then won't we be ok in every situation?"

To just see the good in others without protecting ourselves against the harm others may inflict upon us is foolish. In order to be an elevated person, it doesn't mean making ourselves a doormat for others. If we can, we should protect ourselves from harm by avoiding a harmful situation. This is much wiser than getting ourselves into a situation where our fortitude for seeing and doing good will be challenged. That is not to say that we should become reclusive hermits avoiding people. But it means that if we KNOW for sure somebody or something has a negative impact on us then we should try and avoid or minimise the negative impact that person or thing has on us (if we can).

When we want to live a life of joy and contentment we pursue seeing the good, and simultaneously we guard ourselves and others from elements that could damage us or others, or that hinder our ability to see the good in everything. This is a very important principle, because purely concentrating on the good things in life without guarding against the things that come to harm us doesn't work. We need to do both. It is like making a lovely vegetable garden (seeing the good) and not putting a fence around it (fence = learning how to judge well and distance from not good influences) and letting the sheep, cows, goats etc to have free range in our garden. It is inevitable that the garden will be destroyed and all our hard work wasted. Likewise if we put a lot of effort into cultivating a positive attitude, a good eye and an open and loving heart, we need to protect ourselves from people and things that will destroy this.

Give it a Go!

Look at your life and reflect 'Are there any people I associate with that take me away or drag me down from being positive, happy and giving.'

Identify anybody that drags you down. Make sure it's because the other person is a negative influence on your life, not because of your own inner challenges of being able to see the good in others. Then assess whether this is a relationship that has potential. Can be worked on to be made better and enhance your life? Or is it a relationship that drags you down and will continue to drag you down? Try and do this assessment with completely objective glasses on (i.e. see ALL the good as well as the bad, not fooling yourself or wishing it were different – but see the situation for what it really is). If the relationship is the type that has no potential, then make an objective, informed and fair decision on how to limit/remove this negative drain on your life.

Look objectively and honestly at the people in your life. You need to do this in order to decide which relationships/people to bring closer because they enhance your life and which relationships/people to draw away from because they will cause you pain and suffering if you continue to associate with them.

I tried this exercise _____ times.
I would rate this exercise as:

1	2	3	4	5	6	7	8	9	10
(not so good)				(Average)					(Spot on)

Why Should I?

If we have one rotten apple in a bowl of fruit it will eventually turn all the other apples rotten. If we have one negative, draining influence in our life it can eventually eat away all our happiness. Some of the biggest 'rotten apples' people have in their lives are drugs, alcohol and gambling addictions, crime or emotional illnesses. Some of the smaller 'rotten apples' can be certain friends, jobs or genre of media which drag us down or bring out the worst in us. Being in close contact with people who suffer from 'rotten apples', can also cause us to rot.

We can free ourselves from being dragged down. We don't have to be pitiful victims of circumstance. We can Climb the Mountain of Subjectivity and develop the ability to be Objective.

This exercise will help us pin point people in our lives that drag us down and it will empower us to judge them objectively so that we can move forward in life to a beautiful existence.

Go on – Throw out the rotten apples and enjoy the juicy ones – Give it a Go!

Day 56
Warning Others

"Don't do it! You can't go in there. Stop! Stop! Stop!"

"What are you getting all hysterical about? It's not that dangerous? Anyway, it's my life, and you should mind your own business."

Crash!

"Quick call the ambulance, he's been hit really bad."

If we put out our hand to a wild animal and it bites it off, we don't then put out our other hand and say, "it's ok doggy, I forgive you, now I know you are a good doggy." That's foolish. Being a joyful, upbeat person is the opposite of being a fool. We see the good where it exists, and we also learn to judge the situation well enough to know when to avoid the bad. When we are living with a highly developed sense of joy we have energy and desire to save others from mistakes/people or circumstances that might diminish their enjoyment of life. We need to learn how to lovingly speak up to help others. Of course we shouldn't make their lives a misery by being an out of touch prophet of doom and gloom. But we need to care enough to tell others to watch out for dangerous things or people. We need to give people the information they need, so that they can be good judges.

Until now whenever we have talked about speaking about other people, we have only concentrated on saying good and positive things about them. However there are times when we need to speak up and speak negatively about others. If we have worked very hard on speaking positively of others, we may find it difficult to open our mouths to utter mean words – and that is a great level of achievement. But we need to know there are some times when it is GOOD to run others down, and that is when we can help another person not get hurt. We should only ever speak negatively about another person if we are doing so for a POSITIVE PURPOSE. i.e. We need to tell others about people, places, things etc that can harm them. E.g. "I see you're considering dating Charlie. I want you to know that I know from firsthand experience he has a violent temper."

Since it is such a natural habit to say negative things about people, we find that we have to put in most of our effort to speak positively. However there are some simple tricks to remember. If we run them through our mind before opening our mouths we will be sure to only speak positively about others most of the time, and not fall into the bad habit of speaking negatively about others.

This section is like a Ph.D. in speaking positively and being happy and upbeat in our verbalizations. Here we are learning tools to know when to pass on negative information to others so that they are able to objectively judge for themselves. Hopefully by doing this we will help others avoid being hurt, harmed, embarrassed etc. by the person we are speaking negatively about.

Below there are 7 ideas to think about before we can feel confident that we are speaking negatively for a good reason, and not because we have slipped into a negative frame of mind. These 7 ideas are ways we make sure we are keeping positive, upbeat and always with our eye on the good – despite having to speak negatively.

1. S – SURE - Make sure we saw it first hand, and that we really know what we are talking about. (And if we didn't see it, then say that we don't know if it is true but we heard it as a rumour). This step helps us not start up false rumours.
2. P – POSITIVE – be positive that what we are warning the person about is really harmful, not just our subjective opinion (e.g. there is no need to warn someone that Jayne wears foul smelling perfume, even if we don't like her perfume, because objectively speaking there is nothing wrong with her perfume, it just doesn't accord with our taste.)
3. E – EXPRESS - Express our concern to the person whom we want to speak badly about. Maybe they can correct what they did. Maybe they have a good explanation for their behaviour. However we shouldn't do this if we think the person will hurt us, become sneakier about their wrongdoings, or if doing so is not

likely to cause any positive result. (E.g. Jim approached Scott and expressed his concern. 'I know you wouldn't purposely put slippery oil all over the floor, but it is likely to cause people to slip and hurt themselves.' Jim did this because it was better to 'express' his concern to Scott first, rather than speak negatively about Scott to his boss, which might cause Scott to be fired.)

4. A- ACCURATE - Don't embellish or exaggerate what the person did. (e.g. don't make a person with a bad temper into a mass murderer.) Say it as it really is.

5. KI – KIND INTENT - Only speak up because we care about the wellbeing of the person who we are warning. If we speak up because we want to take revenge, we hate the other person or for any other ulterior motive, then we are not the one to be spreading this negative information. It will only harm us and make us into bitter, negative people.

6. N – NO OTHER WAY - Try and find another way to help the person without having to lower ourselves into speaking negatively about people. For example, if someone set up a practical joke on our friend, and we know she will be embarrassed because of it, we can fix it up so that the practical joke doesn't get performed, by taking it away, or asking the person who set it up not to do it. Then we can produce a better outcome than if w warned our friend that she is about to be the butt of a joke.

7. G – GOOD RESULT - Sharing negative information with others should only be done to affect some positive and good result. If the person warned will take unfair revenge or action on the person he/she was warned against – then we shouldn't warn them. (e.g. "Oh is that right, well how dare he try to overcharge me, I'm going to burn down his shop.") It wouldn't be fair for the person who did this small wrong to be punished so severely. Another situation when we shouldn't warn a person is if the person we want to warn will NOT listen to our warning at all. It's no point telling someone something if they are not going to listen. However, if the person doesn't take defensive action against harm (e.g. break up a harmful relationship), but will still be on guard against being hurt as a result of our warning, then we should warn them - because being on guard against being hurt is positive.

A good way to remember these seven points is by the acronym S.P.E.A.KI.N.G.

These 7 steps are our way of knowing when we need to judge another person and pass down the verdict that we should tell others something negative about them. We need to judge when it is good to spread negativity. Using the seven SPEAKING conditions as a checklist to be completed before we malign another gives us the proper guidelines needed to make sure we are being a good judge, and passing down a fair verdict. So before we speak negatively about another person, try to fulfil all seven SPEAKING conditions.

Give it a Go!

1. See if you can remember. If you are doing this book with a friend then get your friend to test you to see if you can recall what SPEAKING stands for. Otherwise close the book and test yourself.
2. Before you say something negative about another person today (or in another time in the future), try and review the SPEAKING steps to see if it is really worthwhile saying it.

I tried this exercise _____ times.
I would rate this exercise as:

1	2	3	4	5	6	7	8	9	10
(not so good)				(Average)				(Spot on)	

Why Should I?

This exercise will give us clarity in those murky situations when we don't want to lower ourselves to speak negatively about others and lose our positive focus on life, but we also don't want to stand idly by and see others get hurt. If we only speak about the faults of other people after thinking through the seven S.P.E.A.KI.N.G preliminaries then we can be guaranteed never to fall into the grips of useless negativity, gossiping or petty fault finding. We will be soaring the heights of positivity and positive speech. We will be a pleasure to speak with ALL OF THE TIME and we will have these seven preliminaries to guard us from falling into the old habit of running others down for no good reason.

Using these 7 preliminaries is **the best way** to become an objective judge in situations that require us to decide whether to speak negatively about another person or not. These 7 help us to objectively decide whether we should open our mouth to speak negatively or whether we can solve the problem another way. If we can fulfil all 7 preliminaries then we know that our verdict to speak about the faults of another person is good, wise and fair.

It might be challenging to remember all seven to start with, but with practice we'll remember and they will be a help for us for the rest of our happy, positive and wonderful life.

Go on – Master the art of Positive speech – Give it a Go!

Day 57

Occupational Health & Safety (OHS)

"Watch out! There's building and construction going on all around. If you need to be here put on your hard hat, if you don't need to be here then – GET OUT!"

When businesses are involved with potentially dangerous situations, they have Occupational Health and Safety Officers to help assess how to minimise the risk of injury. The OHS team comes up with a set of guidelines designed to protect the wellbeing of all employees.

There are places in this world that should have a sign like 'Enter at your own Risk'.

When passing judgment on places we go to, we need to determine if these destinations are going to be good for us or if they are potentially dangerous. We need to be in touch enough with ourselves to know which places put us into danger and which places we should run to because they provide revitalizing waters.

Imagine two friends invite us to a party. We like the first friend better and her crowd of friends are real party animals that enjoy having a good time. However, we know sometimes her parties get a bit out of control, and sometimes things happen that aren't good for us there. We also like the second friend, but her parties aren't as exciting, although we still have a nice time. The thrill isn't as great and the risk is much less. Which party should we go to? We need to be the judge of this situation.

If we stop to think before we choose, then we have enough time to weigh up all the factors, and we normally make a much better choice.

When we realize that we are very precious, then we will be happy to protect ourselves from harmful situations. We do not need to go to every place in the world. We do not need to live through every bad experience. Some think it is smart to experience pain and show that they can still survive, but it's smarter to avoid the pain altogether, and live a life of happiness and tranquillity.

Sometimes there might be nothing wrong with a certain place, but that place has a very bad effect on us. E.g. A person who is allergic to cats is best to avoid going to a cattery. The places we need to avoid are those that drag us down. For example one person may avoid places/books etc that are really negative and make him/her focus only on what's wrong with his/her/the world. Since everybody is dragged down by different things, it's important to be in touch with what are the triggers that drag you down – and stay away from them.

"I'm a compulsive spend-thrift. So as a part of being kind to myself I stopped going to the mall. Now I order things from home based on a shopping list. I never window shop or randomly search the internet to see what's out there. I have my shopping list and I stick to it. Since I've started avoiding these places that drag me down, I feel so great."

Give it a Go!

It's time to get quiet again. Ask yourself: "What places/things should I really avoid because they drag me down?"

I tried this exercise _____ times.
I would rate this exercise as:

1	2	3	4	5	6	7	8	9	10
(not so good)				(Average)					(Spot on)

Why Should I?

We all do things that are self destructive. We all have places or things that are a trigger to that self destructive mode of ours. If we want to be happy we have to stop doing self destructive things. However, it's really hard to stop old habits. There is a saying 'With strategy you should wage war'. This means we don't have to fight ourselves head on all of the time. If we're always trying to win our internal battles using brute strength and will power – we'll get tired, worn out and bitter. It's a much

4th STEP – HANDING DOWN JUDGEMENTS
Common Circumstances where we need to Judge Others

smarter and a more loving approach to learn how to avoid situations and circumstances that trigger our bad reactions. It's wiser to avoid our triggers than to frequently fight our negative tendencies.

This exercise helps us start to fight our wars with strategy. It will help us identify things that WE KNOW are not good for us, and then plan how to AVOID THEM. It's not courageous to pick a fight with the areas of our character that give us the most trouble. It's much more courageous to admit we have a weakness and plan ways of working around it and avoid having to do battle with it all together.

This exercise will give us the power to control the most powerful negative force we know – Our self destructive side.

Be brave, look closely and carefully at yourself and see what it is that triggers the worst in you or drags you down – Then with a great dose of self love and self acceptance – plan ways to avoid your triggers.

Go on – You're the Loving Boss – Give it a Go!

Day 58
(Not so) good friends

"She's such fun to be around, she has such crazy ideas. However, I'm always getting myself into trouble around her."

Some friends we have are really great people, but somehow bring out the worst in us. They may be the ones that always push our red buttons, they might be the impulsive friends that are fun to follow around to see what action comes up next, or they might be the obsessively caring type who doesn't let us have our own space. Whatever the circumstances, we need to be able to judge whether our friends are good for us or not.

Good friends love us for who we are but are strong enough to tell us 'no' when we want to do something self-destructive.
Good friends care about our feelings and don't purposely do anything to hurt or embarrass us.
Good friends like who we are, not what we can give them.
Good friends will still be our friend regardless of who else is around.
Good friends care about us and will go out of their way to help or protect us.
Good friends know their own self-worth and will not tolerate us abusing them.

The better we treat our friends, the more likely we are to attract good friends. The first stage in staying away from not so good friends is to make sure we are committed to being a good friend. The second stage is to make a conscious effort to CHOOSE who would be a good friend, and do what we can to foster the friendship. (Not everyone we want to be friends with will want to reciprocate. Don't get down if this happens, we just need to think that their rejection is not a reflection on our worth – after all if they really knew us and how wonderful we really are, they would be knocking down our door to be our friend. Unfortunately this person was just blind – blind to our virtues – their loss!) Keep trying to find a good friend or two.

The third step which can be done concurrently with the second stage is to slowly move away from the unhealthy friendships. When we have decided that a friendship is not adding to our lives, then we can slowly pull away. We need to give ourselves enough time to find new friends and get on with life. Ending a friendship doesn't have to be done in an abrupt fashion. It can be done with love and sensitivity for the other person's feelings – assuring them that they are an OK person; it's just that we have different needs or a different focus in our life. It also doesn't have to be a complete severance, we can just 'float' apart spending less and less time with them and more and more time with our new friends. We may find that eventually we'll see our old friends once a year but our new friends every day. However, beware not to give mixed messages (i.e. 'I want to be really close good friends' one day , but the next day being too aloof thereby saying 'now I don't', in a cyclical pattern - that's not kind.)

Try to remember: we aren't rejecting the person but distancing ourselves because of the influence they have on us. The further we 'float' away from our friends the less influence they have on us. We can determine how much distance we should put between us and our old friends by working out how far apart we need to be for them not to have any negative influence on us. With some friends it may mean making the friendship an every now and again 'catch up and re-live old times' type of friendship but with others we may need to completely turn our backs on the friendship altogether.

One important point to remember in this exercise is to never forget the good an old friend has done for us. The first key to happiness was to see the good and be grateful for what others have done for us. If in the past an old friend(s) has done a lot of good for us, or gone out on a limb for us, just remember we owe them one. Being there and available for an old friend in need is something we can't just walk away from easily. It's a balancing act, we need to make friends that are good for us, pull away from the friends that drag us down, but be available to pay back a good turn if it's ever needed – but not to be pulled back into a bad friendship because of this debt of gratitude.

Give it a Go!

Reflect and ask yourself.
Are there any friends I have in my life that drag me down?
Are there any people in my life that I feel positive and uplifted after talking to?
Then ask: "How can I start to fill my life with people who have a positive effect on me?"

I tried this exercise _____ times.
I would rate this exercise as:

1	2	3	4	5	6	7	8	9	10
(not so good)				(Average)					(Spot on)

Why Should I?

This exercise is a must for those who want to build up a life of bliss. We can construct a new, happier life by working step by step to an idealistic reality. We can choose our friends to be people that make us feel good. We don't have to be stuck with the same drag-me-down crowd that we've always had, just because we've never thought it could be different. Life can be different. We're in charge of who we want to have in our life. When we have a strong, positive and giving social circle, we will find that our lives will be full of pleasure.

Most people just haphazardly 'find' friends here and there without much thought as to whether the friendship is a good one or not. This is not a good way to acquire friends, because we'll end up with some friends that really aren't good for us. The best way of developing good friendships is to start with our objective judging hat on. Look at the person that we think might be a good friend, evaluate his/her good qualities and compare them to his/her bad qualities. Does this person have what it takes to be a good friend? If this person was on the shelf at a supermarket, would you pay good money to buy him/her? We need to evaluate our potential (and existing) friends, so that we can fill our lives with the types of people that make life a pleasure to live. Our friends are often one of our greatest sources of pleasure (or pain), so it's important to make sure we only choose people who are made of the right stuff.

Go on – Build up a blissful social network – Give it a Go!

Day 59

Lost Cause

"He's always asking me for a loan, and he never pays me back. He says he will make it up to me and pay me back one day, but this has been going on for 4 years and I haven't seen a cent."

"She's a nice person when we are together and she initiates the friendship, but whenever I want to come over to her house and do things when I'm bored she's always got lots of excuses."

There are people that have never learned to be givers. They are only happy to take, and continue doing so as long as we allow them to. These people are also usually very ungrateful. Be a good judge of character. Learn to see who in our life is capable of interacting with us in a giving and loving way, and who will just try and use us and leave us destitute when they're done.

Some people are not good for us. Not because they bring out the worst in us (as in the previous days examples), but because they have emotional, physiological or other problems that make them incapable of participating in a normal relationship.

We need to be an astute enough judge to know when to avoid someone because they are a bottomless pit of demands on us, and when to reach out and give generously to those that genuinely need our kindness.

Being a judge in these cases means being tough in order to be kind. We have to learn to say no to certain people, and how to replace those that want to use us with those that want to allow us to give lovingly to them in a healthy relationship.

"Please, can't you give me another $10, I'll do anything for you, you're the only one I can turn to, you're the greatest. I'm going to kill myself if I don't get the money. You're totally responsible for this situation so you have to

help me, it's only $10, I'm sure I mean more to you than that. You're so selfish that you never want to help others...."

"No." (I know you use it to buy drugs, I'm not going to do it for you or to myself.)

Perpetuating a relationship where the other person is constantly taking from us, is not doing us any favours nor are we really helping them in the long run. Learning to say no, and walking away letting the other person know they are the only ones that can help themselves with their problem is the best way to keep ourselves positive and together.

When we give and give more than we are capable of giving, it drains us. We need to be able to refuel and we need to take care of ourselves; this will then give us the emotional space to be able to decide what is the best course of action for everyone involved. Although we have an altruistic side, it is important to remember, we are never responsible for another person's problems, nor can we solve their problems; the only thing we can do is HELP them solve their own problems. Problems always need to remain the property of the owner, and can never be handballed to another person. By refusing to be responsible for other people's problems we are hopefully helping that person start to take ownership of their own problems.

The same rules apply to our problems. We need to know with 100% clarity that WE are the only ones who can be responsible for the problems we have, it's no use blaming others e.g. parents, teachers, siblings, friends etc. We are the ONLY ones responsible for our mental well being. Nobody can make us act in an inappropriate way – we CHOOSE to react that way. Nobody can take away our happy outlook on life – we choose to let circumstances/challenges drag us down – it's all OUR choice, not anyone else's fault. Things happen, but we are 100% in control of how we interpret and react to the things that come our way. When we slip into blaming others (e.g. it's your fault that I'm in an unbearable mood), this is a red flag to tell us that we have lost the proper perspective on this point.

Once we have accepted that we can't solve other people's problems, change their personalities or anything else like that, then we should have enough emotional objectivity to decide how to handle this problematic relationship. In order to lead a fulfilled life we need to have healthy relationships with all the people in our lives. If we are involved in an unhealthy relationship, it will inevitably drain out of us much of the good that we are trying to cultivate.

"But earlier you said never to give up on a person."

Yes, we should never give up hope. The hope that the person will eventually change and the hope that the person will be able to live a happy well adjusted life. We can simultaneously see a person's potential, but guard against the damage they are currently doing to us, the two ideas are not contradictory. We can also still have hope that this person will eventually rehabilitate. However, if the person is draining us, then we need to realize that we are not the one to be rehabilitating them – leave it to the professionals or other more objective people.

Give it a Go!

1. Do you have a relationship where the other person refuses to take responsibility for his/her behaviour? If so, then what steps should you take to start freeing yourself from this burden, (including how will you maintain your resolve in this matter)?
2. Ask yourself: "Do I blame anybody for a lack of anything (e.g. money, success, good character traits etc) in my life?" If your quiet voice answers 'yes', ask: "How can I start to take control of my own wellbeing today?"

I tried this exercise _____ times.
I would rate this exercise as:

1	2	3	4	5	6	7	8	9	10
(not so good)				(Average)					(Spot on)

Why Should I?

Taking responsibility for our own life, actions and consequences of our actions will empower us to change ourselves for the good. Trying to take responsibility for the life, actions and consequences of the actions in SOMEBODY ELSE'S life will drain us and will NEVER cause the other person to change. We need to know how to objectively judge the case and when to take charge/responsibility for a situation that we can do something about and when to walk away and show the other person that only they can change the situation.

LEARNING TO JUDGE

This exercise will empower us to change what we can change and leave what we can't. We'll be able to focus all our energies on what we can do something about, and not waste our energy on things we can't alter.

Go on – see where your vitality is being drained, plug up the holes and use that vitality to change your life into an unbelievably pleasurable existence - Give it a Go!

Conclusion

Now we've finished the second key to happiness, which is to be able to judge objectively. When we can climb every mountain of subjectivity and reach the summit, we can then look out on the world with clear objective vision. Imagine if we could make all our important decisions in life with absolute objectivity – what great decisions we would make.

This key brings us happiness because it helps us avoid people or situations that drag us down. It's the protective fence around the happiness we built up with the first key to happiness. In order to excel in our potential to reach the greatest amount of bliss possible, we need to protect what is precious.

The second Ancient Key to Happiness is Objectivity. This key is derived from the second of the seven Commandments given to Noah, which was 'have a righteous justice system.' Just like all societies need to have righteous justice systems to protect its citizens from criminals, moral decline and anarchy, so too do we have to learn to righteously judge others to protect ourselves from things that will bring about a decline in our happiness and well being. Learning the art of objectivity is really learning the art of being able to righteously judge others.

So now with the second ancient key to Happiness, we can circle around our blissful inner-world and erect a formidable protective fence. We can eject anything that will eat away at our happiness, and refuse to let in anything that may threaten to trample our beautiful garden of positivity, kindness and bliss. We can scale the heights of any mountain and stare out victoriously onto the world with the power, strength and inner courage of objectivity.

This second ancient key to happiness gives us control over our lives – we can be super heroes fighting off the negative influences with one hand whilst doing superhuman acts of goodness with the other. We can put on our protective cape of objectivity and fly so fast through the second gate of Happiness that no one will ever be able to catch us.

LOVE EVERY DAY

KEYS #3 TO #7 - LOVE YOURSELF

Introduction

Once we've learned how to see the good in our lives and make a protective fence around that good, the next step is to foster and grow our inner-self so that a deep self love will flourish. Cultivating Happiness is like making a beautiful garden, the first step is to see that our garden plot is beautiful, has good soil and lots of potential, the second step is to erect a protective fence around our garden so wild animals don't come and trample it and throw out any rocks and pebbles that stunt the growth of plants, and the third step is to maintain our garden by planting beautiful plants that will grow and flourish with time making our garden into the most exquisite island of paradise. When we've successfully done all three steps then we have cultivated a glorious amount of happiness and inner-bliss.

In this final section 'Love every Day' we will be focusing on how to cultivate our inner garden. We first start off with an introduction of general principles which show us how to begin to cultivate feelings of self-esteem, serenity and self love. Then we move onto Keys #3 to #7 which consist of, planting five beautiful exotic plants that will be the highlight of our garden of happiness.

In this section 'Love every Day' we will continue the journey towards a blissful life by getting to know ourselves, finding out what really makes us happy, what drains us and to learn to LOVE the absolute beauty of being 'me'. Once we have learned to recognise our greatness, to act in ways that make us feel good and to value ourselves as the great and wonderful person that we really are, then we will have opened up the gates of inner serenity, which is a very high level of happiness.

Getting to know ourselves is a lifelong process. You are a fascinating person! Over time, as we keep in touch with how we feel, think and react to various stimuli, we will start to discover what makes us tick, what gives us a deep sense of pleasure and what helps us maintain high levels of serenity and joy. It's not a process that can be done overnight, it is really part of the journey of life, because the journey of life is often the life long process of understanding who we really are.

The more we get to know ourselves, and shape ourselves into the person we want to be, the more we will come to truly love ourselves. Self-love is very important, we need it to feel energized, successful, independent and worthwhile. A person must work hard to see the good that lies within them, but seeing the good within is not enough we need to learn to value that good, and see ourselves as valuable, likeable, honourable and endlessly loveable.

So how can we love ourselves? After all, we know better than anyone else the terrible faults, failures and things we have done wrong. We put on such a big show to the world about how great we are, whilst all the time hoping no one looks too closely to see the real us, because they might be scared away. In order to love ourselves the first step we need to take is to know we are loveable – the 'real me' is lovable – not that phony me that we pretend to be. We need to get in touch with who we really are. We need to uncover our 'real me' and not run away from who we are to hide under the blanket of 'the phony me'. Once we learn to look in the mirror and see the 'real me' we will fall madly in love with ourselves.

Day 60
Feeling good about yourself

There are two ways to work on feeling great about ourselves. The first ways is to look for an external stimulus, i.e. look for things that aren't the 'real me' but reflect well on us so making us feel good. The second way to feel great about ourselves is to see the real inner beauty that is contained within us and love ourselves for this beautiful part of our personality – we call that the 'real me' part. We will explain these methods below.

1) External

Feeling good about ourselves by doing things that make us feel like a success. e.g. achieving a good result, is the most common way people work on self esteem. A lot of excellent literature that is written about developing a positive self image concentrates on developing goals and achieving them in order to feel a sense of self-worth. If we were to pick up almost any book which is on self esteem or combating depression we'll find many different tools that fall within this category of external stimulus.

The setting and achieving of goals is a great way to bring a quick sense of self-accomplishment and an increased level of self-esteem. However, this type of self-esteem, although very important, is not permanent and it is dependent on being able to always achieve – which is not always the case. Being human, we are susceptible to failure in all different areas of our lives. We have to learn how to value ourselves even when we fail, we need to know even in those times that we have failed we are still loveable, successful and worthwhile.

Another time we can't achieve as much as we would like is when we get older or sick, in these cases our ability to achieve can become diminished due to frailties of body or of mind. Those who have based their entire self-image on external sources or 'achievements' are likely to be overtaken with depression and feelings of worthlessness, when due to circumstances beyond their control, they are unable to achieve.

The main points to know about using external stimulus to build self-esteem are:

a. Use it whenever we can – it will give us energy when we feel we succeed at something;

b. Don't determine our self-worth **entirely** on our ability to achieve our goals;

c. Use an external stimulus such as goal setting and achievement as a springboard to incorporate things that bring us to a more internal longer lasting level of self-esteem such as setting achievable goals in the area of character development (e.g. Setting a goal to do one act of kindness a day.)

2) Internal

There are ways to work on loving ourselves that have nothing to do with whether we DO anything that makes us loveable. We can work on developing an internal sense of self worth, by learning how to appreciate the essence of who we are, peeling off all the layers and seeing the sweet, lovable, soft part of our essence. We can begin to identify ourselves as our essence and our true voice as the quiet voice. This type of self esteem is the self esteem of just 'being'. It's not related to what we do, how we do it, how well we do it, or who knows about what we do. It's about who we are deep down. It's about knowing that we are lovable, good, kind, worthwhile and endlessly valuable.

The more we listen to our quiet inner reflective good voice and act accordingly, the more we come to identify ourselves with this good part of us. This in turn makes us become more in touch with who we really are and the more we become in touch with this part of us, the more we will love ourselves – even if we fail at everything else in life. We will be discussing how to develop this type of internal self-esteem in more depth over the next few days.

Give it a Go!

To feel the power of using external stimulus to develop self-esteem; set yourself an easily achievable goal - something that you would like to achieve by the end of the day (or the end of the week). When setting your goal make it easy enough that it's not too hard to achieve, but challenging enough to make you feel like you are actually achieving something. (e.g. "I chose to eat a healthy breakfast every morning for a week.")

At the end of the day (or week) when you have achieved your goal, pat yourself on the back, feel good about it and start to internalize the feeling that you are a winner and a success in life.

I tried this exercise _____ times.
I would rate this exercise as:

1	2	3	4	5	6	7	8	9	10
(not so good)				(Average)					(Spot on)

Why Should I?

We all need to work on increasing our self esteem and self love We need to work on it so much that we should use any tool we can. Learning to set tiny, little, reachable goals will give a boost to our self esteem, because we are likely to achieve such small goals. Achieving goals, even very minor ones, makes us feel good.

Nobody likes to continuously fail, a person would rather give up than have to face the discomfort of another failure. This is because when we fail, we tell ourselves that we are a failure. We identify ourselves with our actions. It's not true, our worth is not determined by what we do. Just because we have failed at something doesn't mean that we are a failure, however, that's how most of us think. The converse is also true. When we succeed at something we tell ourselves that we are a success. This makes us feel good and positive about ourselves, thus our self esteem increases. In fact whether we succeed or fail really has nothing to do with our self worth. Our self worth is immensely great whether we feel it or not and whether we succeed or fail in life. However, since we find it hard to separate our achievements and failures from our inherent self worth, it is good to use this tool to our advantage and set ourselves up for success – as it gives us an instant self esteem high.

This exercise is great to do whenever we're feeling down, unsuccessful, depressed or like a complete failure in life. We'll see within a short amount of time that we really can achieve so much. The most important thing to remember is not to set our goals too high. If we find it hard to get out of bed because we are so depressed then an 'amazing achievement' might be just to put on our shoes that day. It all depends on where we are at. If we manage to do something that is slightly challenging (but not too hard). Then we are a hero and deserve to be commended.

We should never compare ourselves to what others are doing because they are not us and don't have our challenges so what they do is totally irrelevant to us and our lives. We need to just value our achievements, our wins and our successes – after all we know when we've done a good job and achieved something that was challenging for us.

Go on – Feel like a winner – Give it a Go!

Day 61

Priceless

"I think it's worth $100."

"I'll give you $500 for it."

"I'll give you $1billion for it."

So how much is it worth? Most people will answer that it is worth as much as the highest bidder is willing to pay. This may be the case with regard to goods or services, but it is totally not true when valuing people. However, we tend to value ourselves based on how much the highest bidder is willing to bid i.e. how highly others regard us.

Imagine the following scenario.

8am – woke up, felt depressed, couldn't be bothered getting out of bed.

9am – got up, struggled off to work.

9-11:45am – worked like a slave to finish off the report and handed it in on time.

11:45 – 12:45 – ate lunch at a nearby cafe whilst looking for a better job.

1pm – Boss called me in and said my report was top notch, the best he'd ever seen. He said I'm the greatest and called in the whole office to congratulate me on my efforts.

5pm came home, had a great day, feel like such a success.

———

The person was the same person at 8am as she was at 5pm, but what changed – recognition of her worth by another. When her boss recognised her worth, she felt valuable and this gave her a great feeling about herself. The question to ask is: if her value didn't change – just the recognition of her value occurred – why should she feel any different about herself? Why shouldn't she have woken up feeling like a success – after all she knows she can do a good job? The answer is that we often sit around and wait for others to value us, whereas instead we could be learning to value ourselves – regardless of what others think.

How do we learn to value ourselves?

When someone says something that makes us feel great, then track down what it is about what they said that makes us feel good, and learn to value that for ourselves.

E.g. "The boss made me feel great because he said I did a good job." So what makes me feel good? – the fact that I did a good job. Why then wait for the boss's recognition? – learn how to value doing a good job. Learn how to pat yourself on the back.

We need to be proactive, and look for what makes us great, pause and then praise ourselves for it. To be a self-confident person with high self-esteem we need to be giving ourselves positively encouraging statements constantly.

One important point (which we have mentioned before) is to know that NOBODY in this world can give us value – we have to do it ourselves. So we shouldn't wait around looking for a person to lift us up and proclaim to the world the greatness we know we have – proclaim it to ourselves.

Another related point is that NOBODY in the world can take away our value. No matter what they say or do to us, we are infinitely valuable. We can't even take away our own value - no matter what we have done. Sometimes we do things that make us lose touch with the essential valuable part of us, but that doesn't make us worthless, it just means we need to make a bigger effort to return to our real selves. We are all valuable diamonds – just sometimes we have a bit of ugly rock plastered on top, but when we peel away the rock there is a glorious diamond there.

Give it a Go!

Think of a time that you felt like a success in the past. E.g. I won an award in mathematics, or someone complimented me for being kind, helpful or courageous. Now look and see that you still possess those abilities even when others aren't complementing you on them. This means you still have all this talent and goodness within you, think about this part of you and see it and feel the pleasure of being you.

Alternatively, if you can't think of a time in the past that you felt like a success then try and remember some times that people have complimented you for various things e.g. being intelligent, but you thought they were mistaken. Try and see it from their point of view, try and look at yourself until you can see how and why others thought that about you. Now try and see how that good trait is inherent within you – even when others are not noticing it. Feel good that you have discovered something valuable about yourself. (If you find that you can't find anything valuable about yourself, then you aren't looking truthfully at yourself, there is no person in this world that doesn't have something good about them.)

 Now give yourself 3 honest compliments on what you did right today e.g. times when you used your talents, or gave expression to the good side of your personality.

I tried this exercise _____ times.
I would rate this exercise as:

1	2	3	4	5	6	7	8	9	10
(not so good)				(Average)					(Spot on)

Why Should I?

We all need compliments, we all need encouragement and we all need to be told that we are doing well. But nobody in the world is going to give us the dosages of positivity, unconditional love and acceptance that we so desperately need. We need to learn how to self generate compliments and how to pat ourselves on the back.

Even the most successful people in life need encouragement. In the insurance industry (as with many other sales industries) there are sales conferences where the top selling sales people meet together. We may think they meet to discuss tactics, network, get better marketing ideas etc. but the main point of these yearly conferences is to provide encouragement and motivation. Why do you think TOP SELLING sales people need this? After all, they are the successful ones earning over a million dollars a year. Shouldn't these conferences be for those sales people who just can't sell? The answer is that everybody needs encouragement, everyone needs to be told 'you too can do it', even the most successful people in their field. These conferences work because they motivate already motivated and talented people, so that they become like balls of fire – shooting for success. The more motivated, encouraged and positive a person is about their abilities, talents and inherent value, the better the person will perform. These conferences provide the kick-start to the year for a motivated person, it helps them see their own value and potential. The sales person then takes this message home and replays it in their head over and over "I'm a success, I can do it, I'm a winner, I'm good." The positive self talk and constant compliments are the fuel that help keep their fire of motivation burning, and this in turn leads them on to more success – creating a cycle of more positive talk and more success.

These techniques are used in the sales industry very successfully, but we can use them for selling our own inner value to ourselves and thus achieve true lasting success and happiness. It all starts with knowing we are good. We are valuable. We are a success already, before we do anything. The second part is to reinforce that belief by being able to constantly encourage ourselves with compliments and positive self statements. We need to look within ourselves to see what is good about us and compliment ourselves when we express this good part of ourselves. The more we do this, the more we will be motivated to act in ways that make us feel good about ourselves, and the less self destructive we will be. We can learn to love ourselves by slowly and consistently giving to ourselves the expressions of love, positivity and the praise we need.

It's a good idea to compliment ourselves at least 3 times a day. We need it just like we need to eat three meals a day. If we skip a meal we start to feel slow and lethargic, the same goes for missing a dose of positive reinforcement – we'll start to feel down or flat. So let's look after ourselves and make it a daily routine to compliment ourselves and see the good valuable things that make us the loveable person that we are.

Go on – Feed your need for positive reinforcement – Give it a Go!

Day 62

Inner Coach

We are constantly talking to ourselves. "Will I do this, or that?... What's going to be for dinner?... Uhh, I stepped in some goo ... Get going, you've got to get there by 5pm. ..."

If we listen to the constant babble that goes on inside our head we may notice that there are two voices babbling, sometimes back and forth. One noisy voice is the "I" voice - "I want ... I will... I don't want ..." It's the voice of desire, constantly wanting more and more things, or less and less effort. The other voice is the "You" voice - "You really should get up out of bed. You are always late. You shouldn't eat that." This voice wants us to be the best we can be. It is our inner coach. Both voices prattle away constantly talking to us.

We've learned a lot about the quiet voice – but these two loud voices (really thoughts) are not it. The noisy voices are often involved in superficial or shallow thoughts, whereas the quiet voice is more like a deeper type of thinking.

Now we've identified our noisy inner coach voice (the "You" voice), it's time to teach it how to motivate us using positive talk. Imagine we are training to become an Olympic athlete, and we have a choice of coaches; one coach is loud and mean, telling us how hopeless we are, how we never do anything right etc. The other coach is enthusiastic and positive, encouraging us always to do our best, and pointing out whenever we improve etc – which coach would we choose to train us? If we are sane, we would choose the enthusiastic coach because that coach will bring out the best in us long term. So now we need to train our inner coach to speak to us in a way that we would like to be spoken to. We need to encourage ourselves to greater heights with positive words not with put downs. We can choose to speak to ourselves with a kind, loving and encouraging style and we can start today.

When we start talking to ourselves in a positive way, for example, "That's the way, you can do it, keep going," we will notice that we start to feel good about ourselves. Constantly telling ourselves that we are good and valuable will make us feel good and valuable. When we begin to speak positively to ourselves, we will notice that it will flow over to our conversations with others. We will automatically start encouraging others and motivating them with positive optimistic language. However, if we are speaking harshly to ourselves, we will come to speak harshly to others – even when we wished we wouldn't. A clear sign of somebody with a nasty negative inner coach is nasty negative words being uttered from their mouth. (This insight is good to keep in mind, as it helps us feel sorry for really negative people, because they must be living in an internal hell inside the walls of their mind.)

So let's start today speaking in a way that makes us feel great about ourselves.

Give it a Go!

(These exercises, although similar to Day 10, are a deeper way of learning how to be in touch with and control our inner-dialogue.)

1. Listen to your superficial thinking (i.e. your noisy voices) for a few days, and learn how to identify the 'I' noisy voice, and the 'You' inner coach noisy voice. (If you find this exercise too difficult, don't get worried: the main point is to learn to speak in a positive way to yourself - so try the next exercise anyway.)
2. When your inner coach tries to motivate you in a not so kind way (e.g. get up you lazy bones), try and rephrase it in a positively motivating way (e.g. It's ok, you can get up, it won't hurt that much, you'll feel really good once you do it ... etc")

I tried this exercise _____ times.
I would rate this exercise as:

1	2	3	4	5	6	7	8	9	10
(not so good)				(Average)					(Spot on)

Why Should I?

We have to live 24/7 with ourselves and our thoughts, why not make the time a pleasant one. We have very little control over how others speak to us or treat us, but we do have a heap of control over how we speak to ourselves. We need to respect ourselves, honour ourselves, be kind, encouraging and a good friend to ourselves.

Every person in this world has an inner dialogue, we all constantly think – these thoughts can be empowering or disempowering. The great thing to know is that we can learn to control our thoughts and direct them to think empowering positive messages. We are not bound to always think the way we currently do, we can easily change.

Change however, doesn't happen overnight, it is a slow process of retraining ourselves to think and speak to ourselves positively. The best way to retrain ourselves is to notice when we are thinking disempowering thoughts and then purposely replace those with empowering ones. The way we think affects our emotions and our motivation. If we want to be positive, happy and motivated then we have to speak to ourselves in a way that will illicit positive, happy and motivated emotions.

Discovering our inner coach is like turning on a light in a previously dark room. Before the light is turned on we are likely to trip and fall without knowing what we are falling on. Once the light is on then we can see things that might get in our way and avoid them, walk around them or just pick them up and move them. Our inner coach is able to help us, but we need to know firstly that it is there, secondly that it's worth listening to and thirdly that we need it to speak to us in a way that makes us feel good. We can teach our inner coach to speak to us in a way that makes us avoid all the obstacles in life. We can use this awesome force to help us lead great, motivated and successful lives.

We owe it to ourselves to do this exercise. We need to have a kind, loving and positive internal dialogue, because it will make us feel good. Ignorance of our internal workings and thought processes is NOT BLISS – it can be hell. However, enlightenment, understanding and control over our thought process will lead to bliss.

Go on – (a message from your inner coach) 'You're the greatest, You can do it, I believe in you' – Give it a Go!

Day 63

Doing good leads to feeling good

"I felt great when I organised for my class to visit the old age home. We made some delicious cookies at home and then we bought them to the residents in the home. They were happy to see us, and enjoyed having someone to talk to. The biscuits were a good icebreaker. Although the residents were so pleased to have us come, I was even happier than they were, because I felt like such a good person; it left me on a high for the rest of the day."

"I was so angry with my brother for taking my book and reading it before I had a chance to finish it, I was going to really let him have it. But I decided to hold my tongue and let the incident go as if it never happened. This act of self restraint made me feel great."

"I found $10 on the sidewalk, just after I picked it up I noticed a person with a charity box who was collecting for a really worthy cause, so I popped the $10 in his box. It was such an easy act of goodness to do because I didn't really see the money as my own. Even though I was the one that gave away the money, I felt like a million dollars."

Have you ever noticed when you do something good you feel good? We all work that way (as long as we haven't over- extended ourselves). It is a simple pleasure in life to give pleasure or to relieve the pain of another.

I extend my hand and open my palm
I smile knowing I have the right balm
To be kind, compassionate and full of grace
I know I'll be the winner of first place.

There is no one that has as much joy as me
I'm giving, loving and never stingy
I'm upbeat, happy and full of awesome pride
Because I know I've got a great big good heart inside.

We need to not only do what is good but VALUE what we do. We have to recognise what is good about us and then realize that it is worth a lot, that our goodness isn't superficial, fake or worth nothing. Many people can see the good things about themselves and the good things they do but they discount it by saying 'It's really nothing special'. It's not true, it is really something special, and we are really something special.

Any time we do an act of goodness or refrain from doing something that is lowly we become great, a prime example of a human being, a super, elite person. There is nothing so destructive to our self-esteem than this little voice in our head that says, 'Yeah, so you did something good – so what? Look at all the things you haven't done. Don't pat yourself on the back you arrogant so-and-so." We need to fight this thought and say 'What I did was GREAT, TERRIFIC AND UNBELIEVABLE.'. Arrogance is when we think we're better than someone else, however, enjoying our virtues is not arrogance. Feeling the pleasure of seeing the good that we do has got NOTHING to do with feeling more important than anybody else nor whether we are better or worse than anyone else, it's a completely internal thing– we don't care what others think of our good deed, we're just pleased with what we've done. So feel free to enjoy your own being, it's not being arrogant – it's being self loving, kind and positive.

Another misconception we have is that in order to feel like a great and worthy person we need to do great things. This is also not true. In order to be a great person we need to do lots of little things. Greatness is only built on little things, just like a huge building is made of many small bricks. Small, hidden acts of goodness actually build us into great people. A person needs to appreciate the little things they do, because it's the little things that show how great we really are. It's easy to put on a show of greatness and do a lot of good in a short time, and then when no one's looking to behave like a monster. It's much harder to behave like a good, kind, patient, tolerant and positive person in the confines of our own homes – out of the public eye. When we do the good little things when we don't expect public acclaim, that's when we should celebrate and value ourselves more than ever.

Saying a kind word to a spouse, child or parent is phenomenally more great and valuable than being kind to a stranger – because it's harder to do and we won't get any recognition for it. If we are doing good things for reasons other than other people's approval, then it means that we are acting out our true selves, and not just putting on a show. The more often we can act out this good 'real me' the more in touch we become with ourselves and the more we will love ourselves. We need to value these little things that we do. The more we value them, the more we will feel motivated to do them and the better we will feel about ourselves.

It's not what we do, how much we do or the magnitude of the good we do. It's the value, importance and emphasis we put on this good part of our nature that gives us the feeling of self worth. We all have good things about us, we just need to prioritize these good things to be at the top of our self-definition list. Once we define ourselves first and foremost by these virtues our levels of self love will soar sky high.

Give it a Go!

1. Do something good and kind for another person today, and then reflect back on how that made you feel. Get in touch with how great you feel when you do something good.

2. After doing this above exercise, it's time to update your self-definition to incorporate the good that you just did. Imagine someone asked you: Who are you and what is your essence? Prepare an answer by writing down a self definition with all your good points at the top of the list. e.g. My name is _____, I am kind, generous, loving, patient, courageous, disciplined etc...– Read this frequently. Update this list whenever you do something good and incorporate that into your self definition – up near the top of the list! e.g. a week later you might have done something that demonstrated your ability to be sensitive to another's feelings, so add 'sensitive' to your self-definition list.

I tried this exercise _____ times.
I would rate this exercise as:

1	2	3	4	5	6	7	8	9	10
(not so good)				(Average)				(Spot on)	

Why Should I?

If we want to feel good about ourselves, then we should try this easy 2 step process – Do good and value the good you do. The more good we do the more we will identify ourselves as a good person. We all want to feel like good people, we may have long ago given up on the dream of being this type of person, but deep down the desire is still there.

It's a simple fact of life that the more good we do the better we feel. In fact one healthy way to start to rehabilitate a person who is depressed is to give them situations where they can give or do something good for another person. We don't have to be depressed to use this tool. We can start doing good today and feel the instant satisfaction well up within us.

The second part of the exercise helps us focus on valuing the good that we do. We need to recognise that we make a difference to the world and we can contribute significantly to the lives of others. We also need to view ourselves primarily as a good, wonderful and amazing person. One way of upgrading our self image is to look for times that we did something good, and then label ourselves with a positive label. For example if we didn't answer back when someone insulted us, we could label that as 'Strong, self-assured, dignified or disciplined." Once we've got a list of positive labels for ourselves we can start to identify ourselves as that type of person e.g. I am a disciplined person. It will take a little time before we to start to FEEL that we are these positive labels, but if we can do the exercise often enough we will actually come to honestly see, believe and feel how good we really are.

Go on – See your own goodness and feel great about being you – Give it a Go!

Day 64

The Pleasure of being In-Charge

"I love the feeling I have when I go beyond what I thought were my limits. I like to jog, and I love pushing past that point where my whole body is screaming 'STOP! I can't go on any further, I can't stand it anymore.' When I keep going past this point I reach a point of inner calm where I just do what I want to do without the internal fight."

"I like the thrill of victory when I say 'no' to that triple-decker ice-cream cake because I know it's not on my diet and it's really unhealthy for me."

"There is nothing sweeter than the taste of holding back a nasty comment or criticism which if I said it I know would have really hurt somebody's feelings. When I'm strong enough to be boss over me, then I become such a phenomenal person. It's not easy – but who said life had to be easy? People who take the easy road in life never achieve anything really great."

There is an inner satisfaction every person has when they do something they KNOW is right, even when their body doesn't feel like it. The part of us that wants to quit, desires immediate pleasure or feels they just can't help but act according to old bad habits can be beaten, and this is the sweetest victory a person can ever have. The more we take charge of ourselves and our lives and act in accordance with how we really want to act the more we will fall madly in love with ourselves. Taking the easy way out may appear to give short term pleasure but long term it erodes our self-esteem.

"When I fly off the handle and scream at my family in a big rage, I often feel satisfied that I've shown them in no uncertain terms my disapproval. But later when I calm down and I look at the type of person I had become in that rage I'm disgusted with myself. I know I look really ugly (inside and out) when I lose my temper – that's not the type of person I really want to be."

When we act in a way that is not how we feel we should, we are obscuring our 'real me'. If we try and plan in advance – "how does the 'real me' want to react when I'm angry?" Then when the situation comes up again we will be prepared and will become strong enough to act out the 'real me'.   The more often we have the inner strength to act out our 'real me' the more we become in touch with our loving giving good side and we automatically feel good about ourselves – all it takes is a little bit of planning and some willpower to follow through.

We are not doomed to act according to old negative habits, we can free ourselves from these patterns by determining TODAY that we will live the 'real me.' Every time we make a mistake and slip back into our old habits, we just need to recommit and say – "that was the 'old me' but now I'm living my life as the 'real me'" – then dust yourself off from your fall and get back up and GO FOR IT! If we see a change - even a very slight change - in the FREQUENCY or the INTENSITY of an old habit occurring - then celebrate! Because every little step toward returning to the 'real me' is a major achievement. And the only way we are able to maintain our drive to keep going is to make sure we celebrate every little victory. Our falls should not be dwelt on. Rather, we should just move on by recommitting to our goal (but sometimes using a new strategy).

Give it a Go!

Be the boss today. Do something that you know is right. React the way the 'real me' wants to react, or do something that you've really wanted to do but you've been putting off. Feel the pleasure of living a life the way you really want to live it.

I tried this exercise _____ times.
I would rate this exercise as:

1	2	3	4	5	6	7	8	9	10
(not so good)				(Average)				(Spot on)	

Why Should I?

There is euphoric pleasure in being in control of ourselves. When we have the self restraint to act the way we want to really act, we feel like a super strong hero, tough and confident. The more often we can access this pleasure, the greater we will feel about ourselves. We can do external actions of self restraint to help awaken this strong and admirable part of our real self.

We all know the bad taste failure leaves in our mouths. The taste of failing is so bad, that many people would rather deny they wanted to do better, but just couldn't. This type of self deception doesn't make us feel any better, because deep down there is a part of us that really does want to live life on a more elevated level – this is the part of us that yearns to live out our 'real me' personality.

Once we recognise that part of us which wants to be tough, strong, disciplined and focused then we need to act out this part of us. The more we are able to do acts of self control, the more often we will have the inner freedom to act in the loving, kind, gentle and 'real me' way that makes us feel so good about ourselves. We don't have to let our self destructive side win, we can choose to make every day a day of victory and goodness.

This exercise will empower us to be the person we want to be. Little by little, the more we try out doing this exercise, the more we will build up our 'I'm the boss' muscle. Being in control of ourselves gives us the ability to then behave the way we want. We will have fewer regrets in life, better interpersonal relationships and a hugely upgraded level of self love.

Go on – JUST DO IT! – Give it a Go!

Day 65

Reflective Reality

We all want others to treat us well and accord us with a decent amount of respect. But have you ever noticed that we treat people differently? We don't accord the same amount of respect to one person as we would the next.

"I'd better put on my good formal jacket – we're visiting Mrs C."

"You can't talk like that around her."

"I wouldn't do that to her, nobody would."

Most people treat different people differently. Depending on how a person perceives our value, that is the way they will treat us. But how do people value us? It is extremely fascinating to note that most people will value a person based on how that person values themselves.

Have you ever met that Mr. Nobody, who objectively speaking doesn't seem to be that great, but most people treat him better than we would naturally assume he should be treated? He might not have a great job, be very attractive, have lots of money or drive a fancy car, but there is something respectable about him. Chances are this Mr. Nobody does possess something very valuable – he possesses a good self image, and other people pick up on this and treat him accordingly.

A person with high self-esteem has a certain presence about them that decries to all around – "This is a likable respectable person." High self-esteem is not arrogance. Arrogance is often found in those trying to cover up their low self-esteem, because arrogant people feel that they have to have everything their way, and if things are not 'just so' then it is a poor reflection on them and their worth. People with self-esteem have enough self-love to not need other people to constantly prove that they are good, respectable, honourable etc ...

A rule to remember:
People treat us according to how we value ourselves.

If we don't think we are really valuable, we will allow others to treat us poorly. People who go from one abusive relationship to another, often do this because deep down they don't think they are valuable, and they don't think that they deserve anything better.

We need to know we are indeed valuable, good and likable.

We need to have the self-confidence to not allow others to treat us in a way that is not reflective of our value. At the same time, we need to have enough fortitude and belief in ourselves so that we do not need the approval of others to maintain our self-image.

How do we do all of this? By learning to see what is good and likeable about us, and by getting in touch with the 'real me' and living a life reflective of who we really are.

Give it a Go!

Think of a time that you got upset ("on principle" of course) – but really because somebody didn't accord you with the amount of respect or honour you felt you deserved. Now replay this incident in your mind, pretending you are a self- confident person who doesn't need others to make her/him feel special – how would you have reacted to the same situation in this frame of mind?

I tried this exercise _____ times.
I would rate this exercise as:

1	2	3	4	5	6	7	8	9	10
(not so good)				(Average)					(Spot on)

Why Should I?

This exercise is a big eye opener. It will show us how a person actually brings upon themselves disrespect. When we don't respect ourselves, and we don't act in a respectable manner we open ourselves up to others also not respecting us.

There is a funny trick to being respected it goes like this. If we chase after respect, or demand respect it will run away from us. But if we don't chase after respect and we honestly don't need the respect and approval of others (to bolster us up), then people will run after us to respect us. It may sound funny, but if we want to be respected then we need to learn to respect ourselves and others will follow suit. If we try to do it the other way around and want others to respect us and then we hope to feel respectable - we will never succeed.

Another trick to increasing the amount of respect we get is to make sure that we are always giving it. The rule for this trick is: A person who is respected is a person who respects others. So if we have anyone in our life who is not respecting us, we can ask ourselves: 'Am I speaking to them respectfully?' and if the answer is no, then we shouldn't wonder why they don't treat us well. If however, we do treat them respectfully (i.e. speak kindly and pleasantly to them or treat them as an important person), we then need to ask ourselves: 'Do I really respect myself, and If I don't are they picking up on this?'. These ideas can apply to any relationship (e.g. boss/employee, spouse, friends, children etc.)

The key to treating others with respect is developing the ability to see within another person something good that we don't possess. Every person in this world has strengths or things they can do that we either don't know how to do or struggle to do (e.g. some people are naturally more patient, or outgoing, or intelligent etc.) We need to learn to ask ourselves: "What can I learn from this person? And then keep looking until we find the answer. Once we have the answer, we then need to value or look up to this person because of that positive quality. Only then will we have learned the ability to view every person as respectable.

This exercise will help teach us how to fake feeling respectable until it becomes real. Which means, we will learn how to pretend to be self-confident and full of self-respect so that eventually we will feel that way. Once we honestly feel respectable we start to naturally act more respectably and others will automatically begin to respect us more.

Go on – Respect yourself – Give it a Go!

Day 66

Projecting

The way we talk, walk, dress, the clothes we wear, the cars we drive, the homes we live in are all projecting an image to others. What image are we trying to project?

"I like to dress in clothes that show off my gorgeous figure, after all if you've got it – flaunt it!"

"I like to show (only to people whose opinion I care about) that I have the best of everything – designer clothes, top brand car and luxurious house. I can afford it so why not? You only live once."

"I like to show everyone that I'm such a gifted intellectual. I discuss deep topics, use unusual words and try and best everybody in any intellectual discussion."

We project to others what we think will make them think we are valuable. If we define ourselves as our bodies, then we will take great effort and care that our bodies will be projecting a positive image. If we have an inner need to feel like a success then we will project that to others. If we define our value by our intellectual prowess then we will project this. All of this projecting comes from a lack of self-esteem. We don't value our real selves enough, so we try and get others to approve or value us by some external identity. If others do value us based on this external identity, we may feel good, but this doesn't last, because other people can't give us value, they can only give us the illusion that we have value.

As we said earlier we are projecting an image to others all the time. If we learn to get in touch with the 'real me', then learn to love the 'real me', we will feel safe enough to project the 'real me.'

"I have a great figure. I dress in a way that shows off all of my assets, and I get a lot of social interaction because of this. The biggest problem I have is I never have any satisfying relationships. Although I have a great figure,

I'm actually a really intellectual type of girl. I think by accentuating my body in order to initiate a relationship, I'm actually sending the message that I'm a 'physical' not an 'intellectual' type, so I think I'm attracting the wrong types of people."

People can only judge who we are by how we are projecting ourselves. If we are too scared to show the 'real me' because we are afraid that nobody will like us, then we can't honestly expect to attract people to us that appreciate who we really are. This means we won't have deep and long standing relationships. Because eventually we will want to be ourselves around the person, and that person will wonder what happened – all of a sudden we have changed and became a different person – not the person he/she was attracted to in the first place.

If we dress, act and speak in a way that is not designed to 'show off' an external image, we will find that people will be able to actually see the 'real me'. Externals blind people, they can't see the 'real me' if we are busy trying to loudly project an image. The best way to learn to value ourselves is to have the strength of character to be ourselves then we will see people will love us for who we really are.

Give it a Go!

If we dress too provocatively then we are sending a signal that we want others to view us as a body, and that we don't really think our 'real me' is so great. If we dress really unattractively (e.g. wearing a potato sack dress or sloppy clothes with rips and safety pins), we are sending a signal that we feel we are worthless and nothing. Look deeply into yourself and discover what image you are really trying to project. Be honest with yourself because you will have lots of layers of noisy voice saying 'I do it because I like it', which will cloud the reasons why you are really dressing the way you are, wait patiently and listen for the quiet voice's response.

Then ask yourself: "How can I dress in a dignified way today to show that I value and respect myself enough to project the 'real me' image?"

I tried this exercise _____ times.
I would rate this exercise as:

1	2	3	4	5	6	7	8	9	10
(not so good)				(Average)					(Spot on)

Why Should I?

External actions awaken inner feelings. So if we want to start feeling comfortable living our 'real me' personality, then we need to make a conscious effort to do actions that will awaken this feeling. One of the biggest ways we 'project' is through the choice of clothes we make. We choose clothes based on who we think we really want to be. The problem is, most people don't think about who they really want to be. They might one season dress like their favourite movie star and the next season like their favourite pop star. Either way they are not projecting who they really want to be, they are randomly projecting an image of someone else hoping that image fits them. In order to really love ourselves, we have to want to be who we are, and not wish we were someone else.

In order to feel self-respect and dignity we need to dress with self-respect and dignity. The more refined and dignified we dress the more refined and dignified we act. If we were to take a tramp off the street and give him a haircut, beard trim, shower, a clean white shirt and a dignified suit, black socks and shiny black shoes – he wouldn't act like a tramp, he couldn't do it to himself. Why? Because we are very deeply affected by the way we dress.

This exercise gives us the opportunity to be ourselves - our real self. When we are in touch with who we really are then we are not putty in the hands of the clothing designers. We don't have to try out every style that goes around to test out if it is really me. We can know who we are, love who we are and dress in a way that projects the 'real me'- the dignified, self confident and respectable person that we really are. This gives us an enormous amount of freedom. It's the freedom to think differently, dress in a way that befits our worth and 'project' the 'real me'. We are no longer slaves to fashion, the fashion industry or our own insecurities. Try it out, you will feel the difference almost immediately and you will notice that others will treat you with more respect because of the respectable way you choose to dress yourself and act.

Teenagers who try this exercise out will feel the difference more intensely – their friends will respect them more, their teachers will respect them more, their parents will respect them more and most of all they will feel a sense of self-respect growing automatically from within.

Go On – Love yourself so much that you're confident to project the 'real, respectable, dignified me' image – Give it a Go!

Day 67

Standing up

"Could the real me please stand up!"

When we look in the mirror who do we see? Do we see ourselves as a mass of skin, bones, hair etc? Do we see the 'me' as a hidden spot that is not visible? Who is the real me?

Imagine somebody had their leg cut off, they would say, "Oh, my leg was cut off." They wouldn't say, "Who am I? Part of me is over there where my leg is and the other part of me is sitting on a chair." Deep down we do not identify the 'real me' as our bodies. The 'real me' is something much more deeply within our consciousness, it doesn't have a physical representation.

Imagine someone who had a booming business, millions of dollars in his bank account and the finest of all luxuries. Then one day, due to a bad business deal he loses it all. Do this person's previous possessions scream out 'Help, Who am I? I'm missing the human part of my existence?" Of course not! Our possessions don't care who they belong to, they have no identity of their own. However, some people who identify themselves with their possessions, in this situation may ask 'Who am I?', because their superficial "I" has been ripped away and they are forced to face the mirror, realize that despite the fact that their possessions are not here – they still exist. The real essence of our existence has nothing to do with our possessions. Just like the clothes we wear decorate our bodies, but are not really us, so too any physical possessions we have can enhance our existence but are never an integral part of our being.

If we were asked to describe our 'real me', how would we describe ourselves?
- Would we say, "Brown hair, green eyes, olive skin complexion and oval face." Or would we say, "Kind, caring, a great sense of humour, determined, consistent and loyal?"

- Would we say, "MBA, CEO, successful, leader in my field and sought after intelligent business guru." Or would we say "Hardworking, honest, trustworthy, perceptive, reliable and affable?"
- Would we say, "Mother, wife, good cook and excellent homemaker." Or would we say "Kind-hearted, loving, gentle, organised and a good role model to others."

In each of the examples the first alternative has a person identifying themselves with externalities, and not seeing their 'real me'. But the 'Or would you say' scenario is a person who is looking more internally and seeing their 'real me'.

In order to have a high level of self-esteem, we need to value ourselves as the 'real me' and not base our value on the size, shape and desirability of our body, the amount in our bank account, the number of certificates, trophies, awards or degrees we own, the number of admiring fans we have, the number of employees we are boss over or anything else external.

If we do a bit of self-reflection we will start to realize that the real valuable me is not any of those externals that we show others. This may be a bit scary to realize, because often we have based our whole identity and worth on those externals, and once we realize they don't give us value, we may be worried that we then don't have any value. But this is not true. We all have value, but the true value we have is internal and needs to be uncovered to be seen.

Some people think that they may have had a beautiful inner essence when they were a small child, but now as they have grown up, they have lost this part of themselves, never to be regained. But that's not the way a human works. We can cover up this beautiful inner essence with many layers of 'dirt', but we can't destroy it. It is still there, waiting for us to realize that it is within us. No matter what we have done in our life, how badly we have hurt ourselves, others or society or how badly others have hurt us, we still have this beautiful inner essence. We can reclaim it, we can return back to this state of beauty, we just need to believe we can do it. Once we believe in our ability to uncover this part of us then we'll find ways of discovering our beautiful inner 'real me' essence.

Riddle

"If Kim's body was burned by a fire, rendering her grotesquely ugly, and at the same time she lost all her money and friends, who would she be? "

It's quite a funny riddle because it's obvious that she would still be Kim. So who is Kim? Kim is the same person before her tragedy as she was after her tragedy. Her inner essence hasn't changed. She is still that lovely wonderful person that she was before the accident. One interesting thing to note however is that as a result of losing all of her external identity, Kim may come to look inwardly and start to discover her 'real me'. People in a situation like this, who have discovered their 'real me' will often attest it was worth going through the whole nightmarish accident to learn this lesson – It's so valuable to get in touch with and be able to see and identify with your 'real me'.

You are good and valuable, because deep down you have a beautiful, loving and giving core. You are loveable, because deep inside you there is a very soft spot, a warm gentle loving place – the type you see in the eyes of a little baby smiling – it's there in you, it's just covered over and you can uncover it. You are special and unique because you have never ever met anyone else in the world exactly like you – nobody looks EXACTLY like you, nobody thinks exactly the way you think, just as your fingerprints are individual so is your personality. Because you are so special, and so unique you have an ability to give to others something that they don't have – you can share yourself, your way of perceiving life, or practical suggestions to get the most out of life, you can really make a difference to those people you interact with.

Give it a Go!

1. Pull away all of the externalities. You aren't your body, your bank account, your clothes, your skills or your test results etc. Now look at the real you, the same real you that you were when you were a tiny baby, or a little child. See the love, the wonder, the specialness, the sweetness and innocence that is the real you.
[You may have forgotten what you were like as a child, so you may wish to ask your parents to help describe you in positive ways. Alternatively you can look at little children, at different ages and see the different types beauty in them. Once you see it in other children you will know that you also possessed (and still do possess) this beauty.]

Continued on the next page...

2. Now ask yourself: Who am I?: (write down your answer, and only include positive descriptions)
   e.g. When I was younger (and I still have this deeply embedded in my personality today), I was: sweet, sensitive, trusting, loving, caring, joyful, playful, brave, curious, innocent, giving etc...

   _____

   _____

   _____

   _____

I tried this exercise _____ times.
I would rate this exercise as:

1	2	3	4	5	6	7	8	9	10
(not so good)				(Average)					(Spot on)

Why Should I?

When we learn to identify ourselves as that internal, valuable and good spark that lies under the surface, we begin to love ourselves. This self love is so deep that no matter what happens in our lives we are still able to maintain a feeling of 'Yes, I'm ok, I'm good, I'm loveable.'

When we base our self love on externalities such as how beautiful we are, how wealthy we are or how smart we are, then our self esteem is propped up like a shaky house of cards – any wind can come along and knock it over. There may be times in our lives that these externalities will be ripped away and we will fall into the abyss of despair or depression.

The only way that we can begin to build up a strong and durable self love, is to learn how to love that part of us that is eternally beautiful and loveable. This part of us was present when we were born, and continues to be there with us throughout our lifetime.

One way of getting in touch with our eternal beauty (our 'real me') is to revisit the past and re-discover this part of us. We shouldn't fool ourselves into thinking 'That was me then, when I was young, innocent and stupid...now I'm different.' We may have tried to hide this 'real me' part of us under lots of layers of hurt and disappointment with life – but deep down this is the 'real me'. The more we can give ourselves the permission to be ourselves the more we will come to love ourselves.

Go on – Take a hard look in the mirror and see how loveable you are – Give it a Go!

Day 68
Becoming Acquainted

Once we have become acquainted with the 'real me' we can actually take steps to start developing this part of our personalities. The more we act and give expression to the 'real me' the more we will automatically start to have a feeling of increased self-worth.

"So how do I really start to relate to that 'real me' when I don't have a lot of clarity on who the 'real me' is?"

It's time to do some deep thinking, and reflecting. Let's look back on our life and try and identify times when we felt proud of the way we behaved or reacted, times that brought out the best in us, times that made us feel a real deep sense of pleasure or even something that we read that made us feel energized and alive. Times of deep pleasure often mean that we have touched something deep within ourselves, these times help uncover who the 'real me' is.

"I remember at school I once shared my lunch with a new girl, who had forgotten hers. I felt great to be so self-sacrificing for the benefit of another." Deep down the 'real you' likes doing kind things for others, and also enjoys being in control of yourself enough to allow your altruistic side expression instead of being too weak and always giving into your selfish side.

"I love reading pop-psychology books, I devour books like that in an hour or two, and I feel so good reading them as they help me understand myself and others." Deep down the 'real you' is an intellectual who likes to understand people - probably in order to have more harmonious relationships with others and more internal clarity of who you are.

"I remember when I won the state tennis championships, I felt on top of the world. It wasn't because of the acclaim and recognition I got, it was because I tried and hustled so hard and I broke through and won!" The real you enjoys a challenge, especially the challenge of bringing out the best in yourself.

There are times in our lives that we have expressed our real self. We may have let a person go before us in line, helped an old lady across the road, gone out of our way to help a friend, or said a good word for a colleague that helped him not lose his job. Whenever we act in a way that reflects a more elevated way of behaving we automatically have a great feeling overcome us. This feeling comes from relating and acting like the 'real me'.

"If it feels so good, why don't we act like this all of the time?"

Remember one of the noisy voices (superficial types of thinking) is the selfish one that says "I", I want, I must have, I, I, I, I ... We all have this tendency to be self-absorbed. Sometimes we actually feel that we might be losing out, becoming easy prey for others etc if we don't look after the "I". It's true we need to look after ourselves, and our interests and not let others hurt us, but the only way to truly look after ourselves properly is to allow the 'real me' to have expression - not just giving into the selfish 'I' voice all of the time.

The "I" voice is not our friend. It spends most of the time convincing us to be self-centred. Sometimes it even comes up with ideas that seem really altruistic e.g. "I should invite my abusive friend to come and live with me, so s/he won't be so lonely." If we judged the idea thoroughly we would realize that it would be really destructive for our well being to do such a thing.

This "I" voice is what tricks us to pursue things that don't bring us lasting pleasure, and we get tricked again and again and again. We need to be smart, and rather than acting on automatic pilot, we need to consciously choose to behave in a way that will reflect the 'real me'. Whenever we act out the 'real me' we feel good, not drained, used or abused.

Give it a Go!

Step 1. – Reminisce about what makes you feel really good
Write down some times in your life where you feel you got in touch with the 'real me.' I.e. when you felt a deep sense of pleasure from something you did, read or experienced. Write down each of these experiences, as it will help in doing step 2.

Step 2. – Identify the root of your good feelings
Try and get to the root of what it is that gives you the great feeling.

Step 3. – Define your positive life mission
Once you've identified things that touch deeply on your 'real me' - try and define what you think may be your positive life mission in 1-3 sentences or statements. E.g. My positive life mission is to use my creative flare to bring more joy into the lives of school aged children;

Fill in Your Positive life mission here:
My positive life mission is

_____
_____
_____
_____
_____

Step 4. – Do one thing every day (for at least one week) that comes within your definition of your positive life mission statement.
Take charge of your life and plan opportunities for you to be able to live your 'real me' and accomplish what you would really love to do with your life - every day.

Fill in what you would like to do tomorrow that is in line with your positive life mission
Tomorrow I will:

_____
_____

I tried this exercise _____ times.
I would rate this exercise as:

1	2	3	4	5	6	7	8	9	10
(not so good)				(Average)					(Spot on)

Why Should I?

Everybody has a positive life purpose, or a life mission or something good that they can or want to accomplish with their lives. [Every person also has certain things about their character that need to be worked on – we know what they are because they are the negative character traits that keep tripping us up over and over again. When we do our end of the day introspection (as explained in Day 43) we work on seeing and conquering this negative part of our nature.] But how do we tap into the positive power of our nature and work on making the most of our lives and accomplishing something we value? We do this exercise! When we do this exercise, we start to work on our positive life purpose/mission. Whenever we come into contact with something or some experience that gives us a real, intense or deep pleasure then we know we are touching on a very deep part of our nature. This deep level of pleasure is our indicator of where our positive life goals/mission can be.

Everyone wants to do something valuable with their lives, but what that 'something valuable' is varies from one person to the next. One person's definition of a life well spent is not the same as another person's definition of a valuable life. We all have hardwired into our make up a desire, or tendency for certain good things, or certain ways to express the good part of our personalities.

One person might be attracted to helping people by speaking with them, comforting them and being available for them, and yet there may be a different person, who is also attracted to helping people, but who doesn't enjoy interpersonal interactions. This second person might prefer to express his desire to help others by setting up a charity organization, which involves raising money to help destitute people, but doesn't actually involve personal interaction with those destitute people. Both people are expressing their 'real me' – their caring and giving side, but because their nature's are different they are expressing themselves in different ways. Both people are living their 'real me' and are feeling intense amounts of pleasure doing so. What if, however, the two people swapped roles – the social interactive type became the charity organizer, and the charity organizer tried to comfort and encourage others? - They would both be miserable. In fact they might both doubt that they had a part of them that really liked helping people. In this scenario both wouldn't be expressing their 'real me' in a pleasurable way or in a way that was the right path for them.

So how do we know which is the path in life that leads us towards expressing our 'real me' in a way that we enjoy? Simply, do the exercise above and discover what it is that you really enjoy doing. We can look into our past and see where we felt great when we expressed a certain part of our personality e.g. the good, kind, giving and loving side of our personality or the strong, disciplined and determined side of our personality or the intellectual, thinking and introspective side of our personality etc. We should keep investigating, remembering and analysing until we can put our path in life into a one sentence statement. E.g. My path in life is to be courageous, fearless and brave in protecting those less fortunate from being exploited.

Some people's statements might be more general, whereas other people may find their statement is even more specific than this example above. Some people may find that they have more than one statement that sums up what they really enjoy doing, they may even have 2-3 statements – that's ok. It may take a while for us to define and refine what we think our statement is. Just try and write something down – anything that could be right. Don't wait for perfect clarity because it takes many years to have total clarity on this. The more often we say our statement, the more we will feel where it is correct and on target or where we need to fine tune it. Keep the statement as a work in progress. We may find over our lifetime it may change slightly, because as we grow, so will our ability to see who we really are and what we really enjoy.

The main point of the exercise is to discover what things we enjoy doing/saying/reading etc. that express a deep, real and authentic part of us. Then make a commitment to do something that is in line with our 'real me' at least once EVERY DAY.

Try and live out your positive life mission, make it the direction in life and the part of you that you really identify with. Give yourself the pleasure of doing things you deeply enjoy and you feel are meaningful.

Go on – Give yourself a deeply pleasurable moment every day – Give it a Go!

THE UNIVERSAL ME
INTRODUCTION

There are some things that ALL human beings (if they were in touch with themselves) would find makes them feel good and tuned into their 'real me'. The value of a human is incredible. Imagine if we had created a robot that could see, hear, think, talk, eat, walk, feel emotions, reproduce itself and decompose into dirt when it's useful life was over. Now imagine one day this robot sits down on the couch all day and refuses to get up, we go and ask 'What's wrong' and it replies 'I'm no good, I'm a rotten robot, I just don't love myself and can't see anything good about myself.' Wouldn't we as the inventor of this robot laugh? We would probably try and cheer up our robot and tell it, 'no you're great you are amazing just to watch walk around, you're so terrific and lovable, just because you're an amazing robot.'

If we look at this robot, although it is a terrific invention, however it's nothing compared to a human being. We humans are even greater than that because we have something that makes us awesomely powerful and that's the ability to change our own character traits and inherent selfish nature. We can self program, run our own research and development projects and upgrade our models at any time. No animal in the world can choose to change and improve its inherent character, we are so much greater than animals. We might take dogs to dog obedience school, but that doesn't change their nature, they still like to run, pant, drool and behave like a dog. But the supremacy of a human is that we can choose to rise above the negative side of us and follow that good, positive side. We can change ourselves from a bitter, angry and resentful person into a person full of positivity, love and giving.

But even if we don't choose to work on using that amazing ability to upgrade ourselves, we are still incredible creatures. Just look at the human being with all of his/her various talent and good qualities that are hardwired in – they are beautiful. If we can't see our own greatness, we need to remember that we are being blind to our own strengths and abilities – just like the robot in the above example. The more we see our real selves – 'the real me' - the more we will be able to tap into seeing how truly awesome we human beings are.

THE UNIVERSAL ME

The 'real me' is that part that is unique to the human, it makes us special and it is something we have that we should feel endlessly happy about. We should love ourselves with a deep and profound love because deep down we are very beautiful. Every single one of us!

So we don't need to have externals to prove how loveable we are. We just have to look within ourselves and see that part of us that is adorable.

There are five character traits that we can see within ourselves (and within every other human), which makes us loveable. The more we cultivate these traits, the more our beauty will come to the surface, and the more we will FEEL beautiful, adorable and lovable.

These are:
1. Being Compassionate;
2. Being a Giver; and
3. Being a Bonder (i.e. someone who can bond deeply with another).
4. Being Content
5. Being Truthful

These five are expressions of the human 'real me'. Acting them out makes us feel valuable, and denying we have these takes us further away from being able to relate to the 'real me.' We will now begin to see how to develop these universal good parts of the 'real me'.

LOVE EVERY DAY

THE UNIVERSAL ME

KEY #3 – COMPASSION

Introduction

The first of the Universal 'Me's' is bringing forth our natural desire to be compassionate. Compassion is one of those beautiful plants everyone should want to plant and cultivate in their garden of happiness – it's guaranteed to give them a feeling of peace, beauty and harmony. Compassion is a character trait that all mentally balanced human beings are born with – some have more of it and others have less. However, even if we are not born with a huge dose of compassionate tendencies we can train ourselves to work on becoming more compassionate. Sadly however, we can also choose to train ourselves to be less compassionate.

Compassion is a character trait that brings out the best in a human. It puts us in touch with our loving, giving and soft side. However, some people are afraid to develop their compassionate tendencies, as they feel that compassion is a sign of weakness. They feel that compassionate people are walked all over, give in too much and aren't ruthless enough to get a hard job done. This opinion is based on a misunderstanding of what compassion is.

Compassion is not the opposite of ruthlessness. A compassionate person can be extremely ruthless. For example there is a doctor in our town that is an angel in human guise. He is caring, gentle and always available when we have an emergency. He is the type of doctor that makes other doctors proud to be in the medical profession. It's obvious that he's not in the profession for the money, because he will even come to our home at odd and inconvenient hours, spend quality time helping the patient and leave without even charging a cent. If you were to see this doctor in action, you'd notice he has a fantastic bedside manner, especially with the children. He is so soft and gentle in his ways and he is compassionate because he always tries to find the most loving and pain free way of curing his patients. However, there have been times of emergency when ruthlessness was called for. A child with a gaping wound on the forehead wouldn't remain still for the doctor to glue the wound together. So the doctor very firmly (but without anger or force in his eyes) held the child down so the procedure could be done. Although he was ruthless he remained compassionate. In fact his ruthlessness was a result of his compassion. He cared for the child so much that he was willing to do anything to help that child – even if it meant holding them down and the child thinking (erroneously) that he didn't care about them.

Compassion is seeing the other person, loving them and doing whatever we can to help them and not hurt them – even if they don't appreciate our efforts or hate us for it. Compassion is when we don't focus on how we feel about a situation, event, object or person and instead focus on the how the other person (or animal) feels about it. It takes a tough, strong person to be able to see beyond their own nose and feel for another. Compassion is a strong character trait not a weak one.

Mistaken compassion is when somebody can't be bothered, doesn't have the back bone or doesn't really care enough about the others involved to do what is good and right but just lets others do whatever they want. That's not compassion, it's self indulgence, self-centredness and shows a lack of true care love by taking the easy way out. Compassion is having a soft manner with others but a strong core. Compassion is feeling for another and acting on that feeling. Compassion is a beautiful character trait – one that makes us feel on top of the world if we can master it.

Although this section on compassion speaks mainly about being compassionate to animals, it can apply to humans as well. We can develop our trait of compassion by practising being compassionate to animals and letting that flow on to our interactions with others.

Compassion is most appropriate when we are in a position of power or authority over another. When we don't have a position of power over another and are on an equal footing then the section following this section (Key #4 – Giving) should be referred to.

If we were to look at situations when we have a position of power, supremacy and authority we will discover it is most often when we interact with our animals. We can treat them however we want (within the legal limits of society), and the animals have no defence or recourse against us. Because these animals are so vulnerable, it is in these situations that we need to exercise our elevated trait of compassion. However, in some circumstances some people hold power over others. If we are ever in a position of power over another – we need to make the most of the situation by building up our compassionate muscle. It will make us into supreme human beings, elevated personalities, a credit to mankind and contented, beloved, and empowered people.

Day 69

Compassion

"I heard of a tribe that used to have no refrigeration. They liked the taste of fresh cow's meat, but if they killed a whole cow they couldn't have eaten all of the meat and some of it would have spoiled. Instead what they did is they would cut the leg off the cow, bandage the cow up and let it back into the paddock to graze. Then they would take the severed leg, and eat that. When they were hungry again they would cut off another part of the cow, trying to keep it alive, so that the meat would always remain fresh. It sounds so cruel to use an animal in such a way, but those people must have thought they were justified."

"I saw someone in a restaurant eating a lobster, it was still moving – it was alive! When I asked why the restaurant served its food like that they said 'fresh food tastes best.'"

In order to get in touch with who we really are, we need to be able to visit that soft caring part of our personalities. That caring part doesn't want to inflict pain on another, and certainly doesn't come up with rationalizations to do what we know is cruel.

We are all born with this trait and all of us have this vein of compassion within us. However, as we get older we are taught to 'toughen up', and to some of us that means squashing this tendency. It's true that we do need to be tough, but that means WE shouldn't act like babies and take offense at things easily. However, 'toughen up' does not mean that we should lack compassion for others.

One way of getting in touch with our soft side is to take opportunities to develop our ability to care for all the creatures around us. We don't need to be vegetarians or animal activists, because there is nothing wrong with using an animal. However, what does harm our ability for compassion is when we ABUSE (i.e. cause needless pain) not USE.

"I used to get annoyed with my cat, and I would throw her off the table when she jumped on it. But in order to get in touch with my

compassionate side, I have started taking her down gently and putting her on the floor. I feel this small act has really increased my ability to be a kind and sensitive person, and that makes me feel great about myself."

The more we take little opportunities to express our compassionate and sensitive side the more we will start to feel in touch with our 'real me'.

But how far should we take this idea?

"I heard of someone that was so careful he wouldn't even step on an ant!"

We can't possibly live a normal life worried about stepping on ants or breathing in microscopic organisms. What makes us lose touch with our compassionate side is when we PURPOSELY act in a cruel fashion, not when we accidently step on an ant.

Give it a Go!

1. Resolve to never (again) eat the meat or blood of an animal that is still alive and to never be involved in the purposeful maiming of an animal.
2. Try and do an act of compassion for an animal today. e.g. If you own an animal, feed it before you eat your meal tonight.

I tried this exercise _____ times.
I would rate this exercise as:

1	2	3	4	5	6	7	8	9	10
(not so good)				(Average)				(Spot on)	

Why Should I?

We have within us beauty, sensitivity and harmony. In order to get in touch with this softer side of our nature we need to guard ourselves against doing things that make our hearts hard. People who have hard, cruel hearts may seem tough, strong and enviable on the outside, but inside they are pathetic, bitter and twisted. People with hard hearts are not happy, they can't be because happiness comes from having a happy heart and happy hearts are soft, giving and lovable.

The biggest problem we have with trying to work on softening our hearts is we are afraid. We are afraid of being hurt, rejected or taken advantage of. Softening our hearts however, doesn't mean being foolish. We learned in the previous key (Key # 2 – Objectivity), how to avoid being hurt or taken advantage of. If we keep our head objective and our eyes open to reality then we will start to see that it's safe to soften our hearts.

This exercise gives us some tiny easy steps to help soften up our hearts. It teaches us how to feel mercy and compassion for the defenceless and weak creatures around us. Hopefully with practice, when we learn to allow ourselves to feel compassion for other creatures, we will eventually be able to start to soften up and have mercy and compassion on our fellow humans as well.

Go on – Get in touch with your soft heart – Give it a Go!

Conclusion

Compassion is one of the greatest character traits a person can try to cultivate. It is a trait that takes a person away from their animalistic nature and gives expression to their elevated uniquely human side. We can choose to act out that animalistic side which tears and rips apart its prey, or we can refine ourselves and elevate ourselves to identify with the higher and kinder part of our being.

The trait of compassion is one of those Universal Me characteristics, we all feel good about when we develop. In our garden of happiness that we are trying to cultivate, the plant of compassion is a glorious feature item. It enhances our happiness, brings much blessing into our lives and makes us into top notch, super human beings.

This 3rd Key to Happiness was based on the commandment given to Noah 'Don't tear a limb off a live animal.' At first glance this commandment may seem somewhat incomprehensible. Out of all things Noah could have been commanded to do, this one seems pretty low down on the priority list. But if we put it in the context of historical events it might become more understandable. According to ancient tradition the period of time before Noah, people were vegetarian. Animals were never killed to eat, but only as sacrifices. However, as ancient tradition explains, after Noah saved all the animals from the flood, they owed their lives to him and in order to repay this debt of gratitude to Noah, humanity was given permission to eat animals. Along with this privilege of being able to eat animals came the commandment 'Don't tear a limb off a live animal.' Which shows that along with the privilege of being able to USE an animal came a responsibility not to ABUSE the animal. If this commandment wasn't given there may have been a risk that humanity could have lost touch with its compassionate streak after being given permission to use animals.

Being kind and compassionate to animals is like a fence or a safeguard to that kind and sensitive part of us. We all have this refined side to us and we need to ensure that we don't do anything that makes us lose touch with it. Once we know how to maintain our compassion we are able to

THE UNIVERSAL ME

work on building it up, making ourselves into compassionate, loving and giving people.

This tool is one that could easily be implemented by employers or parents. When a person first has the privilege of having workers work for him/her, that's when he/she needs to work on being compassionate most. The same principle applies to parents who have little children, they may have power over their children but even more importantly they are obliged to learn how to be compassionate towards their young charges.

There is a basic principle of life:
Along with power over others, comes responsibility not to abuse this power.

Learning the ability not to abuse positions of power, but instead learning how to use these times as opportunities to develop that higher, more elevated, soft and caring part of our personalities will transform us into incredibly happy people. We will be happy, because we will know that we are loveable, great and kind people. We will be full of self love and self acceptance, because we will be aware of the extent of our powers and we will know that we could have abused our power but instead we chose to be a compassionate person. Cultivating this part of our personality gives us unbelievable levels of self esteem and feelings of inner bliss. The third key to happiness is to develop compassion. Seize the moment, soften your heart and lovingly embrace those you meet on the way towards the City of Happiness.

LOVE EVERY DAY

THE UNIVERSAL ME

KEY #4 – GIVING

Introduction

There is a part of us that just loves to give, extend ourselves and bestow goodness upon others. We can see it in little children when they hand over their latest scribble and say 'This is for you, I made it because I love you.' Their eyes beam and their smile is adorable, they get such pleasure from the act of giving.

The act of giving creates a feeling of unity and love between people. It's a simple fact, the more we give to others the more we love them. Imagine the local University was running two courses at the same time, on the same day and we had to pick which of the two we would enrol in. The first course was 'How to give to others and love them' and the second course was 'How to get others to give to you and be beloved by them.' Which course would you choose? Which do you think is the greater pleasure – To be the object of someone's giving and love (in which we may or may not feel the love they give), or to develop the skills to be able to give and love others? If we look into the matter deeply, we will notice that it is a greater pleasure to give and love others than to be a passive recipient of others goodwill and affection.

When we plant this 'Giving' Tree in our garden of Happiness, we will see that our lives become more enriched, content and beautiful. There is a beauty and charisma that encircles a person who is a genuine giver. The 'giving type' of personality is forth-coming with a

THE UNIVERSAL ME

smile, not easily offended and a pleasure to be around. They effortlessly give of their time, encouragement and assistance. They may or may not be the most physically beautiful person but their inner beauty shines through so strongly that people can't help but love them.

We can all tap into this natural part of our character. We can look beyond our immediate selves and our lives and begin to see others around us. We can ask ourselves questions that prompt our giving natures to be expressed. We can ask questions such as 'What can I do for this person?' This question makes our focus a giving one. The more we practice giving to others, the more natural it will become and the more we will feel in touch with the part of us that just loves to give.

We were all once that little child that with a heart full of joy gave his/her parent a scribble on a piece of paper. We can revisit this pleasure again and again and again as an adult. It doesn't really matter what it is that we are giving, it's the fact that we deep down love to express that 'real me' part that wants to give endlessly.

Day 70

Eye Opening

When we have mastered the art of giving to our fellow human beings, a force of delight and power will radiate from within. When we turn our focus from ourselves, and instead focus on seeing the needs of others, we have tapped into a deeply wonderful part of our personalities.

Some people are sometimes afraid to give, either of their time, money or emotions. We may be afraid of being burnt, taken for a ride or ultimately losing out somehow. However, when we learn to give in a way that is whole hearted, without wanting anything in return, then we will find that we won't lose. People only feel they have lost when they have given with an expectation of getting something back (e.g. honour, prestige, a favour, a thank-you, reciprocal giving etc).

When we give with a whole heart, with no strings attached, and according to our inner abilities (i.e. without over extending ourselves), then we will feel a deep pleasure, and no loss from any opportunity we have to give. Ultimately we will reach the level where we will tangibly feel that giving to another doesn't in any way reduce us; it only enhances and enriches us.

"Whenever anybody wants something done, they know to call me. I'm always there with a helping hand, but I don't feel great and satisfied all of the time; sometimes I feel resentful and used."

In order to give with a full heart, we need to also know how to say 'no'. Saying no to another's request for help is not a sign that we have lost touch with our ability to care and give. Saying no means we are aware of our other obligations, time restraints, priorities and personal limitations. When we say 'yes', when we really should be saying 'no', we are not drawing closer to the 'real me' but have in fact lost touch with the 'real me', and are not listening to what our quiet voice is trying to tell us.

"Yeah, no-one can hoodwink me into doing their dirty work; I'm tough! Even when they pull my emotional heart strings, I still can say no."

THE UNIVERSAL ME

Turning off our desire to give, with tough self-statements alienate ourselves from our 'real me'. We have a human need to give. If we are turning off this need, or ignoring it we are doing ourselves internal damage. Just like someone turning off their need to eat, will eventually get sick and die, if we ignore our need to give, we will feel our rich internal world starting to slowly wither away.

When we talk about giving to others, it doesn't just mean handing over money to some poor person in desperate need. Giving can be done for anyone, regardless of their wealth, health, age etc... Giving is when we see a need in another person and we do something that can fulfil that need.

The first challenge to giving is to be attuned to the needs of others. It's so easy to go through life without even noticing that others have unfulfilled needs. We all lead very busy, full lives so it's hard to remember to look beyond ourselves and focus on the needs of another.

The second challenge in learning how to give is having clarity of what we can do to help a needy person. However, with a bit of practice, thought and investigation we can often come up with some solutions. The main thing is to WANT to help, even if we can't really do anything for another person we can convey our feeling and desires that we wished we could help, and we can convey our love and concern.

When we were born, all we could think about was how hungry we were or how we needed a diaper change. As we got older we went to school, and judged the teachers on how they treated us. And as we get older still we hopefully mature and started to see past our own immediate world space. Part of the challenge of parenthood is learning to see, care for and prioritise the child's needs and wants before our own. This is really what growing up is all about – it's about getting out of 'me' and into 'you'.

Without consciously trying to work on seeing other people as real entities, with real feelings, emotions and wants, we will tend to only react to others based on how they affect us. E.g. "I like her because she is kind to **me**." Rather than liking her because she is a kind person (regardless of whether she has been kind to us or not.)

In order to draw on that part of us that is giving and kind we need to learn the art of seeing other people for who they really are, and not for how they affect or relate to us. Once we have learned to see another person's feelings, wants and desires as real and valid – just as valid as our own feelings, wants and desires then we can learn to give – not according to what we feel like giving, which is based on a whim or impulse, but giving which is based on trying to satisfy their needs.

Sometimes what another person needs is contrary to what we want to do. E.g. a new girl at school may need new friends, but if we share our friends we may feel worried that she'll take them away from us. When we learn to see past ourselves then we are also able to see past our unreasonable fears, and we will act in a way that is giving and won't cause us harm. E.g. we have the courage to share our friends, knowing that true friends will always stick by us, and knowing that by giving/sharing our friends we are helping another person immensely – it's worth the unlikely risk of losing some friends (who will thereby be revealed to not be true friends) to help another out.

"Why should I bother looking at the world through the eyes of other people? I've got to look after #1."

When we learn to see past our own noses, and really see and feel for another person we are looking after #1. We are becoming a great person, a top notch, elite, superb example of a human being. We are looking after ourselves by developing ourselves into great people, and great people are those that are able to step out of babyhood, grow up and see other people as real.

Give it a Go!

1. Time to get quiet again. Ask yourself: "Am I afraid to give?" – wait for a deep, reflective quiet voice response.
2. Try to remember for a whole day to ask yourself:
   "What can I do for this person?' Whenever you see another person today.
   Notice how many opportunities for giving you will discover that you've never noticed before. You don't have to DO whatever you think would be helpful, but just tune into the needs or want of another person.

I tried this exercise _____ times.
I would rate this exercise as:

1	2	3	4	5	6	7	8	9	10
(not so good)				(Average)					(Spot on)

THE UNIVERSAL ME

Why Should I?

Before we can develop the desirable quality of giving we need to remove any blocks we have that make us think giving to others is not a good idea. If we are not convinced it's worth becoming a giver then we will never have enough inner drive to follow through and achieve this valuable goal.

Some people are honestly afraid to give to others because they feel that when they give, they diminish themselves. For example if we have a packet of popcorn and we give half of that packet away then there is only half a packet of popcorn left for us to enjoy. This type of thinking seems to make sense, but it's missing one very big component and that is what we gain by giving. Whenever we give to another we gain something internally. We can't see this gain, we can't measure this gain nor can we quantify this gain and sometimes we don't even feel that we have gained. But we have gained. When we give to another we have gained a deposit in our internal 'value' bank account. We become more valuable. We become better people, more elevated and people of greater self worth. Over time we will be able to notice that those people who are givers, are people with higher self esteem because they actually feel their self worth more.

People who are afraid to give are like a person who has $1000, but is too afraid to invest the money. Over time he still has $1000, but his money doesn't earn interest and in fact depreciates in value over a number of years. You may ask how can it depreciate in value? It can be explained like this; $1000 one hundred years ago could buy so much more than it can buy today, it may have been able to buy a huge farm with a house on it, but today that same $1000 could only buy a nice framed picture of the farm with a house. Although the amount of money stays the same the VALUE of the money has changed because we can buy much less with it. Going back to our example... If we were to ask this person why he doesn't invest his money, he'll come up with all sorts of excuses of why he's afraid of letting go of it. But to the wise investor his excuses are all foolish – look what he's missing out on. He doesn't need to make high risk high return investments, but to do nothing is just causing him to passively erode his own monetary value. We can all see how he is hurting himself. He is the only one blind to the misery he is causing himself. The same analogy applies to people who are afraid to give, they don't realize what they are missing out on. When we learn to give we become more - our value and our worth increase. It may not be easily seen but we will eventually start to feel a quiet inner satisfaction begin to develop deeply within us.

This exercise will help us work through our rationalizations and other things that are standing in the way of maximizing our feelings of self worth. We can be a giver, we can enjoy it and we can reach levels of self love that we never knew existed by using this key to happiness – the key of enjoying how to be a giver.

The second exercise is designed to help develop that giving muscle. It helps us learn to look beyond our own immediate self and start to see the wants and needs of others. It is an amazingly powerful exercise and it will open up a new world of existence to you – the world of other people. Those who have been able to do this second exercise consistently for a few weeks have found they naturally acquire the ability to see millions of opportunities to help others that they previously didn't even notice existed.

Day 71

Giving

Once we've discovered that we really want to give to others, we open our eyes to see what they need. Now we are in a position to do the next step, which is to actually DO something for another. Giving involves taking something that we possess and sharing it with others. It's really a way of sharing ourselves. The more we share ourselves around the 'bigger' we get.

We all admire those saintly people who devote their lives to worthy causes. We might not want to follow the path they choose, but we admire this ability within a human. Have you noticed that those who are big givers have a serene and peaceful look on their face? Just picture a person whom you admire for their selfless devotion to others – notice their facial features are not hard, bitter or aggressive. The reason for this is that by learning to give we bring forth that part of us that is soft, serene, lovable and endlessly admirable.

We don't have to devote our entire lives to humanitarian causes to get the benefits of living a life of giving. Learning the art of giving can start within our own homes, our own relationships or our own work place. There are many ways a person can build up this altruistic giving muscle. Let's look at a few ways we can begin to give to others.

Giving to others can be done with:
- Our money – either by giving the person money, a loan when they need it or buying them some items that they need.
- Our possessions – we can share what we own. Lend out our books, clothes, cooking appliances or whatever is needed.
- Our knowledge – if we possess a skill e.g. a sales assistant, we can share our tricks of the trade and help another person learn this skill to. Or if we are a lawyer, doctor, accountant etc. we can give free advice every now and again.
- Our time – we can give time to others. We can take out time to listen to another person, there are so many lonely people that feel they have no one that will listen to them. We can take time

to make a healthy soup for a sick friend to help them recover. We can volunteer to help a friend move houses. There are so many ways we can give our time to others.

- Our mouth – we can give encouragement, a smile or words of friendship and love. If others are feeling down this is one of the best gifts to give.

Giving is an attitude. Whatever, we do with our day we can turn that day into an opportunity to develop our giving. If we are at home cleaning the floor or doing laundry, if we focus our thoughts that we are doing this to give to others a clean home or clean clothes, then this mundane task becomes an awesome opportunity to give. If we are going to work, we can look at our day from the viewpoint of 'What can I do to help?' For example if you are a clerk working in an office, the work you do is important (otherwise no one would pay you for doing it). Think about how what you do helps other people, and if you can do your work with these thoughts in mind, your whole work day can be transformed from a day of torture endured in order to receive a pay cheque, into a day of many opportunities to express this elevated giving side of your nature.

With the right attitude we can turn almost every circumstance into an opportunity to focus on giving to others.

"How can you say that I'm giving to others when I'm getting paid for what I do?"

Giving is extending ourselves for another person because we want to benefit them. It's irrelevant whether we are being paid or not. If we don't get paid for our work, we can't afford to eat or feed our families. And if we can't afford these basic essentials in life we won't be able to continue giving. Receiving money for our acts of giving doesn't diminish the act of giving at all, the money just helps us perpetuate our ability to give more. However, it is also important and good for us to give of ourselves for free. The main point to remember here is, if we need to take money for doing this act of giving it doesn't mean the act of giving is voided.

"I only like to give to people I feel I owe one to."

It's a fantastic character trait to have gratitude and to give back to others who have helped us. But this is not the type of giving we are talking about in this section. The 'I owe them one' type of giving is more for working on expressing our thanks and gratitude. The type of giving that brings forth this incredible happiness within us is when we learn to give, no strings attached, not because we owe any one and without calculating if the person we are giving deserves to be given to or not. We are working on developing a feeling within us that wants to outpour and give to others because we have a need to give. It is really irrelevant who the recipient of our giving is.

Give it a Go!

See if you can do this next challenge. Try and give something to another person from each of the following categories (fill in what you did):

Your money:_____

Your possessions:_____

Your knowledge:_____

Your time:_____

Your mouth:_____

I tried this exercise _____ times.
I would rate this exercise as:

1	2	3	4	5	6	7	8	9	10
(not so good)				(Average)					(Spot on)

Why Should I?

This exercise is a challenge to prove to ourselves how giving we can be. It's there to see if we can push ourselves to give in ways we have never even thought of. Once we have experienced doing this, we'll be amazed how confident we will feel in our ability to help others. We all have a lot within us that we can share with others. Just try this exercise out and you'll see for yourself.

When doing this exercise try to remember not to focus on doing big, hard acts of giving. Make the acts of giving small and somewhat easy. The idea is not to push ourselves to the point beyond our endurance (or giving) level, but to give in many different ways. For example if going to an old age home and listening to a resident speak for 1 hour is too much for you, you may want to call up an old aunt and have a 5 minute chat with her.

By doing this exercise we will begin to notice many ways that we can give to others that we previously never knew about. It's a great way to bring out our giving side, it is also a great way to discover which types of giving we prefer to do. Once we know which ways we really enjoy giving we can plan to make opportunities for ourselves to give in those ways more often.

When we learn to give, we learn to love because the more we give the more we love. A parent loves their child much more than a child loves the parent, because the parent has given much more to the child than the child has given to the parent. The very act of giving to another awakens our feelings of love for the person.

The more we give, the more we want to give. Giving is something that is so pleasurable that once we've tasted the sweetness of giving to others we will want to do this the rest of our life. Giving to others is an expression of our 'real me'. Deep inside of every person is a need to bestow goodness and kindness upon all, and if we can give expression to this desire our whole being is uplifted and feels a sense of completion and wholeness.

Go on – Learn how to love giving – Give it a Go!

Day 72
Giving in

Who is a stronger person – someone who insists on having it her way and follows through with her resolve until she has her way, or someone who really wants something but will forgo it because someone else wanted something different?

It's actually hard to answer the question, because it really depends on the person. If a person is a non-confrontational type then it's harder for them to stand up for themselves. If however they like their own way and don't find it hard to push their opinion then giving in is harder. Whenever we do something that is hard for us, but we do it because we really know it is the right thing to do, or it will lead to more peace in the world, then we are truly strong.

So now ask yourself: "Are you being strong if your father yells at you 'take out the garbage' and you feel like walking off and sulking, but instead you take out the garbage?" Of course you are – you have heroic strength.

Giving in is a very strong and courageous form of giving – when we are doing it for the right reasons.

When we give up our own wants or desires and put the needs, wants or desires of another person before our own, and we do it happily, then we really get a taste of the sweetness of living. The key is to find out what is objectively the best thing to do in the situation and then be strong enough to give in and do what we know should be done.

"My best friend wanted to go to a party where I knew there were going to be drugs. I didn't want to go, and I thought maybe I should give in, but then I thought 'If I give in, it won't do me or my friend any good' so I stuck to my guns and refused to go."

There are times that we should not give in. If by giving in we are doing something that may be damaging to us or may harm the other person, then the truly giving thing to do is to not give in, no matter how much pressure we are under. Giving in is only to be used as a tool to bring more goodness into the world. If we find that giving-in will lead to destructive results, then don't use this tool in that circumstance.

"I wanted to go to the movies, but my friend wanted to go to the library. I figured it didn't really matter, and she seemed so excited to go to the library so I gave in and did what she wanted."

Giving in to others is not a form of weakness. It's a sign of strength of character and it is another way to express our inherent need to give. Giving in can be an expression of the 'real me'; it can help us feel great about ourselves and give us a true feeling of self esteem. When we work on increasing our honour rather than fighting for the little honour we think we have then we feel great about ourselves.

Giving in has a very poor PR. Most people just don't see it as a quality worthwhile obtaining. But if we were to ask ourselves 'Should the other person we are arguing with work on giving in more often? Wouldn't it be a noble quality for him/her to possess?' We would answer 'Sure, for other people, learning to be flexible and give in is a very admirable quality.'

We want others to give in, but if we do it then we think it is a sign of weakness. Which means we judge others differently to the way we judge ourselves. This can be explained by playing a game called the 'I, You and He game'. It goes like this. Whatever 'I' do, will be painted in rosy colours and be given the most virtuous adjective. E.g. If I play chicken on the road then I am 'BRAVE'.

Whatever 'You' do, (where 'You' is my friend or the person I'm currently talking to), will be described in a less favourable way, but not so badly as to offend him/her. E.g. saying to our friend 'If you play chicken on the road then you are a 'FOOL'.'

Whatever 'He' does, (where 'He' is this nameless, faceless person or someone who is not there to defend themselves), will be described in the least favourable way as possible. E.g. If 'he' played chicken on the road then he is a 'RECKLESS IDIOT'.

This is part of our in-built, non-objective value system. In key #2 we worked a lot on developing objectivity in order to overcome this problem. But it's important to see how we all play this game to some degree or another – and it can get in the way of developing a desire to cultivate great character traits (such as giving in).

Returning back to 'giving in' – in a situation where a person is ruthlessly sticking to their guns and not budging from their opinion, here is how it goes...I am strong – willed, You are unreasonably stubborn and He is downright pig headed. Which description of the activity is objectively correct? Are we destined to always paint ourselves as 'strong-willed' and the other guy as 'pig-headed' or can we look past our own emotional agenda to find the truth?

The only way to find the truth in this matter is to have a definition and then apply the case to the definition. So what would be a definition of Strong-willed? Perhaps it could mean someone who will do what is good and right in the face of all opposition. What could be a definition of stubborn? Perhaps it might mean, someone who is open to hearing the other position but even when it's unreasonable will pursue their own opinion. Finally, what could be a definition for pig-headed? Perhaps it could be someone who isn't willing to even listen to another's opinion and blindly does whatever they desire regardless of whether it's a good thing to do or not. Now with these 3 definitions, think of a situation where you refused to give in and decide for yourself – were you being strong-willed, stubborn or pig-headed?

Give it a Go!

1. Try out giving in to someone at least once today (if you can do it 3 times – you're doing really well.) *(Note: Never give in and agree to something that is destructive or hurtful to either yourself or to another person i.e. doing something you don't really think you should do. In situations like this it is good and strong to stick to your principles.)*

2. After you've done this, the next day reflect back and feel the pleasure of giving in. Feel how you are a much more elevated person because of this act and how you caused more peace to reign in the world (or in your home).

I tried this exercise _____ times.
I would rate this exercise as:

1	2	3	4	5	6	7	8	9	10
(not so good)				(Average)					(Spot on)

Why Should I?

When we give in to another person we are really telling them 'You are important, your opinions matter and I care for you.' We can look beyond our own personal wants and desires and say 'It's ok, I don't have to have everything my way, there are more important things in life than getting my own way all of the time.'

What are some more important things in life? Some people will say having harmony amongst people, some will say developing the ability to step out of one's own self-centredness, others may say conveying love and care... the list can go on. We need to have our own clarity on why it's more important to develop this ability than to always demand our own way. If we can't find a reason, then just look at what we become when we refuse to give in at all. We become stubborn, bitter, angry, self-centred – like a tantrum throwing two year old, there is nothing admirable about behaving this way.

We don't need to feel afraid to give in because eventually the people in our lives will learn from our example and they too will want to act in such an elevated fashion. Our partner, children, co-workers etc. will have us as their positive role model, and we may be surprised to see in the future those closest to us also giving in just to make us happy. After all what comes around goes around, and our actions will affect the actions of others.

One major side benefit of doing this exercise is to help overcome the trait of anger. Whenever we get angry we have an inner voice that says 'This is not right – it should be the way I want it to be.' If we stand up to this voice and say 'Who says it has to be the way I want?' and then we give in to the other person we will discover one of the biggest and most successful tools for overcoming needless anger. Just try it out to see how it really works.

Another advantage of giving in is we start to realize that the world won't collapse if things don't go our way. We learn to let go. We don't need to feel that we have to control everything that happens in our lives – if things are not under our control, it's liberating to realize that it'll work out well anyway. Learn to let go. This exercise will teach us how.

However the biggest advantage we will find in doing this exercise is that it will cause us to have peace amongst people and attain inner peace. The more we can look beyond ourselves and see other people as real and

THE UNIVERSAL ME

worthy to give to, the more we will have fantastically positive relationships and the more we will feel a sense of inner calm deep inside. Again this exercise has to be practiced in order to reap the results, but we can do it and we'll be glad we did.

It can't be said that this exercise is an easy one – it's not! Depending on your personality, you may even find it the most challenging exercise in the whole book. But don't let that hold you back – according to the effort we put in, so is the reward that we will reap. And this exercise is guaranteed to bring in great rewards and results.

Go on – Discover the beauty of giving in – Give it a Go!

Day 73
It's Murder

"I was so angry, how dare she step on my toes – so I punched her so hard. That'll teach her not to step on my toes."

When we are angry, all of a sudden we tend to become myopic. We are unable to see the other person. All we can see is the BIG ME, and the other person is in the way, and anything that is in the way needs to be DESTROYED. When we are angry we tell ourselves 'this is not right', and we set out to make things right again. Most often if we think deeply about our thoughts when we are angry we will realize we really just want the other person to 'disappear off the face of the earth.' In the height of our anger we could happily wish even our most beloved one to be eradicated.

When we learn to see past our own needs, feelings or desires we are less likely to get angry. If someone steps on our toe and we are not in our self-absorbed mode but are in our seeing others as real mode, we are likely to think, "Oh, it was a mistake; look - they actually tripped on something."

"I heard about an article where many murderers had been interviewed. The murderers had undergone their trials and had been found 100% guilty. They were asked: "Do you have any remorse about what you did?" The most amazing thing about their answers was the majority didn't have a scrap of remorse. When they were asked why they didn't feel remorse, the murderers answered "They deserved it!" That's just incredible – most cold blooded murderers actually think their victims deserved it. Maybe a man murdered his wife because she spoke condescendingly to him – and he thinks she deserved it. Maybe another murdered the shopkeeper because he short-changed him – but he thinks he deserved it."

When we react poorly and don't see another person as real, then we could easily overreact and completely justify our incorrect behaviour with 'well he/she deserved it', or 'what else could I do?' When this is taken to the extreme we could become murderers without any regrets. Nobody deserves to die unless the law of the land has decreed that the person is deserving of the death penalty – and after a fair trial was conducted.

"I'm basically a good person, but when I'm mean and nasty to others it's only because they deserve it."

We need to look at ourselves honestly; if we are purposely hurting another person then we are not giving expression to the good part of our personality. It doesn't mean we should let others walk all over us; after all, if someone is coming after us to kill us and we defend ourselves and kill them first – that's not murder, it's self-defence. If we are engaging in self-defence then we are still in touch with our giving ability – because self-defence is giving life to ourselves.   But if we are the initiator of unkind behaviour or if we overreact to another's actions, even as a reaction to someone else trying to hurting us (unintentionally), then we need to know we are off track and out of touch with our 'real me'. The more out of touch with the 'real me' we are the less we truly value ourselves. Even if we tell ourselves a million times that we are a good person we won't actually FEEL it unless we act in a way that is good and giving.

Seeing another person as real is giving that person the ultimate gift of life. We validate their feelings, needs and very being – and this makes them feel that their life is important. Whereas not seeing the other person as real is on a minor scale like murder because in our minds they are nothing, their opinions, needs and wants are nothing and we eventually treat them like a non-existent reality.

Give it a Go!

1. The next time someone makes you feel upset, angry (even a little resentful) or you feel they are getting in your way from achieving something, try and see the other person as real. In your own mind give them, their opinions, emotions, and viewpoint importance - validate them as a person. (Then see if the bad feeling towards them melts away.)

e.g. I'm angry at my spouse for never putting their clothes in the wash basket - the house always looks messy. But today really was the worst, my spouse said they wanted to invite 5 people for dinner – I can't invite people home here with all the mess around it's too embarrassing.. But I will try and see them as real... They are not as organised as me, they aren't bothered by this like I am, it's not that they don't care about me and my feelings but they just find being neat and clean hard or unimportant. They have so many other wonderful qualities, that in the big scheme of things this is nothing compared to all the good things about them..like how calm and patient they are and.. how nicely they interact with others...

2. Once you are able to see the other person's needs, wants and whole being as valuable and real – GIVE to them something that they appreciate, that will make them feel understood or validated. *E.g. My darling spouse, I really want to make you happy so I'll have the 5 people for dinner, but can you make it in a weeks time so I have enough time to clean the house to a standard where I won't feel embarrassed to have others over? Or maybe we can hire a cleaner the day before to help?*

I tried this exercise _____ times.
I would rate this exercise as:

1	2	3	4	5	6	7	8	9	10
(not so good)				(Average)					(Spot on)

Why Should I?

This exercise helps us practice interacting more positively with people who are aggravating us (or getting in our way.) When we can see the person we are upset with as a real person with real feelings, desires, preferences and valid opinions we are less likely to bulldoze them in an effort to get on with life the way we want to live it.

THE UNIVERSAL ME

We have had a similar exercise (Day 25) trying to see the good in a person that hurts us, but this exercise goes much further. Not only are we working on seeing what is good and valuable about them, but we are working on seeing their wants and needs as important enough for us not to ignore. We are trying to work on GIVING a person what they need even when it is unnecessary, illogical, inconvenient or not something that we can relate to. When we GIVE to another person what they need we are also giving them permission to be who they are, think the way they think and act the way they act - we give them life – their own life.

Seeing others as a real, valuable entity is the ultimate way of giving because it is giving them permission to be themselves and giving them whatever they need in order to live their own lives. For example we can give a person encouragement and words of hope or inspiration when we see they have failed at something – even if we wouldn't need to be propped up like that after a failure. Or we could suggest to a single person someone they might want to meet – even if we have no interest in the single's scene. Wouldn't we all like to be treated this way by others?

Giving others permission or the wherewithal to be who they want to be is a high level of giving. You can be this type of giver. You can access this part of your personality and learn to give the gift of life (their own life), to all those around you. The pleasure you will feel from attaining such heights will fill you with feelings of tranquillity and joy from head to toe.

Go on – Bestow the gift of 'life' on others – Give it a Go!

Day 74
De-humanize

One tool some people use that stops them trying to see another person as real is to de-humanize certain people. If we categorise people as – "these are ones I can relate to and the others don't count", then we are undermining our true ability to give. We are also likely to act in a callous or cruel way towards some people without even realizing we are straying far from our 'real me.'

Some people we find hard to relate to as real human beings with real feelings and needs are:
- People with physical handicaps;
- People with mental/emotional problems;
- People who come from a different culture/country/religion
- Babies or an unborn foetus;
- Little children;
- Very old people
- Parents
- Our Employer
- Teachers

When we fail to see the real person, and just relate to them as an object we are likely to treat them very poorly, or even at times end their lives – because in our minds their lives are not real, they don't have real feelings and their needs, wants and even will to live just doesn't count, especially in comparison to our very real feelings, needs, philosophies or financial considerations.

So how can we see all people as real?
We need to make a conscious choice to live in a real world with real people around us. We need to make the choice that we want to be a giver – not just to those we feel like giving to, but to those who need us to give to them. If we make this choice, and we choose to be a giver, we elevate ourselves and become great people. If we choose that we can't be bothered with other people then we are missing out on a great

opportunity to become the type of person we would be proud to be. The choice is completely up to us and nobody can choose for us. We can make ourselves, or break ourselves – it's up to us.

A great way to practically start to see people as real is to interview them and ask them about their feelings, worries, needs or outlooks on life. E.g. "Nanna how does it feel to be in an old age home?" When interviewing another person it doesn't have to be an interrogation but it can be done in a light conversational manner. People love to talk about themselves and their feelings if they honestly feel they have someone who genuinely wants to hear what they have to say.

Another technique to help see people as real is to pretend to be them. We all have an imagination, and we can utilize this tool to help us feel for another person. Imagine being born with an emotional illness or a learning disability. Imagine the frustration, alienation and feelings of inferiority such a person would have. Now imagine how we would like other people to speak to us or relate to us. Once we feel that we can relate to this person then it's good to think about how we can give to them in a way that makes them feel good. It may be by speaking with respect, understanding or consideration, or it may be helping them do something that they just aren't capable of, because of their disability.

Once we can enter the world of another person that we previously couldn't relate to we have expanded ourselves and our ability to give and we have become an even greater, more enlightened and infinitely more lovable person.

Give it a Go!

1. Think of a person who you find it hard to relate to as a 'real person'.
2. Interview this person (or someone like this person) or just use your imagination. Now try and describe life as if you were looking at the world through their eyes: *e.g. Your boss – 'I am such an overworked hard driven person. I love the business that I built up from nothing. I work hard and expect others to also toe the line. I pay good, hard earned money for the people I choose to work for me and I take a risk whenever I hire a new employee (that they will work out well)...*

I tried this exercise _____ times.
I would rate this exercise as:

1	2	3	4	5	6	7	8	9	10
(not so good)				(Average)					(Spot on)

Why Should I?

Although this exercise is similar to yesterdays, it will help us expand our world and mind to include people we may have never thought to try and include. The more our mind can encompass the minds of others the greater a person we become. A small minded person can only see themselves, but someone with a broad mind can see and relate to many different kinds of people.

This exercise is a practical tool to help develop our ability to enter the internal world of other people. It is an enormously powerful tool. Leaders and charismatic individuals are naturally able to do this, because to become a great leader and liked by the masses it is essential to be able to relate to many different people and give each of them what they need.

Give yourself the gift of greatness – practice this tool. The more people we can convert from the 'I can't relate to' box in our mind, into the 'I understand where they are coming from' box, the better we will be at developing good interpersonal relationships and we will also automatically become a more kind, understanding, forgiving, likeable, happy and giving person.

Go on – Expand your mind today – Give it a Go!

Day 75

Unselfish Giving

We have to learn to give to ourselves. Not the selfish – give me, give me, I'm all that matters type of giving. But the loving - I'm also an important valuable person, type of giving. We can give ourselves words of encouragement, permission to make mistakes while still loving ourselves, or permission to fulfil our deepest needs.

"I like to work a lot. I think people who take holidays are lazy good-for-nothings. I like the feeling of putting in a hard day's work and coming home knowing that I've done a terrific job."

It's good to have ideals, and to try to live up to them, but to fool ourselves that we are machines that can keep going day after day without a break is not being kind to oneself. Being kind to ourselves means honestly assessing what we NEED, and our needs may change. Everybody is different and needs different things. Somebody may need a new outfit every season, and if she doesn't get it she feels terrible. Another person may need time to sit and contemplate and if he doesn't get it he becomes irritable. Needs are different to wants. Wants are never ending and we can do without them. Needs are those things that we have to have in order to feel the vitality of life. We must learn to know ourselves well enough to be able to distinguish between our wants and our needs. And we must love ourselves and see our needs as real enough to be able to give ourselves what we need.

"My life is not worth living, nothing has ever gone right with me. I don't feel really loved by anyone. I'm a hopeless failure, all I feel is pain – the pain of living, the pain of meaninglessness, the pain of rejection, the pain of failure ... I want to end my life, I don't want to live..."

If we ever get to a position where we don't feel we want to live, it is because we have been neglecting to see our own needs as real. We might not even know what our needs are, we just feel down.

Earlier we said that when we don't see another person's needs as real we are likely to commit murder. This applies to suicide as well, when we don't acknowledge our own needs. Suicide is really just murdering our closest relative – OURSELVES! When we fail to see ourselves as real we are travelling down a dangerous road that might lead to murder. Don't go there.

We all need to wake up and see who we really are, find out what makes us tick and discover what drags us down so far that we don't feel like living. If we look into our depression deeply enough we will discover that we are depressed about is ALWAYS an illusion – it's not real. We might be depressed because we feel like a failure – but no one is really a failure, we just need to get up and keep trying. We may be depressed because we feel unloved or rejected – but we are loveable – very, very, very lovable, we just need to start to look for our lovable side and do acts or deeds that bring this side into reality. If we are depressed because our lives feel meaningless – then we need to discover what's meaningful about life and do things that are meaningful for us.

The desire to end one's life can be stopped by learning to see what is good about one's life. Everybody has some elements of good in their life – if we GIVE ourselves the gift of seeing the good in our life, we actually give ourselves life itself. If we refuse to give ourselves a chance to learn how to see the good – then quitting this world won't relieve any pain. Most people will be shocked to hear it, but let's just say it again to give more clarity – quitting this world won't relieve any pain! Why not? Because the emotional pain we feel is really a state of mind that is trapped within our life force. Most people are suicidal not because of physical pain. Some people who suffer from chronic pain don't become suicidal because of the actual pain but because of their interpretation of the physical pain, or depression, despondency or other emotional reactions to the physical pain. When our body dies, it's true that our physical sensations cease however our life force lives on. This life force contains within it our mind set and personality, which means if we have a negative mindset or emotional baggage, this still lives on within us. As we know from science: matter neither comes from nothing or disappears into nothing– the same is true with our life force – it returns to its original source and is not destroyed - it just moves on to a different plane of existence.

We create our own reality – whether it is a good eternal reality or a painful one. But once our life force has left our bodies we can no longer

work on changing our state of mind. We are stuck with what we have.
So it is very important for us not to give into negative emotions and
think by committing suicide we are going to be freeing ourselves from
our inner pain. The only way we can free ourselves from this pain is to
work on it here and now whilst we can.

We need to learn to give to ourselves in a loving, kind and generous way.
We need to look after ourselves, our emotional and internal well being.
The best way to take care of ourselves is to give constantly and
continuously to ourselves in a generous and loving way. We need to
help our inner world become happy, calm and tranquil.

 The more we look after and nourish our 'real me' the more we come to
fall madly in love with ourselves. Also when we feel healthy, nourished
and happy we find that we desire to share our inner goodness with
others and we naturally become more giving and loving to all those
around us.

Give it a Go!

Ask yourself: "Is there anything that I really need, that I am not allowing
myself to give to me?"
Then give to yourself in a loving, guiltless and kind way.

I tried this exercise _____ times.
I would rate this exercise as:

1	2	3	4	5	6	7	8	9	10
(not so good)				(Average)					(Spot on)

Why Should I?

Whatever we want to give to others we have to first possess ourselves.
So if we want to give others anything we must first learn the skill of
giving to ourselves. If we want to unconditionally love others, we first
need to unconditionally love ourselves. Many times we put all our
energy into giving to others because it makes us feel so good, but
eventually we crash and our ability to give dies because we neglect to
give to ourselves. For example imagine a chef who cooks for people all
day long, but forgets to eat. He won't be able to continue cooking for
others if he deprives himself of what he needs.

We need to give ourselves everything that we need. We all need certain
things such as food, shelter, clothes, money etc, these are self evident.

But we also have other emotional needs that we MUST give ourselves, such as; self-love, self-acceptance, encouragement and giving expression to our 'real me' (e.g. feeding our need to be compassionate, give to others, bond deeply with another etc.). If we neglect our non-physical needs we can fall into a heap and sink into depression.

We are our biggest priority in life. No matter how many other people rely on us, or even if the whole world sits at our feet waiting for our help, we need to first make sure we are giving to ourselves. It is not selfishness, because selfishness comes from only seeing ourselves in a small minded way. Looking after ourselves comes from seeing that we are important, needed and worthwhile. It is a pre-requisite for being able to give to others. No one else in the world will be able to nurture us in the way we need to be nurtured, so it is very important that we take ourselves and our needs seriously – and look after ourselves. If we find the whole concept of nurturing ourselves hard, it can be made easier by pretending we are a person we don't know well and asking ourselves "How would I advise this person to take care of themselves?"

This exercise will give you permission to love and give to yourself.

Go on – Give yourself a new lease on life – Give it a Go!

Day 76
Faking it until it's real

We have written a lot about giving and awakening the inner desire to give. But there are some people who may not be in touch with this part of their very being. If this is you, don't despair. Although you may not feel the soft giving part of your nature, it is there, you just need to awaken the dormant feeling. The best way to awaken such dormant feelings is to pretend they exist. Think, act and speak as though you really feel that way, and then this feeling will be awakened within.

"I'm not such a giving person. I just don't feel it; it's more for those 'nice' types – not me"

By giving when we don't actually feel that gush of enthusiasm, we teach ourselves to do what we know will bring us pleasure in the end. In order to awaken our inner force of love and giving we sometimes have to force ourselves to do it, and keep doing it – and with time the good feeling will come.

"I have a heart of stone; I don't think I'll ever feel so loving and kind, no matter how much I fake it."

If we fake it because we want to impress others, or for some other external reason, then it will never be internalized. This is because we are faking it for external approval and not for internal growth. However, if we fake being good, kind, giving and nice, because we want to really awaken something that is dormant inside of us – then we are granted success – GUARANTEED! When we are internally motivated to become a better person, then deep down something changes within us and that giving part of us is resurrected. We just need to be honest with ourselves and consciously choose to become givers – for our own sake only. The success of this technique really lies in the MOTIVATION behind why we are faking it.

"I gave $500 to a really worthwhile charity; it was a great act of giving on my behalf – but I don't feel that different."

It is better to give $1 to 500 people, than one large amount to one person. Why? Because giving is like building up a muscle, if we work out frequently even with a very small weight our muscles will grow, whereas if we work out rarely, but lift one heavy parcel – we may do ourselves damage. We need to assess what is the 'right weight' for our giving muscle to work out with, and then consistently give in those doses regularly in order to work up our giving muscle.

"I tried greeting one person a day with a lovely smile, and an interested facial expression. That was my 'giving muscle' work out. It actually worked really well, because after doing this for 3 months, I find it now comes naturally, and now I'm ready to up my weight and grow some more!"

If we want to grow in any area, we MUST do it in small increments. If we bite off more cake than we can chew, then we'll never enjoy the cake. A small muscle workout can be anything that is a little stretch for us but is really doable. The real trick is persistence – just keep going and looking for small opportunities to give to another person.

Give it a Go!

Set yourself a 'giving muscle workout' exercise that is rather easy but still a slight strain. E.g. say something encouraging to someone once a day. Now try and do this exercise every day until it becomes natural or it becomes so easy that you don't really have to push yourself at all to do it.

My 'giving muscle workout' exercise is:

_____

_____

I tried this exercise _____ times.

I would rate this exercise as:

1	2	3	4	5	6	7	8	9	10
(not so good)				(Average)					(Spot on)

Why Should I?

If we want to reach a goal we need to work for it. We all want to be givers, it just takes a little bit of training, practice and persistence to build up our 'giving muscles.'

This exercise will help us turn the dream of becoming a giver into a reality of being a giver. The difference between people who succeed and those who fail is very small. Both have dreams, both want to follow their dreams and both try to make their dreams a reality – but really successful people don't give up. If we want to build up our 'giving muscle' we have to work out regularly. It's not going to work if we just try it once or twice. But we need to keep going, keep trying and keep setting small reachable goals.

Our need to be a giver is there inside of us. This part of us is yearning for expression. Let's not let a little body resistance or weak 'giving muscles' rob us of being the type of person we crave to be. Sure it might be a bit tough to work on to start with, but once we start to see how we are growing and succeeding we will be inspired to keep going.

There are many demands we have on our time and emotions. We need to prioritise our personal growth to be on the top of the list of things to do. Nobody wants to waste their life away, but the only way we can prevent this from happening is to be pro-active and determined to make the most of every day.

Doing this exercise will enrich you and your life. You will slowly become the type of person that you have always dreamed you can be. Forget all the excuses and the 'Yes, it's a good idea but...' and just try this exercise out.

Go on – You know you yearn to bring out the best in yourself – Give it a Go!

Conclusion

The 4th Key to Happiness is to learn how to give to others. It's about developing the ability to see beyond our own immediate world, needs and desires and notice other people and their need and desires and then to be able rise above ourselves and give generously to others. When we are able to elevate ourselves above our own 'me, me' world, we enter the world of the giver. The more we can live in the world of the giver the more we are able to access supremely high levels of tranquillity, equanimity, serenity, love and joy.

Worlds of pleasure are available to us when we are able to give expression to our inborn yearning to give. Deep down we all want to be givers, we all desire to bring pleasure and joy to others and we all yearn to rise above our own petty selves. We can work at bringing this part of our 'real me' out into the open and integrating it into our lives.

The 4th Key to Happiness was based upon the 4th Commandment given to Noah, which was 'Do not Murder.' So what is the link between 'Do not murder' and 'Be a Giver'? 'Do not murder' is warning mankind not to become myopic and only see ourselves and our own needs. We all need to learn not to discount the real needs and desires of other people. A person only murders another when he/she has lost touch with the fact that their murder victim is a real person with real wants, feeling, desires, and life. A murderer only sees him/herself and their own needs and feelings as real. In fact a murderer places the importance of their own needs and feelings so much higher than others that they are willing to destroy and kill another person just to have their own way. Murderers can be so self absorbed that even after they have committed their crime they have no regrets because they honestly don't think other people count – they feel anyone who gets in their way deserves to be annihilated.

The best way to prevent going down the path of the 'murderer personality' is to develop the opposite trait, and that is the trait of giving. When we develop our ability to give we are really not creating something that wasn't there, we all have this talent and desire within us.

THE UNIVERSAL ME

We just need to remember we want to express this part of us and this 'giving personality' is the type of person we want to be.

It's easy for intense emotions such as anger, revenge, spite, callousness and arrogance to distract us from our real deep desire to be a giver. However, we can work on overcoming these negative emotions by concentrating on building our giving muscles. When our giving muscles are fit and strong we can put up a good fight when we are challenged by our intense negative impulses and we can win.

Learning to be a giver will open our minds up to a bigger and more beautiful world – a world where other people, their needs, wants, desires and lives are real and this new reality will give us an enormous amount of pleasure. We can learn how to become givers in ways that we enjoy and that fit in with our personality. We can be great, loving, kind and elevated people.

If you can take hold of this 4th Key to Happiness and work on your innate desire to bestow goodness upon others, you will be able to enter the inner sanctuary of the City of Happiness with a blissful, calm and serene feeling in your heart.

LOVE EVERY DAY

THE UNIVERSAL ME

KEY #5 – BONDING

Introduction

There is a Universal Me desire to bond deeply with another person. This special relationship of deep bonding gives us overwhelming feelings of happiness, acceptance, love, support, trust and bliss. We all crave a close relationship like this, and even more deeply we crave and desire to express a deep intimate part of ourselves which wants to utterly devote ourselves to another person – completely with no strings attached.

When we were little children we used this desire to bond deeply and directed our need to love, surrender and give to our parents. As we got older we went looking around for another to bond with. The healthiest form of doing this bonding is in a marriage – a long term relationship set up with the purpose of providing the framework for the trust, love, support etc to be present so that this deep bonding can take place.

It is a human need to bond, and it is a Universal Me characteristic to seek and search the world to find that special one to bond with. When we are able to realize this goal and bond deeply with another then our levels of happiness and internal bliss skyrocket.

When we are involved in a stable relationship and we bond with the other person at a deep level, we feel a sense of completeness and stability and our very inner essence experiences a peace, serenity and contentment.

THE UNIVERSAL ME

If we were to look all over the world, throughout all periods of time, we would find that institutions such as marriage are everywhere, and have always been there. If we look around us, we see men and women searching constantly for that special one to be with. It's such a strong inner drive to form a deep relationship, and if this level of relationship is reached we have long lasting happiness in our lives.

The 5th Key to Happiness is to learn how to bond deeply with another person. If we can master this key we are going to experience levels of bliss we never imagined were possible.

Day 77

Love Me

Before we begin to bond with another person we need to make one point completely clear to ourselves, we need to know that we are capable of bonding, and we are worth bonding with. We have to know that we are loveable. We have to be 100% clear that another human being is able to fall madly in love with us.

Earlier in the book we have learned how to work on seeing our 'real me' and falling in love with our real self. This has helped us discover a small well of self love beginning to form. But even if we don't feel it, it is important to know there is a place inside us that is totally crazy about us. It's been crazy about us before we were born and it'll be crazy about us until the end. That is the place of the quiet voice. No matter what we've done, who we've hurt and how unlovable we feel we are – our quiet voice will still whisper messages of love, hope and encouragement to us. Whenever we are feeling down, it's therapeutic to have some quiet time to hear some encouraging messages from our quiet voice. We can ask it: "Am I loveable?", "Why don't I feel like I'm loveable?" etc.

"Why is it important to feel that we love ourselves?"

It's important to feel the love that we have for ourselves because we are about to move deeper into a 'real me' pleasure and that is the pleasure of loving another person.

We are only capable of bonding and truly giving love to another person if we possess love to give. We need to know that we are loveable, and that another person is capable of being in love with us. If we don't feel we are really lovable, then why enter into a relationship? To feel loved? But if we don't think we are lovable, we won't believe anybody when they tell us that they love us. No matter how often or how eloquently our partner tell us that she/he loves us we won't believe them. We will think they are wrong, confused or lying. So we need to know that we are lovable, and if we know we are loveable then we are more likely to believe our partner when they say 'I love you.' Deep down we all want to

THE UNIVERSAL ME

be loved and accepted. We want to, bond and completely devote ourselves to another person.

"I go from one relationship to another. I'm hoping Mr Right will be around the next corner, but there are only people in disguise pretending to be him."

"I'm a great catch, I have everything going for me; I'm intelligent, good looking with depth of personality, but I make foolish choices."

If we feel that we can't find a long term relationship it is usually rooted in the fact that deep down we don't think we are loveable. We thus make a sub-conscious choice to go out with only those people that can't or won't really get close to the 'real me'. We sub-consciously choose a partner that we deep down KNOW is not the type we are really interested in.

 If we would reflect seriously on the relationships we are choosing, we will realize that we push away those types that could really have a good long standing relationship with us, and draw near to only problematic personalities. We may tell ourselves that the types of people that are good for us are boring, unattractive, and not fun. We do all of this because we don't feel lovable.

So the very first step before we can even attempt to bond with another person is to recognize we are lovable, we are valuable and we are top notch, elite, Rolls Royce bonding material. If we can't recognise that we are really loveable then we shouldn't enter into a relationship until we address this problem, because we will never be able to bond with another person if we don't think we are good enough to bond with.

Give it a Go!

Think about this question (on the next page) and don't enter into a relationship until you have a reasonable answer. (If you can't find an answer, then work hard on increasing your self-esteem, seek professional counselling to help you find the answer, or discuss it with your friends who might be able to enlighten you.)

Continued on the next page...

Why should someone love me?
(i.e. What is loveable about me? What can I give another person by being in a relationship with them? What character traits do I have that would make me a 'good catch'? Why am I worthy of being loved? Etc.)

_____
_____
_____
_____
_____
_____
_____
_____

I tried this exercise _____ times.
I would rate this exercise as:

1	2	3	4	5	6	7	8	9	10
(not so good)				(Average)					(Spot on)

Why Should I?

We have to see that we're lovable. We must completely believe we are loveable and feel it in every fibre of our body, because we ARE absolutely lovable.

This exercise helps us get in touch with what is loveable about us. It may require soul searching or confronting some negative self statements such as 'Yes, but... If they only knew me then they wouldn't really love me.' In this exercise we are required to convince ourselves that we are worthy of being in a relationship.

If we don't believe we are lovable, and we find this exercise too uncomfortable to confront – running away from this feeling won't help. The only way to solve a problem is to recognise that it's a problem then set out to fix it. So we need to keep trying to see ourselves as worthy and loveable until we manage to succeed.

However, if we have a reasonable degree of self esteem this exercise will be rather easy – and that's great because it means we're ready to move on and begin to bond.

Go on – Open your eyes to what a great catch you are – Give it a Go!

Day 78

Love You

Now we are ready to fall in love. But before we do this it's time to clarify what it means to love another person.

So what is love?

Love is seeing the beauty, virtue or good in another person and associating that person with his beauty virtue or good.

E.g. "I love my brother because he has a great sense of humour, he is always telling great jokes" or "I love my mother because she is kind and caring and she is always there ready to help out anyone who needs it." We see a virtue e.g. kindness and we associate that person with his virtue i.e. he is kind and for that we love him/her.

If we understand this definition we will come to the realization that we can actually do things that make us feel love towards another person. This is a priceless gem of wisdom. Did you realize that love doesn't have to be a random, unpredictable feeling we have? It can be a feeling we can foster and develop.

How?

We can actually work on loving others by training ourselves to see their beauty, virtue or goodness e.g. write down every day one good thing about the person you want to love more, keep it up for a few months and you will feel the difference!

This is life changing – never again will we need to wait around to fall in love (we can make it happen), and never again will we feel crushed when we realize that we have fallen out of love (because we can re-ignite our love by working on seeing the person's virtues.)

"I think love is that heart stopping, breathless feeling you have when you meet Mr/Mrs Right"

Lust is not love. Lust is a short term emotion that is very powerful, and sometimes it is the spark that starts the bonding process and gets a relationship off the ground, but it doesn't keep it going. Lust can occur with the most unlovable person – but because it is so powerful we don't wake up to who this person really is until much later.

"But there is natural chemistry you feel between some people that others just don't have."

We are more compatible with some types of people than others, but it doesn't mean we should base our choice of partner on chemistry or emotions to the exclusion of using our common sense. Before we get really involved it's important to see if this is the type of person we want to entrust with our most valuable treasure – ourselves. Is this the type of person you can bond with? Just like oil can't bond with wood (no matter how much glue you use), there are certain people that we can never bond with. If the person is not likely to appreciate us, rejects us, purposely hurt us or doesn't really want to bond with us in the first place, then we shouldn't bother trying to bond because it'll just cause us pain. We can look before we leap. We can see if this is the type of person we can bond with. We can see if this person has the qualities we need in order to trust, love and dedicate ourselves to.

"How do you know what she/he's really like?"

In the business world a smart company investigates its clients before agreeing to do trade with them, especially if the trade is going to be an important one and the customer asks for credit. Companies will do credit checks on potential new customers before agreeing to sell their goods to them on credit. Why? Because they want to make sure that this new customer is the type that they can trust and the type that they will benefit from.

We can be smart like these large companies. We can investigate who it is we are thinking of entering a relationship with – BEFORE we start. Why be burnt when it can be avoided? But since we can't ring up the credit ratings bureau for the low down on our next potential partner, we need to find other ways to see if they're worth the risk.

We can tell if someone is a 'good catch' by looking at their 'real me'. Who are they really? Are they the type of material that makes a good spouse? Are they responsible, reliable, dependable, able to give, kind, encouraging etc? Or are they critical, controlling, condescending, overbearing, self-absorbed, unkind etc?

There are different ways of finding out who a person really is:

1) We can sometimes see what type of person they are by observing how they interact with other people, (because for us they may be putting on a show, but how they act with those they are not trying to impress may show their true colours.) See how they treat their relatives, friends, the waiter, the doorman or even a beggar on the street. Would we like them to treat us the way we see them treating others? Because eventually that's how they will treat us.

2) See how they react to stress, distress or pressure – do they become overly self-focused, depressed or hostile? Stress often brings out the worst in a person. If we see someone under stress and they still seem ok to us then this person may be ok. But if we see someone under stress and they become abusive or mean then this may not be a person we want to bond with. For example, how would he/she react if the waiter accidently spills some food/drink on them?

3) Ask around. We may be able to ask old friends, teachers, employees or work colleagues. This can be done with the potential partner's permission. Be brave – ask for references. When employers are thinking of hiring a new employee it is absolutely foolish to do so without a reference. Our relationships are far more important and we have much more to lose by making a poor choice than any employer could by hiring the wrong employee. We should feel confident enough to know we're a good catch and ask for personal references from people who can attest to the character of the person we are thinking of getting involved with.

If we go into a relationship with eyes open and an objective analysing mind then we will often see the warning signs of what will be an impossible person for us to bond with – before we get involved.

"I can't be bothered with complicated, emotional relationships, I never try and get too deeply involved."

If we deny that we want a stable long term relationship, then we don't know ourselves well, and/or we've been burned so badly in the past that we have lost hope of ever achieving this goal. However, if we dare to dream, what would most of us dream? (What does the 'real me' dream about?) A prince on a white horse carrying us off to a palace far away... For how long? You know the ending ... Happily ever after! We dream about having ONE relationship with a special person FOREVER.

So if this is our dream – what are we doing to fulfil it?

"I want it to be like that but my relationships keep breaking up!"

If we want to live our dream, we must make sure that the other person is dreaming the SAME dream. We need to find this out before we let our prince carry us off to the palace. Imagine the princess (you) saying to the prince, "Oh thank you my saviour, where are you going to take me and for how long will we be gone?", and he answers, "I'm taking you to my holiday home for a few months, and then you'll have to find your own way home." You may hesitate to go with him and you may decide to wait for a better offer from a more sincere prince. After all, if you go with the prince to his holiday home you might be missing out on meeting the prince that would have taken you to his palace forever.

We need to have the self-love and inner belief that we will be able to find the right person who will be willing to spend his/her entire life with us. You are a great person, and you will find another great person who will love you – but he/she will only be capable of loving you to the extent that you love yourself.

Give it a Go!

Get quiet, and deeply reflect:
1. Now ask yourself: "What are the internal qualities that I need in my partner in order to have a good, deep, bonding and loving relationship?"

Write down your answer:

_____
_____
_____
_____
_____
_____

What can I do to live my dream of having one long-term stable relationship?

_____

I tried this exercise _____ times.
I would rate this exercise as:

1	2	3	4	5	6	7	8	9	10
(not so good)				(Average)					(Spot on)

Why Should I?

Let's look before we leap! We owe it to ourselves not to get burnt by entering dead-end relationships or getting involved with unstable personalities that we just can't bond with.

This exercise is a MUST to do before we get involved in any relationship. Before we go out to buy a car, we first think about what type of car we want to buy, what we are planning to use the car for (e.g. on-road or off-road driving), how long we want the car to last etc. Only after we have worked out the essential 'must have's' in a car do we actually start looking to purchase a car. The very last things we decide on when we buy a car are the colour or the interior finish – the unimportant things.

Imagine someone going into a car dealer saying 'I haven't thought about what type of car I want, how many seats, how powerful and engine etc. but I want a red car.' It sounds really foolish, because the first red car they see may not be suitable for their lifestyle. They may end up buying a two seater red sports car and when they get home realize it doesn't fit them, the kids and the dog inside.

Just like we need to pre-plan what we want when we buy a car, we also need to do the same for our relationships. We need to have a 'must have's' list. Which is a list of qualities or traits that are totally indispensable, then we might have a 'would like' list, which is a list of things that make the relationship more pleasant and finally the 'unimportant but nice' things which are listed last. If we have such a list for a prospective spouse, then when we meet somebody new we can look at our list and see how well they match up. If we're sharp and in tune with our desires, we will be able to spot a good deal in a relationship from a great distance.

This exercise will help us hone in on what we really want in a prospective spouse. It will sharpen our ability to recognise a 'good catch' and it will give us peace of mind to know that we don't have to settle for a 'bomb' relationship. When we are very clear about what we are looking for in a prospective relationship we will be more successful in achieving exactly what we want.

Go on – Describe your dream partner, then wake up and go find them – Give it a Go!

Day 79

Preparing

"I dream of having a relationship so deep, warm and loving. We will get married, have some children and even hold hands when we eventually sit together in the dining room of our old age home."

"My dream spouse will be full of lots of fun and excitement. We will be lifelong companions on the adventure of life together. Although my spouse will be fun, they will have a deep enough personality to be able to deal with the important things in life that will pop up. My spouse will be strong, dependable and loads of laughs."

When we dream about what our life long spousal relationship will look like, then we know what things we want to look out for in a spouse. We will also be in a position not to waste our time on those relationships that just won't be able to build towards our dream.

"I like going out just for fun. I'm not looking for Mrs Right, that can wait."

Any intimate relationship we enter into leaves an imprint on us. To say we are not affected means we are totally out of tune with our feelings or that we have erected very strong stone walls around our heart. Either way we are in pain. It's painful to be out of touch with our true feelings, and stone walls around our heart are only erected when the heart is full of much sorrow, pain or grief. Relationships where both parties aren't looking for a lifetime commitment are short lived 'fun' for a long term cost, and if we were to look at it honestly, we would realise it isn't worth it.

Imagine you were offered a fantastic weekend away to your favourite holiday destination, free meals at your favourite restaurant and entry to anywhere you wanted to go. You go on the weekend away, enjoy yourself immensely and come back home. A week later you get a bill in the mail for $1,000. You argue with the promoter that the holiday was free, but the promoter points out the fine print, "The holiday is free, don't pay a cent the whole weekend. This terrific offer will cost $1,000 a month for the next 5 years." The holiday was great fun, but was it worth the cost?

When we get involved in a relationship it costs. It costs our emotions, our time (and life is really time), our level of trust in mankind, our ability to love again, our view of our own worth and our very essence. If we are serious about the relationship and the other partner is too, then the 'cost' is really an investment in a good solid asset. If the relationship is not a good investment in the first place – then it's a waste of our limited resources.

Let's imagine we want to buy a house and we have a $20,000 deposit saved up. If we were to give away $1,000, here and $2,000 there, eventually when we find the right house we won't have enough money left to even put down a deposit. The same situation applies with relationships. Every new intimate relationship that doesn't lead to a permanent lifelong companionship is draining us of our loving resources. If we give away a bit of ourselves here in this relationship and there again in another relationship, it erodes us, and then when it comes time for the real one we don't have it left in us to give and build a proper relationship. We're burnt out, bitter, or too emotionally mixed up to be able to develop and have that relationship we have been dreaming about our whole lives. The best course of action is not to get involved at all unless both people have the same dream/goal in mind.

"But I can't not go out, everyone goes out. Maybe I'll be missing out on something."

It takes strength to live the 'real me', and to also know with clarity that we aren't missing out on anything, we are keeping our deposit secure, so we can afford to buy the real thing when it comes up. But the results of living the 'real me' will be quick to see. You will be happy, have vitality and you won't need to go to a psychologist to help you undo the damage you did to yourself by not living the 'real me'.

[322] / 7 ANCIENT KEYS TO HAPPINESS

Give it a Go!

Ask your inner wisdom: "How can I get a support system to help me have the inner strength to live my 'real me'?"

I tried this exercise _____ times.
I would rate this exercise as:

1	2	3	4	5	6	7	8	9	10
(not so good)				(Average)				(Spot on)	

Why Should I?

We all need support to help do things that we want to do but we find hard. Loneliness can be very painful. We need support not to enter into incompatible relationships just to avoid being lonely. There are many single people in the world that can help support each other in their loneliness. Forming a support group with other singles of the same gender and age will help us remain sane whilst we look around for Mr/Mrs Right.

The alternative of jumping into relationships that we just KNOW will go no-where and will never give us long term bonding is inevitably going to hurt us. The hurt we incur will be deeper, longer lasting and more painful than the agony of loneliness.

With a support group, we can have friends, do fun things together, have someone to share our life with and even help each other out by recommending other singles that might be compatible for the other singles in our support group. These types of supporting friendships are so valuable and help us keep our self esteem and self respect intact. In fact by using a support group like this we'll actually find it much, much easier to find our soul mate in the end.

If you are single, this exercise is a MUST. It is the only way you will remain sane and not fall into the trap of desperation and despondency.

Go on – Enjoy being single – Give it a Go!

Day 80

Living it up

Now we've focused our goal – to have a long-term loving relationship. We've removed all the distractions - we've waited until we are really ready and we've worked out what we are seeking in a partner. Now what do we do when we've found Mr or Ms Right? How do we unleash this 'power of love' into the world and build a fantastic relationship?

Loving another can be the greatest pleasure a person may ever feel in his/her lifetime. A true trusting and loving relationship provides the fertile soil needed to grow and become a great person – the 'real me'. Loving another provides the opportunity to release in a safe environment all of that giving, compassion and warmth that we so deeply want to express. Falling in love is actually an exercise in giving – not in getting. When we get married we may feel we are gaining something: maybe more financial security, company, physical pleasure etc, but all of this pales in comparison to the wonderful feeling of joining two kindred spirits and learning to treat our spouse as an extension of ourselves. When we get married we grow – we double, because the other person now becomes part of us. He/she now enters a new relationship called the 'we'.

"I've been married 3 years and I don't feel like my spouse is part of me."

In order to feel this level of bliss we need to work on it. It doesn't come easily and there will be times when we just don't feel connected. Our aim should be to try to do everything we can to give our partner everything he/she would like.

We can try and fulfil our partner's **material needs**, but if we don't have the funds we can still express our desire to fill these needs. E.g. I would love to buy you all the new outfits in the world, but we just can't afford it, so let's try and save up for one special something. Or we can try and fill our partner's **emotional needs** e.g. I see you need to have some time to yourself so I'll go and visit my mother for the day. Or we can try and fill our partners **physical needs** e.g. I see you're in the mood for a good back rub, let me get the massage oil. If we make the effort to do all we can for our partner we will start to feel connected.

When we are there trying with all of our might to do whatever we can to please our spouse, we will have a beautiful marriage and a wonderful life.

"But aren't you afraid, if you always give he/she will take advantage of you?"

If we think that a person is not capable of giving and is purely a taking machine – don't marry them! If we have a normal giving spouse, then acting towards them as their personal cheer squad and loving helper will actually awaken that ability within them. When our spouse sees that we really care for him/her, and that we give 'no strings attached', they will learn from our wonderful example and they will treat us with the same love and dedication that we have shown them.

"I'm worried if I put my spouse first all the time, I'll fade into nothing. What about me? I'm a person with feelings and thoughts different to my spouse. I'm not just a fading shadow of my spouse's image."

Giving and showing that we care and love another person doesn't take away our identity. In fact the more we know who we are, and appreciate our likes and dislikes, the less we feel our identity is threatened by giving to our spouse. Being our spouse's cheerleader, best friend and confidant doesn't mean we have to change our personality. We can still be who we are. We can disagree, have different interests etc and he/she will still love and respect us. Problems arising from one spouse feeling they have to assert themselves over the other, only happen when that spouse doesn't feel loved, respected or lovable. Once a person feels they are respected they don't make a big show about it. It's only when we don't feel that we are truly respected or loved that we start to bang our chest and demand recognition. (Please note: Giving to our spouse doesn't mean that we should tolerate being treated disrespectfully in the hope that he/she will eventually feel our love and respect and reciprocate. We should have enough self-confidence and self-love to say to our spouse 'That's not the way people speak to me. I respect you and I expect you to respect me.")

In order to bond deeply with our partner we need to be focused on dedicating and devoting ourselves fully to them. We need to give our partners the feeling of: "I'll always be there for you, no matter what. I'll always love you, I will work on seeing the good things about you and support you through the good times and the bad. I know you are not perfect (but neither am I) and I accept you and love you for who you are. I want to go through this journey of life together, as a team. I am yours, and you are mine – forever we will be one."

Give it a Go!

Do something today because you know it will bring pleasure to your spouse, and fulfil a need they have.

I tried this exercise _____ times.
I would rate this exercise as:

1	2	3	4	5	6	7	8	9	10
(not so good)				(Average)				(Spot on)	

Why Should I?

One of the biggest pleasures most people will ever have in life is the bonding relationship with their spouse. In order to keep this pleasure alive and well we need to work on developing our relationship. Building a strong, loving and bonding relationship is a lifetime project. It isn't a matter of investing a few good years and then sitting back in blissful bonding. Bonding is dynamic, it needs to be done continuously and consistently all the days of our lives. That might sound like hard work – but it's not because it's so pleasurable to have a healthy loving relationship.

This exercise is designed to help us build up our relationship. The more we work on it the more satisfied, fulfilled and happy we will become. Don't wait for your spouse to make the first move to repair or build the marriage. Take charge of your own happiness and work on it as if you're the only one that can make it succeed. If you do this you will surely see some wonderful positive results.

The happiness and feeling of completion that will be felt after working hard on building a bonding marriage is worth years of toil, tears and trying. Our deep inner 'real me' desires this type relationship more than it desires ANYTHING else in this world.

Go on – Feel the bliss of bonding deeply – Give it a Go!

Day 81

His and Hers

If there is a rule that could enhance any marriage it is:
She needs to be loved. He needs to be respected.

That doesn't mean that she doesn't need to be respected and he doesn't need to be loved, but the main primal need of a woman is to be loved more than she needs to be respected and the primal need of a man is to be respected more than he needs to be loved.

"I noticed an advertisement for a law firm that specialized in family law and divorces. They had two pictures. The first was a picture of a man sitting next to his son: he must have made some funny comment, because the son is looking up at the father admiringly and smiling. The second picture was of a woman: she was surrounded by her children who were giving her a loving embrace. Obviously the advertisement wanted to attract both men and women as clients, but it was eye opening to see how they marketed to each group very differently."

If we want to have a great marriage we need to know how to convey our respect to our husband, or our love to our wife. Often we will find that women try very hard to convey that they love their husbands abundantly when what he really needs to know is that she respects him. Whilst at the same time the husband is slogging away at showing how much he respects his wife and her opinions, when what she deep down wants is for him to show her how much he loves her. In such a case the marriage will be a happier marriage than a marriage where neither partner is trying to convey love or respect. But this marriage could be even better if both parties would treat their partner in a way that they would prefer. Men and women have different needs.

A woman can demonstrate to a man that she respects him by praising his opinions, choices or decisions; not criticizing him when he makes a mistake but ignoring it all together; giving over some matters that involve decision making to him and backing his decision when he makes it; fulfilling his wishes (where possible); asking his opinions; and telling him that he makes her so happy. In summary it means showing him that he is a competent and capable person in her eyes.

A man can demonstrate to his wife that he loves her by showing how much he cares for her needs and desires. He tries to fulfil all of her requests, and if that is not possible he at least tries to accommodate her wishes as much as possible or verbalizes to her that he wishes he could do everything she desired. He expresses his pleasure with her, whether it is what she wears or how well she does what she does. He bites his tongue and doesn't express disapproval of her, but tries to convey to her that he loves her just the way she is. He listens intently and with interest when she wants to talk with him. He takes the initiative to buy her little 'just because I love you' presents, to show he is thinking of her during the day. Basically he needs to show her that she is cherished, loved and the most important person in the world to him.

Although you may say that practically speaking, showing respect or love look pretty much the same, and you would be right, but when a man puts his emphasis on showing her she is loved, and a woman puts her emphasis on showing him that he is respected, the marriage becomes a very happy one.

"I don't really respect my husband much. He's a lovable guy, but he's just not very competent at anything."

Every man has something to respect about him, it's just a matter of trying to focus on what that 'something' is. We can do this if we look for the abilities he has that we don't have. Look for things that he's better at than you are. (Ask yourself 'What can I learn from him?') Once we find those areas where he has strengths, then we just need to focus on how admirable these qualities are and we will automatically start to feel respect for him.

If a woman liked a man enough to marry him, she must have seen something in him that was admirable. Just go back to what you liked about him when you first met him. Those qualities haven't changed – they are still there and you can still respect him for that. The more we look for opportunities to respect our spouse the more we will find such opportunities.

"I love my wife, and she should know it. Why do I have to always prove my love to her?"

We all need positive reinforcement. People need constant reminders that they are loved. The more a husband 'remembers' his wife in speech or actions, the more the woman tangibly feels the love he has for her. Making opportunities to express how pleased we are with our spouse, at least once a week (or even better, every day), will make our spouse feel loved, happy and able to give back to us the love they feel they are receiving.

Give it a Go!

1. Write down a list of things you respect or love about your partner, try and add a new one to your list every day. Try to do this for the next month.

My partner is:

_____

_____

_____

_____

_____

Also

2. Think to yourself: "How can I show my wife I love her?" or "How can I demonstrate to my husband that I respect him?" Then, TODAY, do or say one thing that makes her/him feel loved/respected.

I tried this exercise _____ times.
I would rate this exercise as:

1	2	3	4	5	6	7	8	9	10
(not so good)				(Average)				(Spot on)	

Why Should I?

This topic may touch a raw nerve for some people. Those who think men and women are the same and should be treated similarly may find they are uncomfortable with this exercise. However, if you look for the truth of the matter you will see men and women ARE different. Little boys play differently to little girls naturally without any training. The book 'Men are from Mars, Women are from Venus', explains the differences in communication techniques and needs of men and women. There are a lot of books and material written on this topic. It is conclusive. Just like a man and a woman look different, so too do they think, act and need different things. Different however doesn't mean BETTER (or worse). All because men and women are different and have different needs, it doesn't mean that one is superior to the other. If we look at apples and oranges, we can't say either is superior. They are different and both are great. The same principle applies to men and women. We are both fantastic specimens of human beings.

If we want to give our spouse the most pleasure possible it's a good idea to find out what makes him/her pleased. The insight that men need respect and women need love is a generalization. It's true that generalizations don't apply to all people at all times. That's the downside of a generalization. But the positive side of making a generalization is that MOST of the time this technique will work wonders.

This exercise doesn't imply that women don't need to feel respected or that men don't need to feel loved. That would be completely untrue. Women and men both need to feel respected AND loved. The exercise is just getting us to focus on what will make our spouse feel best. It doesn't mean to exclude showing our wife that we respect her or our husband that we love him. We should do that too.

The best way to actually see the light and truth in this wisdom is to try it out. Experiment with this idea in your relationship. You may discover you have stumbled on a priceless gem of wisdom. This exercise is truly powerful and enlightening. Only more peace, harmony and marital bliss can result from trying it out.

Go on – You have the power to make your marriage blissful – Give it a Go!

Day 82
Withstanding temptation

A few tiny drops of poison can spoil a whole barrelful of wine.

The biggest poison to a life time loving relationship and deep bonding is getting involved with someone else. Straying into the arms of another person will never do anything to enhance a marriage. Some psychologists may even counsel a couple to seek partners external to marriage to try and spice up their lives – don't listen to such foolish advice. Ask your quiet voice: 'What is the best way to have a fulfilling marriage?' –it will never tell us to cheat on our spouse.

So why do people do it? Some reasons could be:
- They don't feel their marriage gives them the emotional support they feel they need;
- The lust has gone out of the marriage so they go looking for excitement;
- They don't feel they are appreciated enough as a good husband/wife, so they go looking for someone who will appreciate them more;
- They don't mean to, but it "just happened";
- They are angry with their spouse, so this is a way they take revenge; or
- They want to get a divorce, but they don't want to be single whilst they look for a new spouse.

If we want to live a life full of bliss, deep pleasure and stability we need to have the inner strength to fight our destructive and selfish desires and to live our ideals and inner truths. Ask yourself: "Is it true that adultery is poison to you, your spouse and your relationship?" (Of course it is.) Our goal in marriage is to provide the framework so that we can bond deeply with our spouse. Bonding can only take place between two totally committed people. If one of the partners starts to pull away from this bond then they are harming themselves (and their partner) because neither person will ever achieve their Universal 'real me' need to bond – and lacking this bonding experience erodes our happiness.

Once we are in touch with our inner wisdom we can tackle the rationalizations that we make. Firstly, if our marriage is not fulfilling then we should try and rekindle the fire of love – and do whatever we can to achieve this. Secondly, if we have tried **everything** to keep the marriage together and it has failed and we are miserable, then we should get divorced. It's not fair to ourselves or our spouse to be in a relationship where we are hurting each other. Thirdly if we do decide to stick it out with our spouse – we need to be strong, resist temptation, and have enough self-respect to act in a way that doesn't go against our 'real me' and our inner truths.

The best antidote to wandering off from our spouse is to make bettering our marriage the primary goal of our life. If we are constantly working on improving it, then it will remain alive, vibrant and rewarding.

"I might work on my marriage for about one month every few years. When I'm concentrating on being a giving and loving spouse the relationship always looks good, but when I forget, things go stale pretty quickly."

We may look at our grandparents or great-grand-parents and think 'they look so happy, it looks so easy'. But know it wasn't easy; every couple has hard times, and goes through rough patches. If we don't give up and we keep trying to bring ourselves closer together then we might eventually merit to make it. Marriage is hard work – don't be fooled by 'happy ever after stories', instead they should read 'and they lived together and both made huge efforts to give to each other, to accept their differences and to appreciate each other's strengths. And their journey together was incredibly enjoyable, despite being lots of hard work...'

Give it a Go!

Time to get quiet and ask yourself:
"What can I do today to start to enhance my marriage?" (E.g. I'll work on speaking more encouragingly to my spouse for the next 3 months)
Try to write down at least three points

- _____
- _____
- _____

I tried this exercise _____ times.
I would rate this exercise as:

1	2	3	4	5	6	7	8	9	10
(not so good)				(Average)				(Spot on)	

Why Should I?

The best defence is an offence. When we are working on improving our relationships then they just can't go sour. But any relationship left on the shelf will automatically start to lose its lustre.

We all want that feeling of love, complete trust and oneness with that special person in our lives. The biggest poison to attaining this is when either partner goes looking elsewhere. The trick to achieving our goal of complete bonding with our partner is to continuously keep applying fresh and new layers of glue.

There are different ways we can keep our marriage freshly glued, but the first step is to commit to making the marriage the number one priority in life. After all when a marriage is done right it is the number one pleasure in our life.

 The next step is to work on doing things together that enhance the marriage. Some people like to have intimate dinners once a week, others like to play sport together. Whatever it is that you enjoy doing, try and do it together where there is just the two of you (no kids, no dog, no friends, no phones, no computer etc...). If you can concentrate on being together and enjoying each other's company this will enhance your relationship. Another way to keep a marriage vibrant is to take marriage courses, or read inspiring books for ideas to help keep the connection alive and well.

This exercise will help you plan for a better future and a better marriage. It is the preventative medicine to take against having a marriage become stale or go completely off track.

Go on – Invest in making your marriage great – Give it a Go!

Day 83
Avoiding it

"I used to be an alcoholic, so now I avoid going to a bar."

"I could never stick to a diet if I went out shopping when I was hungry, so now I make sure to eat a healthy meal before I go shopping, and I make sure to be back in time for my next meal."

If we know something is liable to cause us damage, we will take steps to avoid it. The more precious an object is, the more careful we will be to protect it. The most precious relationship we have is our marriage – but do we take steps to protect it?

"I have an office job and I got along really well with one of the guys in the office. We used to take lunch breaks together and sometimes we even met outside work hours. When I thought about it, I realized that this work relationship was really problematic. It didn't start out that way but I felt I was getting too friendly with my work colleague and that was potentially harmful to my marriage. I stopped the lunches and other outings and I told my work colleague that I didn't feel it was right – he was ok with this, and I felt so good."

We have an internal barometer inside us that starts to flicker when we feel a slight attraction to another person. If we start to feel this, even in a minor way, it is our inner self telling us to put more distance between this person and ourselves, because if we don't it may harm our marriage. We feel it inside when we start to overstep our own inner boundaries. The more we are in tune with this barometer the better we will be able to know when to walk away from a potentially hazardous situation. If, however, we go out and forget to turn the barometer on we could get ourselves into tempting situations that we wished we were never in.

"What about platonic friendships – they're probably ok?"

Platonic friendships are a joke. Either they are not really platonic and one or even both of the friends are fooling themselves, and are really attracted to the other person, or they are not really truly friends, they're just acquaintances. Men and women are attracted to each other. That's the way it's always been and the way it will always be. Continuing "platonic friendships" whilst in a marriage is a huge, potential risk. Is a marriage less valuable than the friendship, that we are willing to risk it just to keep the friend?

"So I need to cut off myself completely from everyone just because I'm married?"`

No, we just need to keep our other gender relationships as businesslike and impersonal as possible. It doesn't mean being rude and unfriendly to members of the opposite sex. It does mean toning down our usual warmth, vibrancy and other parts of us that attract others to us. We all have the wisdom to know when we are overstepping our inner boundaries and we also need to have the strength of character to hold back when we feel we might be going too far.

Our marriage is the vehicle that provides us with the security to give and devote ourselves to our partner. When two people bond, it can be strong and tight. But if a third person enters the scene and one partner starts to pull away from the other, then the marital bonding will fall apart, and this will cause the couple extreme sadness. However deep, loving bonding causes exhilarating heights of contentment and happiness.

We all desire to bond deeply with our special partner, we just need to remember this and take precautions not get distracted and forget that this desire for deep bonding is the 'real me' and it gives us one of the most immense pleasures we feel in life. Why risk losing out on all this potential bliss? – be careful and guard your treasured relationship.

Give it a Go!

Ask yourself: "Are there any times that I'm overfriendly with a man/woman who is not my spouse?"

If there are, then see the pain and heartache this may cause your spouse and ultimately yourself. Know that it is impossible to bond with more than one person at a time. Then resolve to take steps to avoid this ever happening again.

In order to protect my special bond with my partner, from today onwards I will (or will not) ...

_____

_____

I tried this exercise _____ times.
I would rate this exercise as:

1	2	3	4	5	6	7	8	9	10
(not so good)				(Average)					(Spot on)

Why Should I?

This exercise is a must for all married couples. It's so easy to get caught up with somebody other than our spouse if we don't take precautions against it.

Have you ever noticed that big, gorgeous and luxurious homes have fancy security systems protecting the property? Why? Because they want to protect what they have and all of their valuables. Have you looked at old run down shacks? – they don't have security systems. Why not? Because they don't feel they have anything of value to protect.

How much do you value your relationship? Is it like a luxurious home or a run-down shack? The more we value the deep bond of love we have with our spouse the more we will go to lots of effort and expense to stop intruders trying to enter our domain and steal our happiness.

It is of great importance to find ways to protect the special bond we have with our spouse. If we ignore the danger of another person intruding on our relationship we will be the ones to regret it. And if we have been 'robbed' in the past, then we should have complete clarity that we need a high tech. sophisticated and powerful protection system to protect against any future 'robberies'. Both spouses must be committed to protecting their valuable relationship – both spouses need to remember to turn the security system on when they leave home!

This exercise is one that will help us set up our own protective security system to guard the most important thing we have – our special bond of love with our spouse. It is worth all the time, money and effort in the world to do this exercise. We will be saving ourselves a lot of potential heartache and tears by trying out this one.

Go on – Protect your special relationship from thieves and robbers – Give it a Go!

Conclusion

The 5th Key to Happiness is developing the ability to have a deep bonding relationship. We all crave such a relationship and we are driven our whole lives to look for that special bond if we don't have it. The biggest challenge to achieving this key to Happiness is staying focused and on task and not trying to bond with incompatible people or with more than one person at a time.

Deep bonding takes years and lots of effort to achieve, in fact it is more of a process than a result. We are continually trying to rejuvenate our bonding and that in itself is exciting and wonderful. We never really 'get there' enough to sit back and relax, because the pleasure of bonding is having a living, dynamic and alive relationship. It is true as we get older that bonding becomes easier and deeper, but we should never take it for granted. We always need to work for higher and higher levels of this pleasure. And there are endless levels of pleasure we can attain by developing a strong bond with our beloved.

The 5th Key to Happiness – Bonding, is based on the 5th Commandment given to Noah, which was 'Don't enter into 'forbidden' intimate relationships.' It is interesting to look at what some of the 'forbidden' intimate relationships were. Before we analyse this, it is fascinating to note that all of the 'forbidden' relationships were relationships that cannot lead to a true lasting deep bonding experience.

Types of 'forbidden relationships'.
Firstly Adultery – one shouldn't try and bond with another man's wife. It is quite obvious that it is impossible to bond with more than one person at a time. So adultery will never lead to having that deep bonding feeling we all desire.
Secondly Bestiality – It is absolutely impossible for a human being to bond deeply with an animal. Animals have no capacity to bond.
Thirdly Other – in the 'other' category are things like being intimate with people that are too close to us e.g. incest. This may be explained by looking at the following analogy. There are two different types of puzzles. The first is the conventional jigsaw puzzle where all pieces look

THE UNIVERSAL ME

different, and there is the more modern puzzle where all the pieces are the same shape and the sides are flat. In this type of puzzle we just need to carefully place the pieces next to each other to see the puzzle picture. The problem with this second type of puzzle is, if there is a little knock or nudge to the puzzle, the pieces fall apart. They don't have what it takes to bond under the slightest pressure. Whereas with the more conventional jigsaw puzzle, the fact that the pieces are shaped differently gives them stability, so if this sort of puzzle is knocked it is likely to still stay together.

If we apply this analogy to people, there are some people that are too much like us. We are almost carbon copies of the same thing. In this case (like brother/sister or father/mother etc) we just don't have enough differences to make a strong lasting bond. The way a human being is designed makes it impossible for him/her to be able to reach a strong, stable, completely giving and bonding relationship with these types of people.

So after we analyse the 5th Commandment given to Noah we can see it was really good advice to tell us what not to waste our time and energy on. The only way we will be able to access that deep feeling of completion, oneness and bonding is if we devote ourselves to relationships which are stable, healthy and compatible with our 'real me' needs.

Once we have worked hard and dedicated ourselves to finding and building that deep special bonding relationship we will have acquired the 5th Key to Happiness. With this key we will feel overwhelming levels of inner peace, love, acceptance and wholeness. The key of bonding will give us feelings of completeness and deep true eternal love.

LOVE EVERY DAY

THE UNIVERSAL ME

KEY #6 – CONTENTMENT

Introduction

One of the biggest thieves of happiness is lacking the ability to feel a sense of satisfaction and contentment with who we are, or what we have. The panicky feeling of 'I'm missing something', or 'I've got to get 'it'' where we don't know what that missing 'it' is, robs us from enjoying the wonderful things we currently have.

Have you ever bought a new 'something', but on the way home you notice that someone else has and even better 'something' that you just bought? All of a sudden you no longer feel happy and satisfied with your new purchase, you are already looking around for bigger or better.

We all need to learn the ability to be happy with what we have and who we are. This doesn't mean we have to be complaisant and not aim for more. But it means being able to enjoy what we have and not let what others have rob us from our happiness.

If we can plant a contentment plant in our garden of Happiness, and sit under this plant basking in its glory regularly we will find that our lives become one big bubble of bliss. We often create misery for ourselves – we might be experiencing the happiest moment of our lives, but then we see someone else walk by with ONE small thing that we never knew we lacked until we saw them with it and BOOM we are no longer full of happiness and contentment. If we didn't look around and compare ourselves to others we never would have felt a lacking in the first place.

THE UNIVERSAL ME

Keeping up with the Jones' or joining the race for 'he who dies with the most – wins' mentality is guaranteed to rob us of many good lovely potentially happy years. Our lives are full of so many good things, if we can develop the habit of keeping our focus on what we have and not what others have we will merit to lead lives of pure bliss.

Day 84
Too Busy

When a person looks at what another person has and desires it, then they are setting themselves up for misery. We want to be happy, so then we need to do things that make us feel good. Concentrating on what we lack makes us feel down and concentrating on what we have makes us feel up. So since the choice is ours about how we use our mind, which is a more clever choice?

Taking what doesn't belong to us derives from a feeling that we are lacking. Happy people are too busy enjoying what they have to want what others have. Happy people don't want to focus on what they lack – they want to have a life full of joy and abundance.

We live in a society where the media is constantly trying to tell us 'You can't possibly live without my product.' This robs us of our contentment. There are many things we don't need to have and many desires we didn't have until someone came along and told us that we really did want them. If we want to cultivate contentment we need to challenge those enticing advertisements with questions such as 'How will that make me happier?' or 'Why before I saw that product was I perfectly content with what I had?'

The best way to avoid looking out to see what we are missing, is to practice looking 'in' to see what we have. Contentment doesn't come from just noticing the good we have in our lives and learning to appreciate that good – that was the 1st Key to Happiness. Contentment is reaching a place where we feel happy with who we are and what we have and we don't feel a desperate need for more to bolster ourselves up.

Contentment comes from a constriction of self and ego. The opposite of contentment is greed. To have a greedy disposition is to want and want much more than we need. It's like sitting down in a restaurant next to a glutton who piles heaps and heaps of food onto his plate. We feel a natural repulsion when we watch such greedy behaviour. This is because our 'real me' appreciates and feels a sense of serenity when it sees beauty and goodness. And conversely our 'real me' feels a sense of repulsion when we see a deviation from what we know deep down to be beautiful and good. We don't need to be convinced that contentment with our lives is beautiful and good, and we don't need to be convinced that greed and gluttony is repulsive - we naturally feel it.

Deep down we all want to feel contented and deep down we are silently begging for the incessant internal chase for what we don't have to cease. We are not forced to always feel this unending push for more and more, we can break free. All we need to do is work on being satisfied with what we have, who we are, who we married, who our children are, who are friends are etc... and stop looking around at what other people have and comparing our lives to theirs. When we are too busy and contented with our own lives we won't be the slightest bit interested in looking around to see what other people have.

Give it a Go!

1. Reflect and ask yourself: "How can I feel so satisfied with what I have that I don't even want what others have?"

2. When you next desire to buy something trace back in your mind to where the desire for this item came from – Was it a lack that you felt without external stimulus? (which is ok) or Was it because you saw someone else had it or saw it advertised?

I tried this exercise _____ times.
I would rate this exercise as:

1	2	3	4	5	6	7	8	9	10
(not so good)				(Average)					(Spot on)

Why Should I?

Wouldn't we all like to be free from the shackles of having to compete with others? This exercise will help us opt out of the mindless materialistic competition, and by opting out we will discover a new found aura of peace and contentment encircle our lives. What bliss we can feel on this earth, without having to take out a loan, resort to shady business practices or do other things that we really don't want to, but sometimes feel we have to in order to 'get on' in life.

Free yourself from the prison of endless wants and desires and enter into the paradise of enjoying your own unique special and beautiful life.

When we learn the skills for acquiring contentment we will be lifted up above the mundane world, and we will float on a cloud of bliss for the rest of our lives. We will be able look at the pettiness and pain of those around us and wish they too could experience this elevated level of consciousness.

The first exercise is a powerful one if we work on it. No one can give us the answer to the question because every person is different and needs to walk a different path to reach their personal level of contentment. But the answers are there.

Some general guidelines that might help us find the answer are:

1. Keep busy by working on appreciating what we have and who we are and;
2. Discover ways to limit that part of us that wants to take, gain and amass more and more. Don't deny ourselves necessities, because this will only make us feel resentful and lacking. But slowly over time withdraw from things that are not essential. We know we're doing it right if it's done with happiness, joy and a feeling of being 'lighter' or unburdened from our never ending desires.

We can find the answers that are right for us, just keep trying and persisting.

The second exercise is one to help tune into when we are being pulled away from our contented outlook and being dragged into the race for more and more. When we start to look at our purchasing decisions, we will begin to see when we are being tempted away from being content with what we have by advertising campaigns or by looking at what others have.

If our purchasing decision is coming from an internal source, such as we dropped a pile of plates on the floor and now have to go out and by a new set, then that's not departing from being contented, it is just buying things we need. However if we are happily walking along and then notice something in a shop window or that another person has and then we have a desire for that item – we know that we have lost our contented focus. If we really needed what we just saw in the shop window, we would have known about it BEFORE we went shopping.

THE UNIVERSAL ME

There is nothing wrong with going shopping and amassing things if we are happy with our lives and are just buying things we need. But if we are looking out on the world feeling a lack then acquiring, taking and amassing will never fill this void. The second exercise will help us see when we lose our happy focus and start searching externally for fulfilment. Once we recognise this in ourselves we will be able to work on fixing up the void by returning to a mindset of contentment.

Go on – A Contented life is a very good one – Give it a Go!

Day 85

Taking

If we lose focus on being content with what we have in our lives we then look around and notice others have things that we don't have. We think to ourselves 'how dare this person have what I don't have. I want to be happy, I want everything – he's really got what should belong to me.' This type of thinking makes us become takers.

Taking from others makes us feel less or diminished and giving to others makes us feel more or greater. Which would you prefer to be: a person dispensing one dollar coins to everyone down the street, or a beggar trying to gather one dollar coins from everyone? We have an innate feeling that taking from others reduces our worth. People who have just lost their jobs or are on social security living on handouts have a harder time with self-esteem than others. Why? Because deep down we hate being takers.

"I love presents and I hate going out to work. I would be so happy if people gave me whatever I wanted, whenever I wanted and I didn't have to do anything."

That is the sound of our noisy voice. Yes, it's nice to receive things and having material possessions can give us a temporary feeling of elation. But for a deep feeling of self-worth, a person needs to feel they have earned what they have. The pleasure in getting an excellent fake copy of a University Degree is nothing compared to the real pleasure of receiving the real thing if we worked hard to get it.

If we got more pleasure from gaining or winning than from putting in effort and then achieving results, many games and puzzles wouldn't be sold. If the objective of a computer game is to kill all of the enemy invaders, then why not make the game such that we have to press one single button and we win. The game wouldn't sell. Why not? Because if there is no challenge, there is no real pleasure in the result. However, if the challenge is too great this too will not sell, because if people find things too hard and don't see results quickly enough they give up. The trick is to make the work challenging enough, but not too challenging. So the trick in life to maximize pleasure is to make sure that we work hard for what we have (but not too hard), rather than just accumulate everything without any effort.

So why do we want a free ride? Because we foolishly believe, (for a short time), that we will be gaining something by taking it without earning it.

How can we suffer from such temporary insanity? Because we lose focus with being content with what we have. We look up and notice so many things we are lacking and we panic. We panic so hard and so loudly that we go crazy with the thought that we might be missing out, wasting our lives, withering away or missing the boat of life. Nobody wants to waste their lives away, so this panic comes from a deep fear that our lives are amounting to nothing or meaningless because we don't have what others have.

We need to calm this panic inside and tell ourselves that life is not all about what we have, but about who we are. We need to remind ourselves that if others have things that we don't have it's ok, we don't need everything in the world to be happy.

When we are able to calm ourselves enough to realize we have everything that we need then we won't feel the deep desire for taking things that don't belong to us. If however, we succumb to this voice of panic we can end up doing things that make us really ashamed of ourselves. In a panic of thinking we are missing out on something we might become a taker, and thus rob ourselves of our own 'real me' greatness, because our 'real me' hates to take. Our 'real me' really desires to be content with what we have. In the end we feel low if we give into this panicky desire for more.

"A little taking is ok, no one will get hurt, people won't even notice."

Imagine you have a very busy market stall selling fruit and vegetables. Now imagine that everybody who walks by tastes one of the grapes. Some people may come in and buy them, but most people just feel like a grape so they take it. If there is a huge amount of foot traffic, it is possible that if everyone took one grape just to eat, you would be left with no grapes and no one who actually bought any. A little taking is still taking, and although we may feel that it goes unnoticed, it may cause significant financial loss to the person if everyone else does it too.

Also by taking and thinking it is ok because it is so trivial we are hardening our inner core. We start to see the world from a "what can I get perspective" which conceals that sweet good part of us that we really like about ourselves. Also we forget that we have such enormous pleasure in just enjoying what we have. Taking is fool's gold – it glitters, it's golden in colour, and it's cheap and easy but it's worthless and makes us feel that way to.

"Everyone does it; you have to in order to get by in this rat race."

Maybe a lot of people do it, but a lot of people do lots of destructive things. If you had to go to a school only for blind people, would you then purposely make yourself blind because everyone else was? Of course you wouldn't, because you appreciate having sight. If we appreciate the elevated feeling of being content with what we have and not always being hungry for more, then we look at all those people who feel they have to take and amass more and more and more as unfortunates. We feel sorry for them and certainly don't want to be like them.

"I used to like to shoplift; I liked the game of getting what I really liked without having to pay for it. The excitement of the game would last for a few hours afterwards, but deep down I had a feeling that I was rotten, no good and internally ugly. I tried everything to feel good about myself but these feelings kept surfacing. Then I decided to stop shoplifting, and to get in touch with what really makes me fulfilled. As soon as I tapped into the 'real me' I realized that I had been damaging my feelings of self-worth by not behaving in a way that made me feel good about myself. The external part of me had its rationalizations and even had feelings of pleasure but the internal me seemed to be paying the price."

Taking doesn't gain us more, because our internal feelings of self-worth automatically reduce when we become a taker. Taking is a mere illusion of gain. When we take we are actually paying for it. We may not have to pay with something external like money, but if it doesn't come off our external account then it MUST come off our internal account (our internal feelings of self-worth). Isn't it better to lose external value rather than lose our internal values to pay for the goods we have . We are paying for the goods whether we like it or not.

THE UNIVERSAL ME

Using people, not expressing thanks for favours others have done for us, not paying our way, not putting in a good days work when we are being paid for it etc are all examples of taking. If we look at others and see them through the eyes of 'what can this person give me', then we know we have put on our 'taking hat'. Once we have our 'taking hat' on we can no longer feel content with what we have in our lives. Our 'real me' wants to be satisfied with our lives. Our 'real me' doesn't want to be like a wild lion pacing back and forth on edge waiting to see what it can pounce on next. Our 'real me' wants to relax in its beautiful garden of Happiness and enjoy tranquilly all the blessings it has.

Give it a Go!

(If relevant to you) Turn your back on that part of you that panicked and stole.

Have you <u>ever</u> stolen anything (even if it's worth hardly anything), cheated on your work time sheet, not returned something you borrowed, obtained money/good through deception etc...?

If so, resolve to return it or its monetary value. See how good you feel when you've done this.

I tried this exercise _____ times.
I would rate this exercise as:

1	2	3	4	5	6	7	8	9	10
(not so good)				(Average)					(Spot on)

Why Should I?

This exercise is designed for those who have in the past fallen into the trap of being a taker. It is very easy, if we don't work on being contented to fall down into a taking mentality. However, we don't have to stay there we can pick ourselves up, return what we've stolen and get back to developing a contented mind set. Some people may ask 'Why bother returning what was stolen, or apologising etc, just get on with life?'

There is a part inside of us that wants to be free and rid of things we have taken - it wants to feel the burden of other people's belongings lifted from our shoulders. It's an incredibly exhilarating feeling to fix up mistakes we've made in the past. This type of mistake is easy to fix up.

Most people we have stolen from are happy to receive the item/money back. We can do it anonymously, just walk into the shop and tell the shop assistant we owe them money – when people are being given money 'for nothing' they don't usually ask questions. And if we can't remember who we stole from then we can just donate the amount we stole to some community project and that way we can give it back to an unknown member of the community.

It's not as hard as it sounds to rectify this mistake, and we'll feel great and free from being weighed down by it. (And it is weighing us down whether we feel it or not).

Go on- Give yourself the gift of Contentment, fix up the past and move forward into a great future. – Give it a Go!

Day 86
Taking in order to Give

Mr. I.: "That's it; I'm never going to take something from another the rest of my life. I will be content with what I have and I will only be a giver."

(Sometime later)

Mr. O.: "You are such a kind person, and you have helped me so much. I would really like to give you this present to express my thanks"

Mr. I: "No! I don't accept gifts, I'm not a taker – you can keep the gift, I'm content with my lot in life, I don't need presents, I'm just happy I could help you."

Sometimes the act of taking is really an act of giving. If someone wants to give us something, because they have a real need to express their thanks, appreciation, love etc. then it is actually an act of GIVING to take! Giving others the opportunity to give is not losing touch with our contented nature and becoming a taker - it's being a giver. In fact if a person refuses to let another pay a debt of gratitude or express their giving side then they are being the taker because they are taking away somebody's ability and deep desire to give. A contented person wants to give pleasure to others, and if they sense that others will have pleasure by them accepting gifts they want to bestow, then a contented person is happy to accept the gifts. Not because the contented person love gifts, but because they love making other people happy.

The converse can also be the case - giving can sometimes really be a ruse for taking. Imagine somebody gives his wealthy friend an expensive birthday present – not because he wants to make his friend happy, but because he knows when his birthday comes around his wealthy friend will give him a really good present. Now in that case the person is giving in order to take. Why does he want to take? Because he doesn't feel happy with what he has, he thinks if he gets more then he'll be more (either more important, wealthy, happy etc.) This type of scenario is really quite sad, because this 'taker' friend is using this wonderful opportunity to draw close and show love and friendship to his friend and turning it into a cheap, shallow attempt to push himself up the wealth ladder at the expense of his friend. Look how foolishly a lack of contentment with our own lives can make us behave!

'I'll scratch your back and you scratch mine' is a taking mentality. It comes from a feeling of I'm lacking and not content with what I have and I assume you are too, so let's work together to amass more. If we were really content with our lives then we would be happy to be of assistance and scratch another's back but we wouldn't need (or even desire) our back scratched in return.

So how do we know if we are really giving or really taking? The answer depends on our motivations. Are we thinking primarily about ourselves or primarily about the other person? If the other person's happiness is at the forefront of our mind then whether we are doing the physical act of giving or taking we are really giving. However, if the person in the centre of the picture is us, and we feel we are lacking something in our lives, then we are taking – even when we are doing a physical act of giving.

"I made a conscious effort to switch my focus when I give. I try to think exclusively about the person that I want to give to. I don't think about what kick backs I'll get. It's amazing what a loveable person I've become, and how easy I find it to truly care and love others as a result of this small effort I've made."

When we are content and happy with our lives we want to share and give for no other reason than to bring joy and happiness into their lives. When we are content we don't try and scheme or plan ways to enrich or endear ourselves to others for some hope of gain, because people who are content don't feel they are missing anything.

Wouldn't it be nice to have a feeling of completeness, wholeness and utter fulfilment? We can achieve this level by focusing on what good things we have in our life and not desiring at all what others have. If we can reach this level, others will sense that we really care about them. When we give to them they won't be wondering 'what's the catch?' in our acts of giving.

Give it a Go!

1. Today do an act of real giving, focusing totally on the other person and not even desiring a kick back.
2. Next time you think 'What can I get out of this person?' or 'What has this person done for me lately?' squash the thought and think about how wonderful your life is and how you don't really need others to make you more fulfilled.

I tried this exercise _____ times.
I would rate this exercise as:

1	2	3	4	5	6	7	8	9	10
(not so good)				(Average)					(Spot on)

Why Should I?

When we want to live a life of contentment we need to always remain focused on being self fulfilled. Once we feel our lives are not lacking then we are able to make every interaction with others a giving one. We will be free from becoming a 'taker' even when it's a situation that is not obviously taking.

The biggest enemy to a life of contentment is to lose ones focus and become a taker. The most effective way to avoid becoming a taker is to develop the trait of being content. They are the flip side of the same coin. A taker is not content and a contented person will never be a taker.

The second exercise may help us become aware of times in our lives when we honestly think we are giving, but in fact we have become a taker. This will help us identify when our levels of contentment have waned and the 'taker' stepped in instead. We need to be on guard against ruining our happiness by flipping into taking mode. If we are vigilant and guard our contentment and refuse to travel down the path of the taker we will be guaranteed a happy, contented and blissful life.

These exercises will help us learn how to be a 'no strings attached' type of giver. They will also help us avoid anything (e.g. thoughts or situations where we pretend we are giving) that 'smell' slightly of taking, and they will guard our ability to remain in the calm and happy state of contentment.

Go on – Be on Guard for things that might rob you of your contentment – Give it a Go!

Conclusion

The 6th Key to Happiness is to learn how to be completely content with our lives. We can squash that noisy voice that tells us we need more and more and if we don't get it we are missing out on living life the way it should be lived.

Contentment isn't just with physical things, but it can apply to internal matters as well. We can be happy with who we are. We don't have to compare ourselves to our friends, neighbours, relatives or anyone else. Everybody has strengths and weaknesses. If we are always looking around at others we are bound to see people who are better than us at so many things – but that doesn't matter. Even if someone is better than us at something or has more money, power, prestige etc it doesn't make us any less.

Contentment is being able to be happy with who we are and what we have regardless of the rest of the world.

A lack of contentment leads to jealousy, feelings of low self worth and eventually to the desire to steal. In the panic that comes from losing our contentment we feel that taking what doesn't belong to us will fill the void that we feel. In truth we don't lack anything and the void is just an illusion made by looking around at what other people have.

The 6th Key to Happiness – being Content is based on the 6th Commandment given to Noah. This Commandment stated 'Do not steal.' Stealing is the road a person travels down when he's not content. If a person were to travel down a different path in life - the path of contentment, he/she would never come to the place of desiring what others have and then stealing.

Contentment is something we all want to achieve. We don't want to be stuck on the treadmill of 'I must have, I must get, I must....' for all of our lives. We deeply desire to step off this treadmill of never ending desires and sit in our garden of Happiness under the peaceful, calm branches of our Contentment tree. We all want to be happy with our lives, and we all have this ability within us. Just sit back, relax, don't look around, and feel how wonderful and blessed your life is right now.

If we can grab the 6th Key of Happiness – Contentment and run with it, then nothing will ever get in our way from obtaining the magnificent feelings of happiness, bliss, serenity and tranquillity in the City of Happiness.

[356] / 7 ANCIENT KEYS TO HAPPINESS

LOVE EVERY DAY

THE UNIVERSAL ME

KEY #7 – TRUTH

Introduction

The 7th Key to Happiness and a Universal 'real me' need is to be truthful. We all love truthful, straight and upright people. We admire those we sense are truthful and we feel we can trust them.

There is something inside every single person that cringes when we say or do something that deviates from the truth. We may have lost touch with this feeling but it is there. Our deep inner essence is shaken to the core when we don't speak with complete honesty. The scientific device called the 'lie detector' is based upon this deep internal and uncontrollable reaction we have to dishonesty. When a person tells a lie the lie detector can pick up on it because there are small physical changes that occur in our bodies, such as increased blood pressure etc. Our bodies literally 'flip' when we speak lies.

So if speaking falsehoods makes our bodies so uncomfortable, then speaking truth brings about an internal peace. When we are truthful we have harmony, beauty and calmness radiate throughout our bodies. When we speak truthfully we feel good about ourselves, trust ourselves and develop integrity. We are proud of ourselves when we can view ourselves as a truthful, honest and upright person.

When we develop the ability to be truthful, we are tapping into a deep part of our inner essence that wants to be expressed. We all want to be that trustworthy, upstanding citizen.

THE UNIVERSAL ME

The biggest reason why people deviate into lying is because they are afraid. Lying is a defence mechanism, we actually learn to lie. When we were very little (i.e. 1-2 yrs old) we would happily tell our parents the truth, but then we realized by telling the truth sometimes we would get into big trouble we learnt how to lie. People lie to protect themselves from being on the receiving end of other people's disapproval. They lie to avoid getting into trouble. They lie to protect themselves and their self esteem.

The only way to free ourselves of this desire to deviate from the truth is to develop more self confidence. When we are happy with who we are and recognise despite the fact we make mistakes we are still loveable then we won't be tempted to tell a lie to 'save face' when we have done something wrong. Also if we have more self confidence we won't be scared to admit we made a mistake. We will readily admit it and want to do all we can to patch up the mistake we made. We don't need to be afraid of anyone. Other people's disapproval doesn't matter, and if we really did something wrong we don't need to be afraid either. We just need to admit it and fix it up. Most people in this world are nice. Most people are forgiving and will forgive us if we try to make amends. All people in this world make mistakes – but resorting to lying never helps fix things up, in the end it only makes things worse.

Using this Key to Happiness we are going to try and unlock that desire for truth and let it shine forth lighting up our whole essence. When we lead honest and truthful lives we have a good feeling about ourselves. In fact we love this truthful spark in us so much that our levels of self-esteem and self-fulfilment fly sky high. Get ready to learn the power and pleasure of Truth.

Day 87

Getting Deep – inner truths

Everybody has inner truths. These are the things that we just intuitively know are right or are 'just me'. These truths are often echoed in the words of our quiet voice. We may not live these inner truths or even feel at all attached to them but they are there and it drags us down when we don't acknowledge them and try to live our life according to them.

"I used to work in a sales office where I smooth-talked the customers. I was given a really good commission when I could get them to buy the top products. I would treat it as a game, to see how many people I could fool to waste their money on the top products, where the medium range ones were exactly the same, just boxed differently. Although my work was exciting, and my adrenaline would flow freely with the feel of the chase and victory, I didn't feel a sense of deep achievement from my job. One day I was sitting quietly and it hit me: I wasn't living according to my own set of ideals. Sure I'm competitive and I like a good pay check, but there is a part of me that actually cares for other people. When I'm at work I turn off that part of me, and that's why my job doesn't give me true satisfaction. After this realization I changed jobs, this time I was selling things that were really good value and I saw myself as a talented matchmaker – I tried with enthusiasm and zest to match the best product up to my customers needs. I became the best matchmaker in the firm (and the best sales person). I feel such job satisfaction because I am living a life that can give expression to the 'real me'."

"I have a few friends who enjoy the nightclub scene, so I'd often go along with them. I would put on the makeup, wear the stylish clothes, drink a few drinks and dance a bit. If that was all that going to a nightclub was about then I would have loved it. But it's not - I couldn't stand the hunt or be hunted game that goes on there. My friends would say, 'How else are you supposed to meet someone special?' But it just didn't feel right. I thought about what they said, and listened to my quiet voice, deep down I wasn't ready to meet 'someone special', and even if I was, I don't think any 'someone special' I met at a nightclub would ever take me seriously enough to really treat me like their 'someone special'. When I realized that going

to nightclubs was really like going to a meat market, I stopped going and found many more fun ways to fill my evenings – and I felt great about myself. I am happy that I'm in tune enough with myself to be able to differentiate between what makes me really happy and what seems to make me happy but really drags me down."

"My parents wanted to go on a cruise overseas. I know most of my friends would have jumped at the opportunity to go. But I'm a homely type of person, and I don't really enjoy the holiday and people scene. I prefer my own bed, my own home and I like to socialize only a bit - not all day every day. When I explained this to my parents they said it was fine with them if I stayed home with my grandmother. I was so happy. I could imagine that if I didn't know myself better I would have forced myself to go on the cruise and wondered all the time 'why can't I enjoy myself like everyone else here?' But now I'm staying at home I feel pleased that I love myself the way I am, and that I'm happy to look after the 'real me'."

When we start to listen to ourselves, and take our thoughts and feelings seriously, we are on the road to true inner peace. Every person is different, so what our friend, neighbour, sister or spouse enjoys may not be what gives us energy and vitality. When we try and plaster on top of ourselves other people's views of how we should be 'enjoying' our lives, we are likely to lead ourselves to misery and wonder why we are not happy. We can only be happy when we live a life of who WE are, not who anybody else is. We need to have the trust and belief in our own opinions and feelings to say to another person: "That's ok for you – go and enjoy, but I really like doing ...." Having strength of character to be the 'real me' will bring unbelievable pleasure.

Give it a Go!

Reflect deeply and ask yourself: "Is there anything I do that I don't really enjoy deep down, but pretend to enjoy because I feel that is what is expected of me?"

I tried this exercise _____ times.
I would rate this exercise as:

1	2	3	4	5	6	7	8	9	10
(not so good)				(Average)					(Spot on)

Why Should I?

We might be able to fool the whole world into believing we are something that we are not, but why fool ourselves? We need to get in touch with our inner truths, with who we are, what we like and what makes us really happy. Inner truths are deeply embedded in our nature and when we act against what we know is an inner truth we feel deep down that something is 'wrong' or 'off'. We might push away this uneasy feeling, or even block it out, but it's there. Now is the time to uncover our inner truths and run with them. If we can do that we will unleash a power of self-awareness, self-love and true inner happiness.

This exercise will help us uncover those areas of our lives where we don't live fully with who we really are. When we live a life that is completely the 'real me', we are happy. When we don't know who we are and we try to fit ourselves into somebody else's 'real me' we feel cramped and uncomfortable. We can get in touch with who we are by trial and error. We can see what makes us feel good and track down when we are doing things that we think should make us feel good but don't. This exercise involves being in touch with who we are. It involves introspection and learning to recognise when we feel good and when the good feeling we think we should be having is just not present.

When we live our life according to who we are and our inner-truths, we will become self confident, self assured and happy. People will look at us and wonder how it is that we have such high levels of self esteem and joy. But we will know the secret to our success is uncovering our 'real me' and living with our inner truths.

Go on – Attain inner-peace – Give it a Go!

Day 88

Being true to yourself

One of the biggest drains on our internal serenity is living our lives as a lie. When we are not true to ourselves and don't recognise who we are and what makes us happy we are bound to be miserable. Imagine someone with two identities: married to two different women in different countries. Neither of his wives knows about the other. This guy on the outside may think he's smart – after all he's fooling two people and doing a really good job of it. But is he really smart? Will leading a double life, a life of deception and dishonesty ever bring him an inner calm and happiness?

We are all looking for happiness. It is the biggest human drive. The only way we can ever achieve true and real happiness is to be honest with ourselves and live a life that we know is true and correct.

Many of us live with untruths. We may even think they are cute or funny. Living with things in our lives that are not true robs us of our internal integrity and the ability we have to trust ourselves. Even if we are in a situation where we feel we have to tell somebody something that is not true, it is important that we don't believe it ourselves.

"I told my friend that I couldn't come to her party because I had a headache. I didn't really have a headache - I just didn't want to come. But the really funny thing was that I lay in bed all night pretending to have a headache – I even believed my own made up story!"

""It's not my fault", "I couldn't help it", "It's got nothing to do with me" – I would often defend myself to others with such words, but I found that I actually believed what I said. This was a big problem because it meant that I never looked hard at myself to see how I really was causing a lot of misery to others and myself. As soon as I resolved not to fool myself, I discovered that I grew strong and responsible. Being truthful to myself has been the best step I've ever taken in my life."

So how do we learn to be truthful to ourselves?

First step – learn to ask ourselves the question: 'Is this true?" Whenever we make a statement or comment we need to ask ourselves if it is really true. When we cross-examine ourselves we will come up with the right answers. We also need to evaluate what others are saying and determine if their words are true. Basically we need to be turned on, and committed to living a life that is truthful.

Second step – learn to feel that 'untrue hunch'. We have something inside us that doesn't feel right when we say things that are not true. It may take a while to learn to feel this, especially if we speak untruths regularly. But if we try to avoid any type of falsehood, we will have an internal uncomfortable feeling when we do accidently utter something that is not 100% correct.

Imagine we were a rich owner of hundreds of slaves, living a thousand years ago. Now imagine somebody said to us 'All people are equal. Slavery should be abolished. But if we can't free our slaves, we should at least treat them kindly – like family members.' Would we be willing to listen to their advice? Probably not, after all, a thousand years ago slavery was considered completely acceptable and normal. Why would anyone give up their slaves when society saw nothing wrong with it and a person could feel like a good, decent and likeable person even if they frequently beat or killed their slaves? Most of us have a hard time stepping out of 'the world as we know it' and don't feel comfortable re-considering the truth and correctness of our values or social norms.

In order to be a truthful individual we need to be constantly re-evaluating ourselves and the ideals we live by. We must be willing to step out of our comfort zone of what we thought we knew and pursue what is true and correct. E.g. do you still believe in the tooth fairy? If we don't believe it exists, why pretend we do?

Give it a Go!

1. For a whole day listen to yourself speak. Try and pick up anytime when you feel a hunch of 'This is not true.'
2. When you feel this hunch, see if you can change what you said to be expressed truthfully and feel the hunch disappear.

I tried this exercise _____ times.
I would rate this exercise as:

1	2	3	4	5	6	7	8	9	10
(not so good)				(Average)					(Spot on)

THE UNIVERSAL ME

Why Should I?

The more truthful we become the happier we will be. Everybody loves the feeling of inner integrity. Everybody wants to see themselves as a good person. Deep down we all want to be truthful. It's a Universal drive. Deep down the 'real me' part of us is full of self respect and pleasure when we choose to walk the path of truth and honesty.

These exercises help us get back in touch with that truthful part of ourselves. We all have a compass inside that directs us towards truth. We just need to hone in to the messages it sends us. The more we can practice tuning in to our internal truth compass the easier we will find it to navigate truthfully through life. The skill of feeling an untrue 'hunch' can become second nature to us. We can eventually learn to live a life of complete truth and honesty and we will feel great about ourselves. A life lived truthfully is a life lived happily.

We can access great levels of self love, integrity and bliss by following our deep need to attach ourselves to truth. A well developed feeling for truth will lead us towards things that will provide us with bliss and will repel us away from things that drag us down. The more truthful we become, the wiser we will be and the more satisfied we will feel with our lives.

Go on – Feel your value and integrity grow – Give it a Go!

Day 89
Partial truths

The best and most believable lie is one that is based on a large amount of truth. This is where we have to be the most discerning.

"I got caught up with a cult; at first what they said made a heap of sense. They taught me how to meditate and how to get in touch with parts of me I didn't know existed. But what got me suspicious, and eventually got me out, was that I liked to question. The cult leaders didn't like questions. They wanted me to just accept what they said. The more I questioned, the more upset they got with me – so I left. Now, looking back, I see that I was attracted to the things that were basically truthful, but I didn't want to park my mind and accept all the other garbage they were throwing at me."

We've all heard the expression, "Ask no questions and be told no lies." This applies to things that are propped up by falsehood, even though there may be kernels of truth within.

In order to get to the truth in things we need to ask lots of question and hear the lies, know they are not true and move forward taking out the good, and leaving the untruthful husks.

Many centuries ago it was widespread for people to go to a shop, purchase a wooden statue, take the statue home, cook a good meal for it, place the meal in front of the statue, bow to it and say 'this is my god'. Such practices, to the Western mind, seem absolutely foolish. Just as foolish as getting our garden rake out, cooking it a meal, and saying it's a god. But if it's so foolish why did people do it? Some might say it was cultural – so it was mass foolishness! Some might say it was symbolic or a channel to achieve spiritual elation – so why call it 'my god'? Call it a piece of wood I look at to help my concentration. Such wood doesn't need homage and reverence. The most likely reason they did it was because they weren't willing to question why they were doing what they were doing. They just did it. If they seriously asked themselves why they were doing such a thing, and really wanted to live a life of truth they would have thrown out their idol, ate the meal themselves and thanked The Source of All Goodness for such delicious food.

In our search for meaning, a deeper inner life and a happy existence there will be many well meaning groups offering to provide the answers to all our needs. Before getting hooked up to anything, we need to be objective, and ask ourselves if what they are saying is 100% true, or is it falsehood intermingled with elements of truth. Always ask questions, analyse the answers, see if there are any contradictions in what we are being told and if it feels correct according to our quiet voice. Asking questions is the only way to eventually find the truth.

"I used to do drugs; I wanted to just escape it all. But I also had a desire to be in touch with 'it'. I didn't know what 'it' was but I knew that it was something beyond me. The drugs almost killed me, but what saved me was finding someone who taught me how to get what I was really looking for in a non-destructive way. I met a person who showed me how to escape from my horrible existence, and live in the world of goodness. She taught me to see the world and myself in such a great way that I didn't want to escape but rather I wanted to live life fully. She also taught me to be in touch with myself and how to have a real spiritual connection with a force that is so powerful, loving and full of ecstasy that I now live with 'it' constantly in my life (the real thing not the cheap hazardous imitation.)"

Anything that is truly good and meaningful can be found in its true, pure and harmless form.

We only need to look for the truth – the real product - and not get caught up in the harmful, cheap imitations. When we are internally strong enough to live a life based on truth, we are being kind and giving to our 'real me'. Because our 'real me' has inner peace when it leads a life it knows is true.

Give it a Go!

It's time to get quiet. Reflect deeply and ask yourself: "Is there anything that I don't really 100% believe in, but I do it anyway?" If the answer is yes, then find a way to get what you are really looking for in a true and good form.

I tried this exercise _____ times.
I would rate this exercise as:

1	2	3	4	5	6	7	8	9	10
(not so good)				(Average)					(Spot on)

Why Should I?

This exercise is similar to Day 87, however the earlier exercise was designed to help us track down the times when we do things we don't enjoy because we don't know ourselves well enough or we are just following the crowd or what other people like. This exercise is different, it's designed to help us start thinking about the things we do that we know are false, but have never thought to look for an alternate way of getting the pleasure we have from pursuing these false things. On the one hand we have pleasure from this thing/activity etc but on the other hand we know it's not true and it's draining us.

Since there is no pleasure in this world that cannot be obtained in its true and purely good form we can feel confident that if we search hard enough we will be able to uncover the truthful part of what we desire and leave the husk of falsehood behind.

The first step is to look deeply into ourselves and try to discover what pleasure we are really seeking. Deep down, what are we hoping to gain from doing what we are doing? Once we have identified that, then the next step is to do research. We can look for ways to get the 100% truthful product. It's out there, we just have to look to discover it. We don't have to live our lives with falsehood just because we are ignorant of how to get the real truthful pleasure. If we are determined to live truthful lives we will eventually discover the best way to get what we really want – with no negative side effects.

Go on – Reach for the stars – don't settle for second best – Give it a Go!

Conclusion

We all need to have internal integrity. We need it just like we need to breathe air and drink water. If we by our own actions cause our internal integrity to be harmed or soiled we feel it deep down, and this drains us of our happiness.

Conversely when we live lives that are pure, good, honest and upright we feel great about ourselves. We feel we are strong, trustworthy and respectable. The best way to feel self respect is to act in a way that makes us respect ourselves. When we are basically truthful and honest people we respect ourselves for this.

Truth is one of those plants we all want to plant in our Happiness garden. It's a strong, tall, imposing and awesome plant. It brings a sense of wonder to the eyes and delight to the heart. We are all born straight and honest, we just need to cultivate this part of our nature in order for it to blossom within.

The 7th Key to Happiness is Truth. This key is based on the 7th Commandment given to Noah, which was 'Don't engage in idol worship.' It is against all logic to bow down to idols. No thinking person can honestly believe that an object made from wood, stone or plastic made the world (including itself) or has any independent powers. The only reason people worshiped idols is because they got distracted from reality and lived lives of falsehood. A person who is committed to seeking truth and being truthful would never get hooked into idol worship.

We all internally desire to live a life of truth. We love the feeling of honesty, integrity and pure straight forwardness. Our hearts are created straight and truthful, and our bodies are so intimately attuned to the truth that one single (little) lie cause us to shudder internally.

The more we can accustom ourselves to always pursue truth and speak words that are truthful, the more we will admire ourselves for being the type of person we want to be.

THE UNIVERSAL ME

Go on grab this last 7th Key to Happiness, hold it in your hand and don't let go. It is your compass in life, it will guide you to all the doors leading to bliss, tranquillity, elation and much more. With the 7th Key to Happiness – Truth, you will be guaranteed to make it promptly, safely and securely into the Awesome City of Happiness.

Keep it Alive with Team work

All great things are achieved through teamwork. There is nothing like having a team of people to help the whole group stay focused and on task. A friend can help us when we fall, and we can help our friend when he/she falls, and together we will both get further than if we tried it on our own.

"I want to keep positive and upbeat, but sometimes I just have days where I feel down."

We all have days that drag us down. Having others who are working towards the same goal can strengthen us at the times of our weakness; they can prop us back on our feet and encourage us to keep going.

"I find it so hard to stay positive; I live in such a negative environment. My family are pessimists, my friends are pessimists, even the weather forecaster can't tell the weather in a positive way – he said it was going to be a stinking hot day, whereas I thought it was a gloriously warm day, perfect for ice-cream by the pool."

We need to hear and see positive messages regularly to keep up our positive attitude. The best way of achieving this is to have a group of friends who are all committed to becoming more positive. Then when we speak to our friends our conversations will be positive and uplifting. We all need an island of sanity to run to, so if we can make some like-minded friends we will find that living a positive life becomes much easier.

"I wanted to have an upbeat group of friends that didn't sit around and moan but were positive, caring and supportive. So I created a club. Anybody was able to join, as long as they kept to the club rules – the rules were the 7 Ancient Keys to Happiness which included speaking in a positive way, being a giving and caring person and guarding against doing or saying things that hurt others.   We had a motto 'see the good and be a giver not a taker'. This was the best thing I've ever done in my life."

If we don't have a support system, or even ONE single friend who wants to work on being more positive, we can always be proactive and create one. We can create the world that we want to live in. The more positive and happy people there are in the world the easier it is for us to be happier. Somebody's happiness doesn't take away from ours, it enhances it.

Give it a Go!

See if you can get two or more friends together and commit to working on becoming more positive, happy and loving as a group. (If your group has a meeting once a week and learn one 'DAY' of this book every week, then you'll have almost 2 years worth of material for meetings.)

I tried this exercise _____ times.
I would rate this exercise as:

1	2	3	4	5	6	7	8	9	10
(not so good)				(Average)					(Spot on)

Why Should I?

Teamwork is the best way to keep anything we want to work on alive. There are many different types of support groups in the world for people trying to work on overcoming bad habits e.g. Alcoholics Anonymous etc. By establishing a Happiness team, we can actually work on developing good traits and habits. Why not try making a good life even better?

We all need support to keep going. Life is busy and it also has its ups and downs – we need others to help us keep going. We also need to be there for others to strengthen them. When we are able to help another person become happy, we find that we also become happier. The more we can help others the more clarity and will power we will have to achieve higher and higher levels of bliss.

One small group of people has the ability to change the world. We all affect each other, because we are creatures that live in groups and societies. We can affect the world to be a happier place, just by working on doing this with a small group. The growth and happiness that comes from that group will have a ripple effect on those who come into contact with its members, and this will then affect those who come into contact with them, until eventually millions or even billions of people can be affected for the good just by one small group.

Go on - Do yourself and the world a favour – Give it a Go!

Final word & summary

There are a lot of great tools for life written in the pages of this book. There is no way that all the tools will be able to be implemented in one reading. The value of this book will be greatly enhanced if it is re-read. You may even find that it would be a great new year's resolution (each year) to read it once a year until you feel you have tried all the ideas, incorporated them you we don't need to be reminded of them.

The contents of this book can be summarized into 7 major Ancient Principles.

Summary of 7 Ancient Keys to Happiness.

Step 1 – Smell Every Rose

1) Recognise and focus on the good. Use your quiet voice to help you see all of the good in your life and trace it back to where the good comes from - say "thank you". Failing to see the good in life may lead to denying the good exists or worse still – it may lead to ingratitude and wishing bad upon the one who provides us with the goodness in our lives.

Step 2 – Climb Every Mountain

2) Judge people fairly – have both the defendant and prosecutor there – try and see the whole picture (OBJECTIVELY from atop of the mountain) and see every person as a whole with good and bad. The second part of this principle is to protect ourselves and others from bad influences and people. This is what a court system does for humanity.

Step 3 – Love Every Day

3) Be compassionate. We can use but not abuse. An example of lacking compassion is tearing a limb off an animal whilst it is still alive.

4) Be a giver. See other people's wants and needs as real, and try and accommodate them as much as possible – even when it costs

money, time or effort. Failing to see beyond oneself can ultimately lead to murder.

5) Bond deeply with another – Bonding can only be done with one compatible person via total dedication and devotion. Don't get involved in intimate relationships with people who are impossible to have a deep bond with.

6) Be Content – Feel a deep pleasure of being who you are and with what you have. Avoid looking around at what others have to decide whether you have enough. A lack of contentment can lead to stealing and rationalizing theft with excuses such as - they won't mind, it's not much, they won't notice, it's my lucky windfall, they're not a person but a business, they're rich, it's only 5 cents etc …

7) Be truthful. Enjoy the feeling of internal integrity. Don't fall for illusions, don't park your mind, follow cults, do drugs or try to find an escape or a different reality. Doing this is as foolish as bowing down to your garden rake and calling it 'my god'. Follow your inner voice to help you get to real meaning and lasting pleasure.

Final word

Whenever we are in a bind and we don't know what to do, remember to turn to that deep reflective quiet voice. It is this quiet voice that is the voice of love. It is the voice of care and compassion. It is the voice that leads us to everything that is good, because it is connected to the Ultimate Source of all Goodness.

Tracing it all back

It is always good to acknowledge the source of one's wisdom. The wisdom contained within this book is gleaned from the Ancient teachings and consciousness of Jewish belief. Given this is the source, many may be surprised that God was not mentioned. That is because when most people talk about God, they are thinking about an old man with a long beard sitting in the sky somewhere. This is not the Jewish definition of God.

The Ancient teachings describe a power that is the Ultimate Source of all Goodness - a fair, true and good Judge, compassionate, giving not taking, trustworthy, faithful, content, truthful, kind, and full of joy and boundless love. This 'Power' is the originator of everything in the past and whatever will come in the future, it is the one guiding and controlling the principle of what goes around comes around. It is the 'Power' that continuously propels every sub-atomic particle and the same 'Power' that is continuously maintaining the universe. It is the 'Power' that gives life to everything. A 'life force' like this 'Power' is found in every human being in the world and we can tap into it by getting in touch with our quiet voice. (This human 'life force' is often referred to as the soul). If we learn to listen to our quiet voice, and appreciate all of the good in our lives we will discover this 'Power' on our own, because it is self evident and doesn't require religious doctrine to prove its existence.

Others may be sceptical at this point thinking – so you really are pushing religion. The answer is NO. According to Jewish teachings every person in this world can lead a life filled with happiness, joy and elevation, and you don't have to be Jewish to do so. Living with the 7 Ancient Keys to Happiness, which were given to Noah and are applicable to all humanity is all the guidance you will need to lead such a great life – no religious adherence needed.

So feel free to enjoy this book – no strings attached.

Acknowledgements

I would like to thank:

My wonderful husband who is so supportive, loving and encouraging. Thank you for being everything a woman could ever want in a husband – and more! Thank you for sticking in there in editing this book.

My special children, who are so lovable, inspiring and fill my life with lots of love and pleasure.

My parents for teaching me to think, dream and to follow my dreams.

My friend Jacqui who encouraged me to keep going, when I was writing this book.

Mrs. Miriam Cowen, an author and special person, who thoroughly reviewed this book and polished it into a beautiful diamond.

Rabbi Noach Weinberg, (especially his audio series called 'The 48 Ways') Rebbitzen Tziporah Heller, Rabbi Aryeh Nivin, Rabbi Yisroel Greenwald, Rebbitzen Yiti Neustadt, Rabbi Zelig Pliskin, Rabbi E.E. Dessler, R' Chaim Luzzatto, R' Abraham J. Twerski and Rabbi Shalom Arush/ Rabbi Lazer Brody from whose audio recordings, books or classes I have quoted and/or drawn an enormous amount of wisdom to write this book.

Most of all HaShem, there are no words that can describe how much I owe You and how good You are. Thank You for always being there for me and giving me the honour of writing this book – I hope You like it.

Note to the reader

A note to my dear reader:

There are lots of wonderful tools I've presented to you. You may be tempted to look at me and say "You don't do them all, you're not perfect." And what you would be saying is true. But don't look at the faults I have, although they are many. I am human and I am not perfect. However, the wisdom I've shared with you is eternal, it is true. Don't let my faults detract you from the truth. Just let me hold your hand and help you smell the roses, walk up the mountain path and love yourself. Together we can enjoy this journey of life. I know that if you can live by the wisdom written here you will be so happy and fulfilled.

Your happiness and fulfilment will be in direct proportion to which you can and have applied yourself. I too am working on applying the principles, and sometimes I forget or succumb to old habits. The main thing is to get back up again and keep trying. The effort is so much worth the results of what you will undoubtedly achieve.

Try not to get discouraged, and never give up (especially on yourself), because you are great, beautiful, and a wonderfully lovable person. Remember how loveable the 'real you' is and never lose faith in how great you can be. Listen to your quiet voice as it has all of the answers and will always lead you towards everything that is good.

CPSIA information can be obtained at www.ICGtesting.com
Printed in the USA
LVOW121704071212

310628LV00020B/731/P